S0-CCW-358

TRAHERNE IN DIALOGUE

Traherne in Dialogue

Heidegger, Lacan, and Derrida

A. LEIGH DENEEF

Duke University Press Durham and London 1988

Printed in the United States of America
on acid-free paper

For Heather

whose presence has been an unqualified delight

CONTENTS

ACKNOWLEDGMENTS

Among the "voices" that have helped to shape this dialogue are several that deserve special acknowledgment. John Morey's troubled fascination with Traherne has been a forceful presence in my own attempts to come to grips with him; Wallace Jackson's troubled response to my "unhistorical" tendencies has been a constant challenge to the strategies I have adopted here; and Frank Lentricchia's positive response to my attempts to deal with Wally's troubled one has been a welcome support. Joanne Ferguson has, once again, done more than one has a right to ask or expect of any press editor; and Nancy Margolis has suffered more than any copyeditor should have to in coping with both my own inconsistencies and the imperfections of WordPerfect. Finally, for encouraging me to write the kind of work I wanted to write and for providing the countless private benefits that made that writing so pleasurable, I owe most, as always, to Barbara.

CHAPTER ONE

Traherne in Dialogue

I hope . . . the reader will not censure me for attempting to state what I have proposed to myself to perform; and also (as far as the limits of a preface will permit) to explain some of the chief reasons which have determined me in the choice of my purpose: that at least he may be spared any unpleasant feeling of disappointment, and that I myself may be protected from one of the most dishonorable accusations which can be brought against an author; namely, that of an indolence which prevents him from endeavoring to ascertain what is his duty, or, when his duty is ascertained, prevents him from performing it. —WILLIAM WORDSWORTH

The author can never entirely offer himself and his verbal work to the complete and definitive will of present or immediate addressees . . . and he imagines . . . a sort of superior instance of responsive understanding, which may extend or recede in different [temporal] directions. Each dialogue takes place, in some manner, on the basis of the responsive understanding of an invisible and present third, holding itself above all the participants of the dialogue.
—MIKHAIL BAKHTIN

1 OF DIALOGUES AND HISTORICISMS

The title of this study demands an explanation. What kind of dialogue could Thomas Traherne have with Martin Heidegger, Jacques Lacan, and Jacques Derrida? What would any one of these twentieth-century thinkers have to say to him? Why should a reader or critic of Renaissance literature seek to imagine such an exchange? And, supposing for the moment that it were imaginable, what purpose would it serve?

Posed in this manner, the four questions survey the grounds that would call for a theoretical justification of the project proposed here, and that is a demand no critic writing today can avoid or evade. In trying to define, therefore, the task I have set for myself, I accept as a prerequisite the need to make explicit the methodological choices that have led me to write this particular kind of work at this particular time. To bring one's own critical agenda into the open, however, is also to place unusual demands upon the typical scholarly audience. That audience will expect to learn something new about Thomas Traherne and to learn it fairly quickly. To insist that my own interpretive choices in approaching Traherne also say something new about him may strain more than audience patience. A subtler demand is also at work, for to the extent that I foreground my own orientations as a critic, I risk subverting the authority and the ostensible objectivity of my description of Traherne's writing. The notion of an "objective" criticism, of course, has been under widespread attack for several years, but those critiques have never licensed any arbitrarily "subjective" reading and the fact remains that most Renaissance studies published today still present themselves under an objectivist banner. This is especially true, I think, of the two subfields that concern me most: criticism on Traherne in particular and the increasingly dominant mode of New Historicism. Since I intend to situate the present study in polemical relation to both the old historicism usually brought to bear upon Traherne and the New Historicism which has yet to address him, I will need to begin by categorizing what I see as the unique claims of these two methodologies.

The mere fact that we have a poet named Traherne in the canon of seventeenth-century literature is an uncontestable triumph of traditional literary history. It is also fair to say that virtually everything we have learned or said about Traherne in the eighty or so years since Dobell finally reclaimed and proclaimed him as author of his anonymous manuscript is the result of archeological retrieval. Individual critics may disagree, of course, upon which general tradition Traherne should be aligned with or which specific authors he is most influenced by; but all would agree that the figure we call Traherne becomes knowable and accessible only insofar as he is situated in a particular historical context.

This claim, of course, is not unique to Traherne criticism; the notion that the meaning of a literary text is determined by its context has long been an historicist cliché. But the consequences of this view have been especially severe in the case of Traherne precisely because, first, we know so little about the historical situation of the man himself, and second, it has been universally assumed that his writings are simply not accessible on even on a superficial level in the same way that Donne's, or Herbert's, or Vaughan's are accessible.[1] The latter point may explain why the New Critics, despite their general predisposition toward metaphysical poetry, left Traherne pretty much alone.

Most traditional criticism, then, argues that Traherne's poetry demands a special historical background—sometimes that of Christian mysticism, sometimes that of Cambridge Platonism, sometimes a more focused knowledge of Augustine, Bonaventura, Ficino, Hermes Trismegistus, or a few other identifiable sources or analogues. Regardless of the form such arguments take—that is, whether they propose the influence of a generalized tradition or cite individual precursors—they all assume that a reader coming to Traherne unfamiliar with the theological, philosophical, or cultural commonplaces that shaped his writings would not be able to appreciate or understand those writings. The task that traditional scholarship has set for itself, therefore, has been to find in the literature available to Traherne himself structural patterns for the *Centuries of Meditations* and the Dobell poems,[2] similar thoughts on the expanses of space and time,[3] or lineages for his prominent literary symbols.[4] There can be no doubt that scholarship has been successful at this task, but its success has been achieved by means of a rather obvious blind spot—the historical situation of Thomas Traherne himself. To read through the criticism that has so far been written on him is to discover a Traherne who is distinguished from his seventeenth-century peers by the fact that he is blissfully untroubled by the tensions, doubts, and anxieties that (we are repeatedly told) mark the age in general. Whether this criticism ascribes Traherne's felicity to a theological mysticism, a psychological fascination with childhood, or a philosophical conviction of a unified existence, there is little sense that Traherne ever suffered from the kinds of alienation that besiege either his own contemporaries or his subsequent readers. To this extent, traditional criticism has never seriously challenged Gladys Wade's early pronouncement that Traherne is "one of the most radiantly, most infectiously happy mortals this earth has known."[5]

In a very real sense, I would argue, the old historicism has constructed a Traherne that is blatantly unhistorical. To this extent, it seems to me that traditional scholarship is open to the charge leveled by Dominick LaCapra:

> The attempt to return a thinker to his own times or to place his texts squarely in the past has often served as a mode of abstract categorization that drastically oversimplifies the problem of historical understanding. Indeed, the rhetoric of contextualization has often encouraged narrowly documentary readings in which the text becomes little more than a sign of the time or a straightforward expression of one larger phenomenon or another. At the limit, this indiscriminate approach to reading and interpretation becomes a detour around texts and an excuse for not really reading them at all.[6]

This may seem a fairly harsh critique of previous scholarship, but LaCapra's point is not to question the importance of the terms that scholarship makes available to the modern interpreter, but rather the extent to which it has adequately understood the consequences of its own historical assumptions or to which it has actually dehistoricized the subject of its own study. In the case of Traherne, I think LaCapra's points are correct. The "contexts" within which Traherne's work has been situated are themselves assumed to have monolithic coherence; the relations between Traherne's texts and those contexts have never been "problematized" in any significant way; and Traherne's own texts have rarely been subjected to close critical scrutiny.

It could be argued, I think, that to the extent that the old historicism failed to historicize Traherne it also kept him conveniently alien to modern readers. If Traherne had nothing to say to his own age and time, what can he have to say to ours? Alienated from his contemporaries, radically idiosyncratic in both his thinking and his writing, and wilfully committed to reimagining a childhood innocence that is either blatantly unrecoverable or simply absurd, Traherne can hardly compete with figures like Donne and Milton for the attention of a modern reader. As a sign of the sort of alienation I am trying to describe here, one might compare the impact of such titles as "Shakespeare in Our Time" or "Donne in Our Time" with "Traherne in Our Time." Never having been situated in any time, Traherne is preemptorily excluded from an attempt to situate him here and now.

Although it is possible that Traherne scholarship is a genuine anomaly in historical criticism in general, I think it more likely that the unhistorical tendencies in such criticism are simply seen here in starker and clearer form. And if this is so, then the challenge to the contemporary critic would seem naturally to be to adopt the practice of a New Historicism in order to reconstruct both Traherne and his texts in their more specific and concrete sociopolitical contexts.[7]

In a recent essay in *English Literary Renaissance*, Louis Montrose tries to articulate the critical/theoretical agenda of the New Historicism. He argues that both the Renaissance poet under study and the modern critic studying him are historical constructs, that our "comprehension, representation, interpretation of the texts of the past always proceed by a mixture of estrangement and appropriation, as a reciprocal conditioning of the Renaissance text and our text of the Renaissance."[8] If we bracket, for a moment, the relationship between poet and critic, we can see that both are subject to and made subjects by a multiplicity of historical contexts. Montrose, like other New Historicists, is particularly emphatic about that multiplicity. Whereas old historicism assumed that "history" could be recognized and summarized in a stable, coherent, collective, and monolithic "world picture"—Elizabethan patriarchy, Tudor-Stuart ideology, reformed Protestantism—the New Historicism follows Frank Lentricchia in positing any number of histories, each of which is characterized by "forces of heterogeneity, contradiction, fragmentation, and difference."[9] Thus, where an old historicism would situate Traherne's text in, say, the context of Cambridge Platonism, the New Historicist would problematize that ostensibly unified or totalized context by demonstrating that it is always already contaminated and fragmented by traces of competing and alien contexts, both discursive and nondiscursive, literary and social, traditional and novel.

By "problematizing" contexts, the New Historicism means primarily the interplay of culture-specific practices which both produce and are produced by the literary text. As Montrose rightly acknowledges, this emphasis is a reaction against a positivist reading of history and a formalist approach to an autonomous literary work. Thus, in his essay "The Elizabethan Subject and the Spenserian Text," Montrose shows how the queen's political and sexual rhetorics constrain and determine how Spenser is able to present or figure her in his poetry; at the same time, once she has been re-presented in the poem, her own options of self-figuration are measurably expanded.[10] If this interplay, however, is the ideal of one side of the New Historicist agenda, it is an ideal rarely achieved in current practice. Most New Historicism clearly focuses on the text as *product* of a set of cultural practices rather than as *producer* of those practices. And to the extent that this observation is valid, the "histories" that New Historicism has reconstructed are at best partial. The New Historicist, of course, is perfectly willing to concede that argument since all history is partial. But the concession masks the deeper problem that an "unknowable" complex of histories and contexts is more often than not merely a rhetorical gesture toward the unexplored side of the textual dialectic which then allows the critic to proceed, in relatively traditional fashion, to describe one cultural context within which the text must be situated. That context may well be more complex than those of the old historicism—perhaps because more broadly cultural than literary, ideological than generic —but it is not presented any less objectively.[11]

There are, consequently, two problems on this side of the New Historicist agenda: a tendency to substitute for a questionable notion of history an unquestioned notion of context; and a tendency to privilege the social pressures upon the text rather than the pressures the text itself exerts on cultural practice or ideology. Hayden White calls attention to the first of these issues when he writes: "Nor is it unusual for literary theorists, when they are speaking about the 'context' of a literary work, to suppose that this context—the 'historical milieu'—has a concreteness and an accessibility that the work itself can never have, as if it were easier to perceive the reality of a past world put together from a thousand historical documents than it is to probe the depths of a single literary work that is present to the critics studying it."[12]

We see this most clearly, I think, in the recent wave of feminist revisions of Renaissance texts. There is no question that the work of Leah Marcus, Janel Mueller, Mary Ellen Lamb, Tilde Sankovitch, Mary Nyquist, Mary Beth Rose, and others has changed radically the way we now understand the difficulties and complexities of gender relations in the period. At the same time, however, certain of the enabling contexts of this work—an ideological patriarchy, for example—assume a concreteness and a specificity that are hard to justify theoretically. As Jean E. Howard notes, it is far too easy to "objectify" this context with a smattering of Lawrence Stone, Keith Thomas, or Joan Kelly-Gadol.[13] One recent collection of essays, *Rewriting the Renaissance*, devotes the first third of its contents to "The Politics of Patriarchy." Although the remainder of the volume illustrates ways in which various writers, male and female, work within and against this context, there is little acknowledgment that the context itself is being read or constructed provisionally; indeed, it seems rather to be taken as objectively and as historically specific as Tillyard took his Elizabethan world picture.[14] The unproblematized concept of contexts, in short, is somewhat paradoxically a blind spot in the New Historicism.[15] To this extent, I agree with LaCapra that what has been proposed as a solution to the problem of an "unhistorical" old historicism needs to be reformulated as itself a problem within New Historicism. Context as such must be posed as a question: of what value or necessity is it to the historicist project and upon what grounds can one context or even a series of contexts be privileged over another or others? LaCapra himself is worth citing on this point:

> An appeal to the context does not *eo ipso* answer all questions in reading and interpretation. And an appeal to *the* context is deceptive: one never has—at least in the case of complex texts—*the* context. The assumption that one does relies on a hypostatization of "context," often in the service of misleading organic or other overly reductive analogies. For complex texts, one has a set of interacting contexts whose relations to one another are variable and problematic and whose relation to the text being investigated raises difficult issues in interpretation. Indeed, what may be most insistent in a modern text is the way it challenges one or more of its contexts. In addition, the assertion that a specific context or subset of contexts is especially significant in a given case has to be argued and not simply assumed or surreptitiously built into an explanatory model or framework of analysis.[16]

To continue with my earlier example, Mary Ellen Lamb has written powerfully and persuasively on the constraints under which women like the countess of Pembroke worked as translators, the principal role the patriarchal system allowed.[17] But Lamb also shows how the countess's translations, though produced by the male-dominated literary system, make possible "a more positive option for future literary women" and thus produce change in the system itself. As in the most recent work of Montrose and Greenblatt, the literary text assumes here a subversive and contestatorial function in relation to its cultural context(s). Still, I think it fair to say that the pressures of context upon text are far more prevalent and specific in the New Historicism than the pressures of texts on contexts. The ways in which particular literary works "produced" an equally particular sociocultural effect have proved far less recoverable, more tentative and suggestive, than the forces of contextual constraints producing those texts.

If one side of the New Historicist agenda situates the literary text within a product/producing dialectic of sociocultural practice, the other side situates the critic in the same condition: "this project of historical resituation is necessarily the textual reconstruction of critics who are themselves historical subjects." Or, as Montrose puts it a bit later in the same essay, "integral to this new project of historical criticism is a realization and acknowledgment that the critic's own text is as fully implicated in such an interplay as are the texts under study."[18] Clearly Montrose is right about this crucial point and he emphasizes, again correctly, that "interplay" means that the modern critic is both product of and producer of the various contexts within which he or she is situated. His clearest example is the split internal to New Historicism itself between the American practitioners, who have focused mainly upon "a refiguring of the sociocultural field in which Renaissance texts were *originally* produced," and the British practitioners, who have focused more extensively "upon the uses to which the *present* has put its versions of the past."[19] While the example is clear enough in its broadest configuration, it disguises the deeper historical/contextual issue. If we think again of the various feminist revisions currently under way, we might well inquire about the extent to which patriarchy is an historical "context" of the Renaissance or of the late 1970s and early 1980s. Indeed, the most persistent topics of the New Historicism—gender relations, the various appropriations of power and authority, the complex structures of identity configuration, the subversions of a literary subversiveness by a dominant ideology—would seem much more *our* contexts than ones we have "discovered" in the Renaissance.

There are two ways to think about this problem, neither of which finds much voice in current practice. Jean Howard, trying to ask why the Renaissance in particular has proved so rich a field for the New Historicism, argues that the age has been appropriated in the name of history in order to allow a kind of transhistorical narcissism. Howard, of course, does not put her objection quite as baldly as this, and she eventually, and too easily, clears New Historicism of the charge. She writes that the New Historicist reconstructs the Renaissance

> as *neither* modern nor medieval, but as a boundary or liminal space between two more monolithic periods where one can see

> acted out a clash of paradigms and ideologies . . . which resonate with some of the dominant elements of postmodern culture.
>
> In short, I would argue that the Renaissance, seen as the last refuge of preindustrial man, is of such interest to scholars of the postindustrial era because these scholars construe the period in terms reflecting their own sense of the exhilaration and fearfulness of living inside a gap in history, when the paradigms that structured the past seem facile and new paradigms uncertain.[20]

Even if we are willing to concede Howard's "monolithic periods," there is, I would posit, little new in such narcissism: it is the same "historical" reflection that led Grierson and Eliot to seize upon John Donne many years ago. And it is by no means certain that the self-consciousness of the modern critic is any more willing to interrogate its own presuppositions than that of our predecessors earlier in the century.

Nowhere is this clearer, I think, than in the recent work of Gary Waller. Waller concludes his New Historical *English Poetry of the Sixteenth Century*[21] by asking us to think about reopening the canon of the age and he points specifically to the mass of writings by and about women that we are just beginning to explore. Certainly Waller is right to urge this kind of recovery, but the question is the status of the "history" we assign to it. Whose history, in short, will that recovery be? As Waller writes elsewhere, again invoking the spectral context of the patriarchy against which women were "struggling into discourse," "what is it like to read and be read, to write and be written, as a woman?"[22] If this is an historical question, it is Waller's own, not one that was raised in the Renaissance. At the very least, it is historical precisely insofar as it defines our historical filiation with the Renaissance. The point here is that historical fact, as fact, becomes so problematic and unstable that we must begin to wonder about the meaning that history, as a term, can carry at all or the conditions under which it can become meaningful. To grasp the terms of the New Historicist's doubled discourses that make it possible to see certain phenomena as "historical," the notion of history itself must be more openly problematized. Failure to do so will leave the New Historicism as blindly dehistoricizing as the older historicism it seeks to replace.

A second way of thinking about the historicity of the contexts now being deployed might be to posit a more thorough critique of the relations between past and present in terms of deep and surface structures or unconscious and conscious pressures. The questions to which Waller directs us—what is it like to read and be read, write or be written, as a woman—have obviously been thematized and brought to the surface in contemporary theory and practice. Does the fact that we can find precursors to such thematizing in certain Renaissance texts mean that the questions occupy the same historical site or exert the same historical pressure? I think not, and only by articulating more carefully the differences among such pressures can we approach anything like "historical" understanding.

If, then, the history of old historicism is called into question by its blindness to competing claims and counterclaims against its monolithic fictions, the history of the New Historicism is equally called into question by its failure to pursue its own insights into the complexities of those competing claims. In such a discursive scene, any and all history can be only a provisional effect of a certain arbitrary cut, a referential context wilfully privileged at the expense of and by excluding other contexts. The critic simply cannot specify everything at once. If, moreover, the subject is literary, then the status of history, however deployed, becomes even more questionable. To what ground extrinsic to itself does literature refer? To what ground extrinsic to itself does history refer? What, exactly, are the relations here? If all literature is historical and all history is literary, what privilege can the notion of history or historical have at all? Or, as Howard more tellingly puts it, without, it should be noted, following up her own question: "If one accepts certain tendencies in poststructural thought, is the possibility of an historical criticism even conceivable?"[23]

I would not be misunderstood here. I am not arguing against an historical approach to literary texts, but against a certain blindness that seems to me to have surrounded the reliance on that term. History, like power, writes Montrose, and also, I would add, like context, is in danger of hypostatization.[24] My concern, therefore, is how to guard against this tendency that threatens the New Historicism as forcefully and insidiously as it did the old. I am not convinced by the New Historicist's easy acknowledgment that the critic's work is as historically embedded as the text he or she is studying, for that acknowledgment rarely goes beyond a facile gesture. Until the critic puts his own pressures into play as concretely and precisely as those he is uncovering in the past, acknowledgment remains purely rhetorical. Nor am I sure that foregrounding those pressures would, in itself, provide any clearer sense of history. In short, history as such is the contested field.

Let me use another illustration from Waller to clarify the point I am trying to make here. In defense of his New Historicist revision of the tradition of sixteenth-century poetry, Waller argues that "one important function of the literary text—perhaps, it is often argued, what constitutes 'greatness' in a work—is that of bringing out the multiplicity, contradictions, and tensions that a dominant ideology tries to ignore or cover over." A few pages later, he repeats this assertion in even bolder terms: "The most interesting [the next sentence says "the best"] poetry of the whole period is written in the last twenty years of the century *precisely because* it is torn among conflicting ideological pressures that fracture its apparent serenity" (my italics).[25] Whether we accept Waller's reconstructions of the context(s) of sixteenth-century poetry or not, we must not fail to understand that his presuppositions about the function and value of literature itself are derived not from sixteenth-century "historical" contexts but from ours. "Precisely because," in short, is the mark of the present's appropriation of the past in its own terms; and the present has then imposed those terms upon the past in order to render a judgment upon that age's "most interesting" or "best" poetry. I cite this example not so much to call into question the historicity of Waller's study, but to question whether he is sufficiently attentive to the complexities of his own historicism. I am perfectly willing to concede the New Historicism the point that text and critic are historical constructs, but for historicism itself, the real question is the relation between those constructs. To the extent that Waller remains blind to his own historical pressures, his revision is considerably less "historical" than it claims and certainly less "New Historicist" as well.

At this point pragmatic considerations begin to exert their own kinds of inevitable pressures, and we might redirect the issue by asking whether the New Historicist agenda is capable of being carried out. This is not an idle question, and the fact that the American and British practitioners have sharply diverged in their critical practice only raises its stakes. To reconstruct the cultural conditions producing and produced by a Renaissance text is no small feat; to reconstruct the conditions producing and produced by the critic's own text is no less demanding. Clearly the two subschools have made a choice to privilege one side of the agenda over the other, perhaps out of a recognition that both cannot be substantiated at once. Whether that assumption is correct or not, the status of the claim either makes to historical recovery is seriously undermined or, at the very least, rendered partial and provisional. Within the theoretical positions of the method itself, moreover, the choice of emphasis—past contexts or present—can be seen only as arbitrary.

II SITUATING THE CRITIC

It is into this critical situation and under the pressures of this kind of pragmatic choice that I would insert anew the situation of the contemporary critic as I experience or conceive it. In so doing, I have already restricted that situation, arbitrarily now on my part, to the current academic intellectual scene.[26] I do so not to deny competing scenes and with full acknowledgment that even this scene is a product both of filiations I choose for the most to ignore—the demands of society at large that literary studies justify themselves, the apparently widespread desire within the profession to address an audience wider than students or colleagues, even the more restricted and personal need simply to find something new to say about texts we may have grown weary of teaching over the last twenty years—and of filiations that I do not yet understand or recognize. But I would also broaden the contemporary situation beyond the New Historicist's limited focus on how we appropriate Renaissance texts, for the present scene is, in several respects, period blind.

Many critics writing today, I assume, were trained during the 1950s and 1960s under the then-dominant New Criticism, which shared a somewhat uneasy alliance with traditional historicism. We learned to appropriate that historicism where necessary as the enabling fiction or authorization for our more-or-less intrinsically formalistic readings of the otherwise isolated literary text. Increasingly, however, over the next twenty-five years the excitement of the profession shifted radically to contemporary theory—to structuralism, to deconstruction, to poststructuralism. There can be little question, I think, that the new theory called substantively into question all the "objective" relations we thought we had to the Renaissance texts we were studying. We came to understand that our connections to those texts were broadly intertextual, and the burden such knowledge brought forced us to uncover the terms by which that intertextuality could be specified and rendered concrete. History, or even histories, quickly became the privileged term of this enterprise, even though now surrounded by their concurrent characteristics of heterogeneity, contradiction, fragmentation, and *différance*. The Renaissance text became an Other before which, with which, we were forced to refigure our own situations.

A hasty and simplified summary, to be sure, but not, I think, an unfair or unfamiliar one. In my own case, there is no question that the theory I was reading was considerably more challenging than the literature and that the primary need became a revalidation of the significance of the literature by demonstrating that it was every bit as complex and unsettling as the theory. This was long before I realized that my own situation was precisely in that gap between theory and text, between the contemporary exhilaration and a literature that had all but played itself out.

Even if I have stated the predicament in somewhat negative terms, the fact remains that the Renaissance criticism that compels my attention today is that which that seeks to negotiate these gaps between present and past, theory and poetic practice.[27] And the figures, past and present, that I choose to work with are those that seem to me most able to make sense of the dimensions of those gaps. I have not given up my sense of the importance of studying Renaissance texts, but I have come to expect that if that importance is to be uncovered it will have to be in terms of contemporary theory.

The most challenging, unsettling, of the modern theorists for me have been Heidegger, Lacan, and Derrida; as a consequence, they become the context within which I want to situate my own text as well as that of Traherne. Why privilege this context over another? Why not Bakhtin, Foucault, and Jameson; or Iser, Genette, and

Fish? There is no objective answer to such a question. I choose to make my synchronic cuts where they suit the task at hand and according to the urgencies that compel my thinking and my writing. If I argue that certain questions of being, identity, desire, and supplementarity are marks of my own historical context, I do so not to deny other strands or to insist that these questions should dominate modern criticism.[28] What I do argue, however, is that these questions and the figures who have most persistently raised them *are* signifiers of my historical moment—whether or not I expose or explore their own historicity.

Let me define this orientation in slightly different terms. I said above that certain questions of being, psychic identity, desire, and the discursive economy of supplementarity are marks of my own historical context. I am also prepared to argue, on the basis of my examination of Traherne, that they are on some level marks of his historical situation. To this extent, and only to this extent, I will posit them as transhistorical. To some readers, no doubt, that argument will constitute an attempt to evade history altogether, to emancipate certain ideas from the particular necessities that may have summoned and employed them at any given historical time,[29] or to set them free within a fictive paradise of intellectual *jouissance*. This, I fear, is a reading of my own text that I must risk in order to force a broader question.

I would thus pose my own position in somewhat bolder terms: that only by a refusal to specify or concretize the historical conditions of my textual figures can I keep in question the nature and the pressures of history as such. As soon as I begin to particularize under the force of a delimited notion of history the objective contexts I can draw around such figures, I have lost the very challenge to which my own history is constantly drawing me. That challenge, as I would now perceive it, is to keep constantly in question the conditions under which any of the facts or figures I treat can be represented and experienced as historical. History does not situate—not me, not the texts I treat. History is that field from which I ask questions about my situation and strive, as best I can, to work out some form of action.

At issue, then, "is the process of recognition and even of naming with respect to various approaches to history. One important question facing us is that of the type of research that should be called intellectual history, indeed that of the type of research to be recognized as historical."[30] One has only to reread Richard Helgerson's 1986 *SEL* review, "Recent Studies in the English Renaissance," to understand the importance of this question. Helgerson's decision that some of the work he reviews is historical and that some is not seems perfectly confident; his decision that that which is not historical is of questionable critical value is even more confident. But if the "recognition and even . . . naming" of the "historical" is itself problematized, the issue is not so simple. And if there are, legitimately, "various approaches to history" or to an historical criticism, then one might at least begin to argue that a contestatory ahistorical dialogue could serve the necessary function of keeping the question of history itself open to reconsideration. I would again call upon LaCapra, appropriating his text to my own purposes by a few strategic alterations:

> the reconstruction of . . . dialogues [with] the dead [or the living] should be self-consciously combined with the interpretive attempt to enter into an exchange with them that is itself dialogical only insofar as it actively recognizes the difficulties of communication across time [no matter how long or short] and the importance of understanding as fully as possible what the other is trying to say. To the extent that the past is investigated in terms of its most particularized aspects, dialogue with it becomes minimal. But the subsequent question is whether historical research should be directed primarily to aspects of this sort, which restrict the historian's use of language to predominantly informational . . . functions.[31]

To escape these informational constraints—what LaCapra elsewhere calls the documentary recovery of a text—I have here tried to establish a dialogue that operates on at least two different levels. One level involves the participants I have called upon to speak in person across the temporal gap that separates them. There is no question of a transhistorical or ahistorical dimension to this level of the dialogue. And yet, as they are made to say the same, the four authors continually speak difference and it is precisely in the gap between difference and sameness that the crucial question of the historical as such begins to be heard. At the same time, a dialogue emerges at a different level between the *me* through whom these authors speak and those who decide to listen. LaCapra once more: we "are involved in the effort to understand what something meant in its own time and what it may mean for us today. The most engaging, if at times the most perplexing, dimensions of interpretation exist on the margins, where these two meanings are not simply disjoined from one another, for it is at this liminal point that the dialogue with the past becomes internal" to the critic and his invisible but present reader.[32] Michael McCanles makes a comparable point: "Instead of viewing the scholar's enterprise as merely the recovery and explanation of an already constituted Renaissance text, Renaissance studies should recognise that its [I would prefer *a*] central task lies in the constitution of that text through an intertextuality whereby two texts are brought together and fused: the constituted discourse of the Renaissance and the constitutive discourse of the scholar."[33] Here, I think, is where we can begin to debate which approaches to Renaissance texts are permissible and valuable to our own historical enterprise: here the critic must put his own voice and his own evaluations at risk, but here too is where he tries to join and to shape the dialogues of the future. On the margins of his own text, he tries, as best he can, to make an historical difference.

So I return to two of my initial questions: why try to imagine the kind of dialogue I invoke here and what purpose will it serve? My answers are hardly novel: to disclose purposes, structures, and pressures in the Renaissance text that we have not seen before; to make that text accessible to contemporary urgencies or issues by demonstrating how it deploys the kinds of strategies modern theory has so usefully charted; to revalidate that theory by showing the extent to which it is capable of explicating a prior text; and to make, therefore, the theory itself more accessible by compelling it to speak to a particular literary figure. At each level of such a dialogue, questions of history inevitably arise. The critical choice is whether to thematize those questions. Unlike either the old or the New historicist, I have not. That choice, I would argue, leaves open the broader discursive and nondiscursive fields within which both my own text and those of my four authors are constituted. Rather than avoiding or foreclosing historical interrogation, such openness compels it by refusing to specify any particular "objective" context. The dialogue I wish to incite initiates a clash of several competing contexts, and the filiations each can establish with the others will mark the extent to which history as such is both available to and continually evading us. If both history and the criticism that can legitimately claim to be historical are the contested fields, then it is surely a misdirection of energies to constrain ourselves to only such methodologies as appropriate "historicism" to their claims or names.

III TRAHERNE THROUGH OTHER VOICES

Having thus far foregrounded my methodological choices, let me turn for a moment to the choice of Heidegger, Lacan, and Derrida in particular. I have said already that certain questions of being, identity, desire, and economy have assumed a privileged thematic place in contemporary thought. To this extent they offer a prospect from which we can begin the task of revising and refiguring the Traherne that the old historicism has offered us. Insinuating the three moderns into the Renaissance text will allow us to see things in that text—pressures, themes, structures—to which traditional scholarship has necessarily been blind.

In the work of his final period, roughly from 1951 to 1976, Martin Heidegger grounds his continuing explorations of the nature of Being on the relationship between thinking and poetry.[34] Although Heidegger recognizes that proper thinking—and by this he means, of course, thinking that tries to move outside the normative and concealing structures of western metaphysics—and important poetizing are not identical, he remains convinced that the two were necessarily related, that Being as well as beings can be meaningfully spoken only in the Saying of poetry and thinking in dialogue with each other. Heidegger's insistence is a crucial reminder for the critic who would do justice to Traherne, for the truth is that no modern scholar has ever considered Traherne a serious or original thinker.[35] He does not, to most scholars, offer an intelligent view of the present world or of man with which we, as modern readers, must come to terms. As a poet of luxuriant, sometimes wanton, mysticism, he cannot be judged or criticized according to the coherence, the rigor, or the logic of this thought;[36] as a late redactor of traditional theological or philosophical commonplaces, he has little to add of genuine or original intellectual consequence.[37] Each of these views seems to me an indefensible consignment of Traherne to a second-class intellectuality: when he is appreciated, it is more likely for a kind of stylistic bravado than for a systematically argued idea.

To bring Traherne into dialogue with Heidegger is thus to try to reveal the thinking that validates and authorizes his poetry. Traherne does not, of course, use Heidegger's unique terminology, but his poetry is nonetheless an attempt to think Being-in-the-World. Indeed, it is striking how many of Heidegger's principal notions can be shown to structure Traherne's thought as well: the nature, being, and usefulness of things; the apartness that determines a continual absence/presence in the time/space continuum; the constitutive being of language; the gathering of appropriation by which all beings are called into Being; the Clearing in which thought allows Being to shine forth and be seen as such. Chapter two, therefore, attempts to instigate this Traherne-Heidegger dialogue by allowing some of the key issues of the philosopher to disclose significant verbal and ideational centers of the poet.

Chapter three invites Jacques Lacan to join this conversation, initially because Lacan's analysis of the *stade du miroir* opens Traherne's own treatments of childhood, of the Image and Similitude, of the reflexive Eye, and the desired/desiring Other to far more serious consequences than have yet been thought. I assume that criticism has moved well beyond viewing Traherne's emphasis on childhood as a preromantic quest for trails or traces of vanished glory, but it has not appreciated the philosophical complexity of this theme in Traherne or its particular psychological implications for his poetry.[38] Lacan, I think, offers entry into these issues, and especially entry into the thoughtful relations between the Eye and its Image, the "I" and its objects, the self and its Other. Thus, while chapter three brings additional centers of Traherne's thinking into play, it also extends the dialogue of chapter two by following the conversion of Heideggerian things into Lacanian objects and thereby raising the issue not of the thingness of beings but of the structures of desire that articulate the relations between a reflected and reflecting Eye-I and its reflecting and reflected Image-Other. These structures, moreover, will encourage a closer examination of a whole range of alienating differences which shape Traherne's own sense of human-nonhuman relations: absence/presence, word/thing, desire/object, part/whole, essence/act, lack/fulfillment.

In chapter four I have made use of Jacques Derrida's meditations on the supplement to extend the structural implications of chapters two and three. In particular, I try here to show how Traherne's imagination, continually returning to either a Heideggerian lack or a Lacanian want, must obsessively attempt to fill such abysses with "more." The supplementary more is then itself extended in order to expose Traherne's continual employment of what might be called a rhetoric of the superlative: great-greater-greatest, bright-brighter-brightest, good-better-best, and so forth. The Derridean supplement, therefore, serves as a convenient model not only for the kind of imaginative effort that must constantly fill a space—either sensible or logical—perceived as empty, but also for the imaginative rigor which recognizes that all such filling and fulfillment is grounded in a gap that can be measured only by the continual interplay of trace-structures: presence/ absence, inside/outside, body/spirit, finite/infinite, creature/Creator. Ultimately, the aim of this chapter is to define the economy of Traherne's discourse: the poetic and intellectual investments that generate all sense of worth and value. In a sense, chapters two and three establish some of the generative structures of Traherne's imaginative text—contexts in which items "mean"; chapter four shows how that meaning is produced and appropriated specifically as wealth, as a discursive coin of investment, interest, commodification, and exchange.

So again, why Heidegger, Lacan, and Derrida? The first answer to this question would see in the three moderns development of a single linguistic/philosophical line of inquiry. There can be little question today that Lacan is deeply indebted to Heidegger[39] or that Derrida is indebted to Lacan.[40] Both Lacan and Derrida, of course, offer broad critiques of Heideggerian phenomenology, and the relations between Lacan and Derrida have frequently been acrimonious. But the fact remains that Heidegger is a crucial precursor to Lacan and both are essential grounds for the work of Derrida. Part of my own task, then, is to open Traherne to this progressive and developing intertextual inquiry. The second reason for the choice of these particular authors discriminates among them in such a way as to argue that they offer both a critical vocabulary and a critical agenda for three levels on which Traherne's work might be examined or reexamined. That is to say that no study of Traherne can claim to do justice to his writings without confronting as squarely as possible the rich philosophical, psychological, and poetical questions they raise. For my purposes, Heidegger offers the most useful entry into key questions of Traherne's philosophy; Lacan provides the language and the structures with which to explore his psychology; and Derrida charts the discursive logic of his poetic.

To put Traherne, a poet squarely in the tradition of Christian logos-centricity, in relation to a series of thinkers whose express purposes include calling that very tradition into question is, if not simply odd, then at least to risk collapsing discrete, even antagonistic, philosophical endeavors.[41] I have tried to be alert to this danger and to avoid such strategies as would silence or elide historical differences. One could, for example, follow several of Heidegger's detractors in simply substituting "God" for "Sein" in his primary texts and thereby close the vocabulary gap between the twentieth and the seventeenth centuries. Similarly, one might translate Traherne's occasional distrust of man's "mortal words" into a Derridean subversion of logocentric language in general. But such rewritings would surely be unwarranted. The modern thinkers do not think as Traherne does, and he is not here posited as a specific predecessor to them. I have tried, therefore, to keep in clear and constant view this common poststructural maxim: only by allowing difference its full and alienating say can sameness be heard. If the end is a genuine dialogue between the past and the present, then the terms of either side cannot merely be rewritten into those of the other.

IV SITUATING TRAHERNE

It will be helpful at this point to focus more narrowly on Traherne himself in order to establish the prospect from which I wish to view him. At issue in this preliminary sketch are the principal filiations of what I have called Traherne's "text": the intertextual network that sketches the outlines of his imagination. To that end, we can glance briefly at three passages from different works.

> Yet the Sun is but a little spark, among all the Creatures, that are made for the Soul; the Soul, being the most High and Noble of all, is capable of far higher Perfections, far more full of Life and Vigour in its uses. The Sphere of its Activity is illimited, its Energy is endless upon all its Objects. It can exceed the Heavens in its Operations, and run out into infinite spaces. Such is the extent of Knowledge, that it seemeth to be the Light of all Eternity. All Objects are equally near to the splendor of its Beams: As innumerable millions may be conceived in its Light, with a ready capacity for millions more; so can it penetrate all Abysses, reach to the Centre of all Nature, converse with all Beings, visible and invisible, Corporeal and Spiritual, Temporal and Eternal, Created and Increated, Finite and Infinite, Substantial and Accidental, Actual and Possible, Imaginary and Real; All the Mysteries of Bliss and Misery, all the Secrets of Heaven and Hell are Objects of the Souls Capacity here. (*Christian Ethicks* [*CE*], 40)[42]

> My Naked Simple Life was I.
> That Act so Strongly Shind
> Upon the Earth, the Sea, the Skie,
> That was the Substance of My Mind.
> The Sence it self was I.
> I felt no Dross nor Matter in my Soul,
> No Brims nor Borders, such as in a Bowl
> We see, My Essence was Capacitie.
> That felt all Things,
> The Thought that Springs
> Therfrom's it self. It hath no other Wings
> To Spread abroad, nor Eys to see,
> Nor Hands Distinct to feel,
> Nor Knees to Kneel:

But being Simple like the Deitie
  In its own Centre is a Sphere
  Not shut up here, but evry Where.

  It Acts not from a Centre to
    Its Object as remote,
  But present is, when it doth view,
  Being with the Being it doth note.
    Whatever it doth do,
It doth not by another Engine work,
But by it self; which in the Act doth lurk.
Its Essence is Transformed into a true
    And perfect Act.
    And so Exact
Hath God appeard in this Mysterious Fact,
  That tis all Ey, all Act, all Sight,
    And what it pleas can be,
      Not only see,
Or do; for tis more Voluble then Light:
  Which can put on ten thousand Forms,
  Being clothd with what it self adorns.
("My Spirit," ll. 1–34)

The Heavens and the Earth serv you, not only in shewing unto you your fathers Glory, as all Things without you are your Riches and Enjoyments. But as within you also, they Magnify, and Beautify, and Illuminat your Soul. For as the Sun Beams Illuminat the Air and All Objects, yet are them selvs also Illuminated by them, so fareth it with the Powers of your Soul. The Rays of the Sun carry Light in them as they Pass through the Air, but go on in vain till they meet an Object: and there they are Expresst. They Illuminat a Mirror, and are Illuminated by it. For a looking glass without them would be in the Dark, and they without the Glass unperceived. There they revive and overtake them selvs, and represent the Effigies from whence they came; both of the Sun and Heavens and Trees and Mountains, if the Glass be seated conveniently to receiv them.

> Which were it not that the Glass were present there one would have thought even the Ideas of them absent from the Place. Even so your Soul in its Rays and Powers is unknown: and no man would believ it present evry where, were there no Objects there to be Discerned. Your Thoughts and Inclinations pass on and are unperceived. But by their Objects are discerned to be present: being illuminated by them. for they are Present with them and Activ about them. They recover and feel them selvs, and by those Objects live in Employment. Being turned into the figure and Idea of them. For as Light varieth upon all objects wither it cometh, and returneth with the Form and figure of them: so is the Soul Transformed into the Being of its Object. Like Light from the Sun, its first Effigies is Simple Life, the Pure resemblance of its Primitive Fountain but on the Object which it meeteth it is quickly changed, and by Understanding becometh All Things. (*Centuries of Meditation* [*CM*], II.78)

The principal subject of all three passages is the astonishing capacity (meaning both power and volume) of the human soul. We must take special care not to undervalue either the intellectual conception of that capacity or the wonder with which Traherne senses it, for both are distinctive features of his poetry. At the moment, however, we can focus on the conception. Traherne attempts to define the soul's capacity by means of several key relations: relations between a confined place and an infinite space, between a present moment and an eternity of presence, between a perceptual center and the sphere of its perceiving, between an interior Eye and its exterior object, between an essence and an act, between a simple origin and a complex end. These relations, furthermore, are all extensions or elaborations of a single three-part analogy: as the Sun is to the world, so the Eye is to its object, so the Deity is to the soul. Although this last relation is present only fleetingly in these three passages, it is the essential ground upon which the others are constructed. Some hint of its importance may be seen in the fact that it is easily reversible: since the Eye perceiving its object may be either divine or mortal, the object either man's soul or God himself, Deity is to the soul as the soul is to the Deity. Indeed, we might argue that this reversible relation between the soul and God is the sole object of Traherne's imagination and that it is precisely because that relation is reversible that Traherne can insist upon the infinite capacity of the soul.

From the assumption that the soul is to the Deity as Deity is to soul, it is but a short step to argue that the soul is an image of God. Such an argument, of course, is hardly surprising or novel for a Christian poet. What may be surprising, however, and even a bit disconcerting, is the extent to which Traherne insists upon a literal and optimistic coordination of the divine and the mortal. In fact, it often seems that, to Traherne, man is divine.[43] Thus, unlike most if not all of his seventeenth-century peers, Traherne seems never to be haunted by the radical otherness of God or the inescapable mortality of man. And perhaps these two lacks distance his poetry from modern readers as well. What I mean here is that most Renaissance religious poetry draws man into relation with God by proposing metaphoric correspondences. For the modern reader, it is the very awareness of those metaphors *as metaphors*—as hypotheses about the unknown and the unknowable on the basis of the presumably known—that makes the imagined relations intellectually or even emotionally credible, which is to say, plausible. But Traherne patently eschews this strategy by insisting upon a relation that is radical in its literalness: the soul is divine, not by metaphoric hypothesis, but by logical demonstration of its essence and its acts, its necessary capacity. This is not to say that Traherne's poetry is nonmetaphoric, but rather that its claims do not allow the comforting *alterite* of metaphor as such. That Traherne is himself conscious of this maneuver might be seen in the amazement with which he experiences his own thoughts and in the astonishment his poetry constantly incites in the reader confronting those thoughts. The challenge the poetry thus raises for a modern reader is to be genuinely surprised at its blatantly literal terms. It may seem especially odd to call Traherne's poetry disconcerting in this sense, for his vision of man seems more often the wishful thinking of a naive or arbitrarily simplistic idealist.[44] My contention, however, is that Traherne carefully and deliberately undermines such a judgment by both the literal logic of his arguments and the surprise he himself registers in regard to his own conclusions. That dual strategy requires that the poetry be taken in full seriousness: that it astonish us as powerfully as it seems to astonish him, and that its claims be confronted as literally as they are posed.

In the appendix to *Christian Ethicks*, Traherne argues that "Godliness is a kind of GOD-LIKENESS, a divine habit, or frame of Soul, that may fitly be accounted *the fulness of the stature of the Inward Man*" (*CE*, 285). To be "like" God, of course, is susceptible to two distinct interpretations: to be similar to God or to be equal to God, difference or sameness. Traherne is well aware that calling man the Image or Similitude of God usually results in emphasizing difference more than identity, otherness rather than sameness. His strategy is to employ the same terms in order to reverse the focus. "GOD-LIKE-NESS" names the radical oneness of the soul and the Deity, and "Image" defines the exact nature of that oneness. As our present passages suggest, that nature is grounded upon the operations of sight.

"My Spirit" opens with a significant pun: "My Naked Simple Life was I" (Eye). The pun is made explicit as the poem continues: "The Sence it self was I"; "tis all Ey . . . all Sight"; "it had a Power to see"; "O Living Orb of Sight"; "Thou which within me art, yet Me! Thou Ey." The centrality of the Eye to Traherne's imagination has often been noted,[45] but it is important to understand how his conception of the mechanics of sight directly conditions all of his major conclusions about God, the soul, and man himself. In the passage from the *Centuries*, Traherne argues that beams from the Sun pass vainly through the air unless and until they meet an object. As the Sun's light illuminates that object—lets it be seen and thus known for what it is—so the object itself illuminates the light that shines upon it—lets it be seen and known for what it is. Traherne names this reflexive illumination a mirror, the optical convergence of intra- and extramission, as well as Image or Likeness (or, as here, Effigy). The Sun is thus imagined as a metaphoric Eye, the Sun's object as the glass wherein that Eye perceives itself. In the object-mirror, furthermore, the Sun's rays both over-take (sur-prise) and ex-press themselves.

A simple substitution of God for Sun reveals part of Traherne's intention. God creates and looks upon the world—and especially man—so that He might see Himself reflected in the mirror-image that man, as image-of-God, is. Man is the object, the "apple of his Ey," not because he is of some particular nature or essence, but purely by virtue of the fact that God observes him. "What is man that thou art mindful of him," David asks in Psalm 8; Traherne answers, "the object of God's Ey." As object, man is effigy and mirror, that thing wherein God both expresses and surprises himself. As mirror or glass, man is that object which God's sight lets be seen and known, as well as the ground which lets God's sight be seen and known.

As I have already suggested, and as the passages from *Christian Ethicks* and the *Centuries* reveal, this optical relationship is exactly reversible. God is the object of man's Eye, not because man can necessarily see God, but because he requires a mirror-object in order to see himself. What he sees, in fact, is himself reflected in the sight of God. If we understand "the sight of God" as God's operation, activity, of seeing, not as the object seen, then the power and capacity of man's Eye is the precise mirror-image of God's Eye. As Eye is to object, so Deity is to soul and so soul is to Deity. The reversibility of the optical operation structures all of Traherne's most important ideas and images: center and sphere, spring and fountain, origin and end, self and other, essence and act. Traherne calls the capacity of reversibility "circulation" or "communication."[46]

It is difficult to express the radical end of Traherne's circular logic, but perhaps his conflation of perceiving and knowing will clarify it. In a discussion of knowledge and its proper objects in chapter five of *Christian Ethicks*, Traherne offers this provocative assertion: "For not to *be*, and not to *appear*, are the same thing to the understanding" (*CE*, 37). If we assume that the positive version of this negative is equally valid, God *is* only as and insofar as He appears, becomes visible or makes Himself manifest, as an object to man's Eye; man *is* only as and insofar as he appears, makes himself manifest as an object to God. What each appears to be is both Eye *and* object to the other. It is exactly this desire or concern to see and be seen, to be present with and present to the other's sight, to mirror each other's perceiving, that defines both the essence and the act of Being itself.

But man *is*, of course, not only in his relation to God but also in relation to all other things: "All Eternity," "All Nature," "All . . .

Mysteries," "all Secrets." Once again Traherne takes the most radical stance to make his point—that man is the sole object of every other thing and that every thing is capable of being an object in man's Eye. And he means *every* man, each and any individual man. Thus the astonishing, even for the seventeenth century, privilege accorded the perceiving "I." But every "I" is an Eye, and the Eye is All: center and sphere, spring and fountain, origin and end of being, instrument of seeing and the object seen. Furthermore, if the capacity of that Eye is to extend its sight to all other objects in order to see and to be seen by all other Eyes, then that essence *is* only as it *appears*, only as it makes itself *visible* in the activity of seeing. At stake here is the optical dimension of what has frequently been called Traherne's "expanded voice" or "expanded self."[47] Interestingly, Traherne's favorite figure for that expansion is fluidity: the Eye-I overflows, flows out of the center of the self and circulates amidst the sphere of its perceived/perceiving others; emits, transmits, and receives remission from the objects of its sight. As we might expect, Traherne's principal example for this circulating process is love, colloquially expressed as making the object/other "the apple of his Eye."

"There is Room enough for all Objects in the esteem of the Soul," Traherne writes in *Christian Ethicks*, and he immediately defines esteem as the middle term between seeing an object and enjoying it. The Eye sees in order to enjoy, to be delighted by, and to take delight in. Indeed, to "take in" those objects that are delightful is another principal action of the properly perceiving/understanding Eye. In the Dobell manuscript poems, Traherne names this activity "re-collecting." To recollect is to gather together the infinite variety of creation into a single "conjoyned" sphere of sight—the center of the Eye, the "end" of the "I." That center or end is the human soul, or rather, not man's soul in general, but *my* soul in particular: "all *in one fair Order* move / And joyntly by their Service End in *me*" ("The Improvment," ll. 21–22). Thus Traherne brings the meditation on metaphysical optics full circle. The Eye makes I ("My Soul my only All"), all that *is*, "Whose Power, whose Act, whose Essence was to see" ("The Preparative," ll. 11–14).

Admittedly, this hasty summary of Traherne's optics vastly oversimplifies the subtle texture of his argument, but it does suggest both the surprising twists in and the radical nature of his thinking. In the chapters to follow I will try to flesh out this sketch in order to demonstrate not only the overall coherence of Traherne's imagination, but also some of the principal threads it weaves into what I have called his intertextual network. Though only one chapter will be devoted extensively to the processes of sight, it is necessary to keep this basic model in mind at all times. Equally important to bear in mind is the larger question of how the privilege accorded the Eye and sight affects Traherne's entire imaginative effort. Previous criticism has tended simply to assume that such privileging is an inevitable consequence of Traherne's mysticism, an assumption that is certainly valid given the centrality of vision in mystical literature generally. My own interest, however, is not in accounting for Traherne's initial choice of such visionary imagery, but rather in understanding the extent to which the imaginative concentration on the essence and the act of seeing provides the structural ground upon which his philosophy, psychology, and poetry necessarily rest.

If these comments suggest the thematic scope of Traherne's text, the passages in question reveal even more about its essential urgencies. The citation from *Christian Ethicks*, for example, is generated by a telling sequence of superlatives. The soul, as the "*most* High and Noble of all," is capable of "far higher," "far more," "illimited," "endless," "infinit" perceptions. It both "exceeds" and "run[s] out," always desiring "more." At the end of the passage, that more has become an insistently repeated "all." Although we can see this rhetoric of the superlative structuring the other two passages as well, perhaps the most revealing of Traherne's works is the short poem entitled (by Margoliouth) "Insatiableness II":

> This busy, vast, enquiring Soul
> Brooks no Controul,
> No Limits will endure,
> Nor any Rest: It will all see
> Not Time alone, but ev'n Eternity.
> What is it? Endless sure.

In this opening stanza, Traherne attempts to define the soul's precise nature, and immediately collapses any distinction between essence and act. The soul is "busy, vast, enquiring"; it strives to see "all."

The paradoxical conclusion, that the soul is "Endless sure," is the product of a slippery syllogism: the soul has no perceivable limits; the soul's objects of perception are infinite; therefore the soul must itself be infinite. So far, the poem repeats the theme of the passages already cited.

Stanza two brings one of Traherne's central terms into play:

> 'Tis mean Ambition to desire
> A single World:
> To many I aspire,
> Tho one upon another hurl'd:
> Nor will they all, if they be all confin'd
> Delight my Mind.

Ambition, driven by and registered within what might be called the mechanics or force of desire, clarifies the notion of a "busy" soul. Inquire, desire, aspire: the rhymes announce in miniature a typical Trahernean progress. In the final line Traherne again seems to collapse categories as the vast soul becomes the "enquiring" mind. Significantly, now even the "all" that either soul or mind sees is not enough. The "more" that both desire is here defined as "delight."

The third stanza, then, returns to the opening definition in order to announce yet another registration of desire:

> This busy, vast, enquiring Soul
> Brooks no Controul:
> 'Tis hugely curious too.
> Each one of all those Worlds must be
> Enricht with infinit Variety
> And Worth; or 'twill not do.

We might argue at this point that Traherne initially situates the solution to the poem's principal question—the question of what exactly *is* the soul's being, "What is it?"—in the relationship between the individual soul and the world, whether that be imagined as single or multiple. In stanza one that relation focuses upon limitlessness or endlessness; in stanza two the relation is a multiplication of desires and delights; in the present stanza the concern is to generate or impute worth or value, to "Enrich" what was already an "infinit Variety." Unless the soul conceives its many objects/worlds as valuable, they (and it) "will not do." This conclusion may be more significant than at first appears, for in light of the argument of stanza one, the soul that does not *do* is the soul that *is not*. To do is to be.

The final stanza charts the economy of such doing and being:

> 'Tis nor Delight nor perfect Pleasure
> To have a Purse
> That hath a Bottom of its Treasure,
> Since I must thence endless Expense disburse.
> Sure there's a GOD (for els there's no Delight)
> One Infinit.

Divorced from the rest of Traherne's poetry, the last two lines must come as something of a shock, for nothing in the poem has led us to expect that any question about God's Being is at issue here. Within that broader context, however, the conversion of even a perfect pleasure to an enriched treasure, the endless disbursing of an always full purse, and the resolution of aspiring desire in a conflation of "infinit Variety" and "One Infinit[y]" inevitably suggest again the process of circulation binding man and God, the soul and its most proper object. Looking back over the poem as a whole, we can rechart the movement as beginning with a question about the soul's being, progressing, by stages, through the world as the soul's/mind's initial object of attention, through the motivation of that attention by desire and its deployment in an economy of riches, and ending in a revalidation of the infinity of Being. In a general sense, these stages will also mark the progress of the present study: the central questioning of being and world, the various urgencies of desire, and the economy that seeks always to generate a surplus or supplement that can be either taken in or given out as richness, wealth, and worth. At times we will see the stages compressed into the narrow, if complex, movement from pleasure to treasure or from soul to God; at others we will see them stretched broadly across the entire Trahernean text, determining its course and identifying for us its primary structural units. To this extent, then, "Insatiableness II" opens the clearest prospect on the Traherne I intend to keep in view.

V A POSTSCRIPT ON TEXTS

As a postscript to this chapter I would add a brief comment on the problem of the Trahernean "text." Since new manuscripts are still being discovered, discovered manuscripts still in the process of being published, and published ones still in a hopeless muddle of both precise order and other hands, the difficulties in determining Traherne's texts are legion. Ironically, much the same situation prevails in the case of my modern writers.[48] With Traherne, the textual complications mean that any conclusion drawn from the texts must remain somewhat provisional. That provisionality does not seem to me particularly worrisome, especially since I am not concerned with any discrete text but rather with the texture that is the imagination of Thomas Traherne. A new *Centuries* manuscript or a new Commonplace Book might force some minor adjustments in what I have to say about that imagination, but if the new work is recognizably *Traherne* then it ought, by an admittedly circular logic, to conform to the intertextual network I have here called by that name.

It is important, however, not to underemphasize this provisionality. The "Commentaries of Heaven" would remain largely unknown even if we had available now the full texts of Traherne's Commonplace Book, the Church's Year-Book, the Ficino Notebook, and the "Select Meditations." And yet we are told that the "Commentaries of Heaven" contains more poems than the Dobell and Burney sequences put together.[49] Under these conditions it would be sheer folly to claim to describe the Traherne corpus in anything approaching definitive terms.

At the same time, it is both important and provocative to remember that virtually everything we now have of Traherne's was written in the short gap between 1668 and his death in 1674.[50] Traditional scholarship has often lamented this compression because it allows hardly any adequate recovery of poetic development or progress.[51] To me, it offers a unique opportunity, for I presume that whatever subtle changes may chart the differences between the Trahernes of *Roman Forgeries*, *Christian Ethicks*, the *Centuries*, and the Dobell or Burney poems, the imagination shaping those works is, at a certain level, fundamentally unchanged and consequently retrievable as a provisional text. Thus, while I will return from time to time to make particular arguments about a given work —usually the Dobell sequence[52]—I cannot emphasize enough that it is the texture of that five-year imagination that most concerns me.

CHAPTER TWO

Traherne and Heidegger

The Questioning of Being

But it is also possible and at times even necessary that there be a conversation between thinking and poetizing, and this because both own an especially distinctive although distinct relation to language.

But there would be, and there is, the sole necessity, by thinking our way soberly into what his poetry says, to come to learn what is unspoken. That is the course of the history of Being. If we reach and enter that course, it will lead thinking into a dialogue with poetry, a dialogue that is of the history of Being. Scholars of literary history inevitably consider that dialogue to be an unscientific violation of what such scholarship takes to be the facts. Philosophers consider the dialogue to be a helpless aberration into fantasy. But destiny pursues its course untroubled by all that.

—MARTIN HEIDEGGER

I THINKING AND POETIZING

In lecture five of *What Is Called Thinking*, the published version of his 1951–52 university course, Martin Heidegger makes the rather startling claim that "every thinker thinks one thought only."[1] Two years later, in a discussion of George Trakl, Heidegger repeats this assertion with a significant variation: "Every great poet creates his poetry out of a single poetic statement only. The measure of his greatness is the extent to which he becomes so committed to that singleness that he is able to keep his poetic Saying wholly within it."[2] This convergence of thinking and poetizing signals a crucial turn in Heidegger's ongoing attempt to reconsider the nature of Being, for from this point on in his career, thinking and poetry become the two principal ways Being is spoken by and speaks to man. If, for the sake of argument, we take Heidegger's statements seriously—that is, not as simply a nostalgic wish for conceptual or poetic unity—they compel us to maintain a careful distinction between thinking and poetry at the same time that we draw both into direct relationship with that Saying which is language. It is necessary from the start, therefore, to reconstruct as best we can Heidegger's sense of these two activities and their appropriation by the language that names Being, that lets beings come to be in the flash of presence that is Being. Only in this way can we begin to understand why a great poet must also be a thinker and why his poetic thought is committed to a single Saying.

Before beginning that task, however, let us extend the context of the remarks on Trakl. Heidegger opens this essay, "Language in the Poem," by confessing that he is trying to "give thought" to "the site of [Trakl's] poetic work." The word "site," he continues, "suggests a place where everything comes together, is concentrated. The site gathers unto itself. . . . Its gathering power penetrates and pervades everything. The site, the gathering power, gathers in and preserves all it has gathered, not like an encapsulating shell but rather by penetrating with its light all it has gathered, and only thus releases it into its own nature."[3] Behind this passage lie several of the principal concerns of Heidegger's later years: the Overwhelming and the Arrival, the Gathering and Releasement, the flash by which the Concealed becomes present in Unconcealedness. Although Heidegger normally privileges the sense of hearing over that of sight, it is clear that his notion of a poetic site involves an in-sight.[4] The poetic site grants sight: it lets Being as such be seen, brings both beings and Being into the visible clearing (truth, or *aletheia*) he calls the Open. This granting is the primary function Heidegger assigns to language insofar as it gathers Being and speaks it.

Heidegger usually characterizes the gathering and speaking (naming, saying, etc.) of language as the Call and the Summons, but their relation to the poetic site and to the thinking that such a site occasions is deeply enmeshed in the interconnections between a number of Heidegger's complex terms: gathering, releasement, saying, clearing. Heidegger forestalls the most obvious misdirections such terms might give by proceeding: "The poet's statement remains unspoken. None of his individual poems, nor their totality, says it. Nonetheless, every single poem speaks from the whole of the one single statement, and each instance says that statement. From the site of the statement there arises the wave that in each instance moves his Saying as poetic saying. But that wave, far from leaving the site behind, in its rise causes all the movement of Saying to flow back to its ever more hidden source."[5] The hidden source, for Heidegger, is Being itself, revealed only in a play of difference as that which remains concealed. That interplay of concealed/unconcealed also structures the poet's saying of Being and the site of his saying. The place of gathering is not, therefore, a localized imaginative core, and especially not a key phrase or theme or mood. Nor can we say that the poet speaks from or in this site; rather, the site is a certain rhythm we sense in his attempt to bring to saying what must remain, by its very nature, unsaid.[6]

If we try to avoid Heidegger's own poetizing terms, we might argue that the site is a given poet's situation, a situating of himself in relation to language and to Being. Such a site can be discussed, Heidegger cautions, only by means of "a dialogue between thinking and poetry." That discussion, moreover, neither reports a poet's outlook on the world—or on man or on God—nor "take[s] inventory of his workshop." Instead of these two traditionally analytic modes—Heidegger elsewhere names them exposition and clarification[7]—the discussion that results from the dialogue between thinking and poetry releases us from what he calls the writing that smothers imagination into a "listening" to the summons of Being as it recalls us to the gathering site of language itself.[8]

Although Heidegger's remarks here betray both the cryptic density of his unique style and a view of poetry that seems sometimes naive at best, they do point the direction I want to take in the present discussion of Thomas Traherne. Like Heidegger, I prefer to orient that discussion by a kind of indirection. Although some "inventory" of Traherne's verbal, imagistic, and thematic workshop will be necessary, I am not trying to identify his key notions or terms. Nor will I assume that we can locate anywhere in his various texts a site of seminal (in all its senses) importance. Of more concern is the vaguer rhythm or movement of imagination that urges Traherne toward the Being he cannot quite define and that draws Being itself toward the poetry that tries to speak it.

In less oblique terms, I am assuming that Traherne's poetry has something serious to say to us. If I provisionally accept Heidegger's own term, Being, as naming that "something," I do so only because his analysis of Being provides a model for the kind of questioning—both thinking and poetizing—Traherne himself seems to engage in. In other words, I am positing a Traherne who is constantly interpreting the conditions and contexts of man's existence: what allows him to be, what grants him being, and what does the sheer fact that he exists suggest about the manner in which he should exist or about how he should comport himself in relation to every other existing thing? As Traherne puts these questions in "Thanksgiving for the Soul," "Who! how! what is thy Creature" (l. 150). To this extent, the textual site that we almost unconsciously call Traherne can be analyzed as an attempt to bring to thoughtful saying that which by its very essence and existence cannot be directly thought or said.[9]

We need not assume, of course, that all thoughtful poetry speaks of or to Being in Heidegger's sense in order to understand the intellectual challenge of his manner of questioning. Heidegger himself, we recall, openly confronted the technological explosion, which he saw as increasingly hiding from man the essence of his being and closing him off from his openness-to-Being (*Dasein*); repressive political systems, which threatened both man's concern for and caring about other beings; and a method of philosophical thinking that constantly steered human thought exactly away from the very things most necessary to be thought. Heidegger thus issued an intensely personal challenge to his own age, a call to return to and to rethink the central issues of man, language, and authentic humanity.[10]

We have not, obviously, escaped the threats Heidegger saw, and their impact on our present concerns need not be rendered in such global terms as oppressive technology, exploitive politics, or abstruse metaphysics, for we confront it everyday in our insular classrooms. And whether we openly acknowledge it or not, the challenges that we, as professors of literature, would like to issue to our audiences are not very different from his. Unless I teach Traherne solely as a literary object, an historical curiosity that my students need to know in order to pass a final exam, score well on a pending GRE, or successfully leap the hurdle of a Ph.D. comprehensive, I must assume that Traherne has something essential and important to say to them. Even if I teach Traherne as somehow vaguely necessary to my students' intellectual and moral well-being, I suspect I have not really brought them to hear what he has to say or convinced them that he is worthy of being listened to. To lecture on the notion of an Infant-Ey, an infinite God, or an endless space is not to enter into a seriously or challengingly thoughtful relation with Traherne's poetry, no matter how textually centered my lecture is. For the center of that poetry is not a text in the students' normal understanding of that term. It is rather a textual gathering of a particular saying of language, the site of a dialogue in which man questions his own being and nature's by attempting to converse with all things exterior to him. How and where, then, does the thoughtful poet I announce and present as Traherne situate himself in relation to human life in this world and to the language that allows him to think and to say what that life is, authentically and essentially? In the most general of terms, this is the question Heidegger brings me to ask. It is not, of course, the only question that could be asked of Traherne, and Heidegger's approach to it is not the only meaningful course; but if it can lead us to see in Traherne a seriousness hitherto unexamined, then we will have responded, at least in this small context, to the challenge Heidegger posed and will have listened more intently to the philosophical issues Traherne's poetry tries to speak.

Let us return, then, to Heidegger's relation between Being and beings so that we might better understand his dialogue between thinking and poetry. As Heidegger insists from his monumental *Being and Time* on, Being itself cannot be either thought or said; it can only be questioned.[11] In fact, only man can question Being and only insofar as he immediately and constantly endeavors to question Being can he himself authentically be. Man's (*Dasein*'s) distinction is as the only being (*Seiende*) who thinks, is open to, or referred to by Being (*Sein*).[12] Three terms are at issue here—human beings, being in general, and Being—and because it is only in their necessary relatedness to one another that they are at all, their very difference is what must first be thought. A step may be taken by means of Heidegger's assertion that Being is that which grounds, being that which is grounded.[13] Being, that is, is the context within which human beings must determine what it means to be. More radically, beings *are* whereas Being *is not*: "The Being of beings . . . is the fact that all . . . objects and persons *are*. Being does not identify itself with any of these beings, not even with the concept of being in general. In a certain sense, Being is not. For if Being were, it would in its turn be a being, whereas Being is, in some way, the very occurrence of existence in and of all beings."[14] Or again: "Being is not a being, because it is that which enables beings to be (present) to man and men to each other. It is nearest to man, because it makes him to be what he is and enables him to enter into comportment with other beings. Yet it is farthest removed from him because it is not a being with which he, structured as he is to deal directly with only beings, can comport himself."[15]

Being, therefore, is the systematic relation between man as one particular kind of being and every other thing that can be said to be. Being is not a "whatness" or even a "thatness," but rather the situational context of all essence/existence, the way in which anything, as what it is, takes its course and holds sway in its ongoing presence, the manner in which it endures and persists in its presencing.[16] In Heidegger's designation man is that being that is openness-to-Being, a site or dwelling in which Being can be set free and preserved in its concealing/unconcealing presence. Man is appropriated by Being insofar as he is granted existence and he appropriates Being in turn insofar as he attempts to understand that existence. Heidegger thus rewrites his early conception of man as a thrown-being, as being-there (*Da-Sein*) or being-in-the-world, to man as an hermeneutic relation between or relatedness to the "twofold" of Being's hidden presence and present beings: "Dasein has set for itself the task of giving a primordial Interpretation for its own Being and the possibilities of that Being, or indeed for the meaning of Being in general."[17] This necessary openness-to-Being Heidegger names *Dasein*'s nature as *sign*: "Drawn into what withdraws, drawing toward it and thus pointing into the withdrawal, man first *is* man. His essential nature lies in being such a pointer."[18] Man is open-to-Being in that he continually points out and points to that Being which opens itself to him even as it conceals itself from him.

The relationship between what a given thing is and the sheer fact that it is—what Heidegger calls its facticity[19]—governs much of his thinking and writing. That relationship is in turn grounded upon a twofold distinction: an ontological difference between Being and beings and the metaphysical difference between essence and existence. But even this is not quite accurate, for difference, as Heidegger uses it, implies a belonging-together or a belonging-with, so that difference itself can be thought only in its relation to sameness.[20] Indeed, it might be argued that it is only by maintaining the difference/sameness of relations *between* that Heidegger can think at all. At this methodological level, it does not matter whether he is thinking about Being and beings or some smaller subset of the ontological question. What Heidegger's characteristic manner reveals is the structural ground of a significant portion of all human thought: a model of difference/sameness which tries to interpret man's sense of belonging-together with something that is other. The urgency that motivates this model seems also characteristically human: a decisive distinction that belonging-together is susceptible to manners that can be called either authentic or inauthentic, fully human or something less than or other than human.[21]

Heidegger's distinctions between authentic and inauthentic existence are attempts to recall man from in-difference to his own potentials for being and to those beings that surround him. As mentioned above, it is precisely this reformative urgency in Heidegger that I find particularly suggestive in approaching Thomas Traherne. But in order to appropriate Heidegger for this purpose, we will need to explore a bit further a few of his central discussions. While Heidegger's constantly infolding or interfolding method of meditation will hardly countenance any rigid differentiation of themes, I have selected five topics as especially relevant to the purposes of the present chapter: the relations between equipment, thing, and the work of art; relations between the clearing, world, and the notorious fourfold; language itself as the "house of Being"; the analysis of *Dasein*'s Being as care; and the late dialogue between thinking and poetizing.

Some of Heidegger's most accessible writing concerns the relations between equipment, things, and works of art. These three may be called the modes or manners by which any entity—Heidegger's more neutral designation of the sheer fact that something exists—appears to man. The basic feature or manner of equipment is usefulness. As an entity that can be used, equipment comes into man's presence or presents itself as "readiness-to-hand": equipment is handy (with all the implications of close by, convenient, easily grasped and handled, having practical utility). As equipment is used, however, it becomes more inconspicuous; it disappears, as entity, within its own usefulness.[22] A thing, on the other hand, is an entity that is not so used up. In being "present-at-hand," the thing stands out and stands forth, presents and presences itself, as this or that thing.[23] Heidegger's favorite gloss involves the notion that the thing things: it gathers and preserves the being-alongside and belonging-together of the fourfold (earth and sky, divinities and mortals). Thing-ness is appropriating the fourfold: allowing a site for the four which brings or gathers the fourfold's stay into something that abides, dwells, for a while—into this or that thing.[24] Use of a thing, therefore, does not utilize or use up. Handling a thing that is present-at-hand, we release the thing into its essential nature and keep it there. This handling is a summoning, a presencing and safekeeping of the thingness of the thing.[25]

Heidegger's famous illustration of the distinction between equipment and thing (as well as work of art) is a pair of shoes. To a peasant woman, shoes are ready to hand as useful and reliable. As the shoes are worn, they connect her to the earth, they make her sure of her world, secure in that world. At the same time, as soon as the shoes are put on, they themselves become inconspicuous in their very usefulness. The peasant woman is no longer conscious of the presentness or the existence of the shoes, for they have disappeared, withdrawn behind, the service they provide. When confronted in a painting by Van Gogh, however, the same shoes are reclaimed into thingness. The shoes in the painting are presented and thus come to presence as a gathering site of world in a far different sense (not the peasant woman's workaday world, but the mutual belonging-together of the fourfold). Van Gogh reveals, therefore, the thingly character of the shoes, lets us experience them as thing. And insofar as the painting lets the thing thing, the painting becomes itself a work. To be a work means to set up or open a world and to keep it abidingly present. In the simplest of terms, the work sets the thing free to do its own work by clearing a site for its gathering of the fourfold. The Van Gogh painting thus discloses the shoes' relatedness to earth and sky, to the divinities that grant, to the mortal who uses. That relatedness is the worlding of world in the thinging of the thing.[26]

However misleading, or even wrong, Heidegger's treatment of Van Gogh may be, it does suggest his fundamental intentions. The central distinction between equipment and thing involves use, the manner in which a given entity is used. A hammer, as an entity, has the potential for being either equipment or thing, but the use proper to hammer-equipment is not the same as use appropriate to hammer-thing. Although Heidegger at times charges modern man with a consumptive use of all things as equipment—exploiting entities by using them up and immediately passing on to other supplementary and substituted objects—the utilization of equipment is not, in itself, a negative act. The hammer-equipment does exist in order to be used and in its use it does effect an existential relatedness between man and his world. But if man wants to understand such relatedness ontologically or to be conscious of the hammer as a thing, then equipmental use of it inevitably withdraws or conceals its thingness in utilization. Thus withdrawn from the manner of things, the hammer can no longer gather or disclose the relatedness of world or the Being of beings. To be experienced as a thing, the hammer would have to be reclaimed from its potentiality for equipment and renamed so that it can stand forth, be present at hand, once again as a thing. That reclamation is the effect of what Heidegger elsewhere calls a step-back from the use of equipment, and it is the function of the work of art and, more originally, of language itself: "Only where the word for the thing has been found is the thing a thing. Only thus *is* it. No thing *is* where the word, the name, is lacking. The word alone gives being to the thing."[27] By summoning the thing back into its being, language makes possible the working of work—the presencing, disclosing, opening of the thing and the preserving of it as a thing. Language and work open things to man, who must, insofar as he is man, be also open to both the thing as thing and the Being that lets the thing be.

The thing cannot be experienced or understood outside of world and the fourfold. Although the fourfold is the most mythologized of Heidegger's central notions, it is absolutely essential to his exposition of relatedness. Earth and sky, divinities and mortals exist as the dimensions or regions within which everything exists. They represent Heidegger's attempt to create a conceptual model of man's belonging-together with all that is. We might initially take the fourfold, then, as a methodological strategy for presenting and representing difference/sameness. The earth as earth (ground, etc.) *is* only in relation to sky as sky (horizon, etc.); mortals *are* only in relation to divinities; earth-and-sky *are* only in relation to divinities-and-mortals. The oneness of the fourfold is thus a difference/sameness of striving relatedness.

We have said that the thing things. *What* the thing things is world. And the world *worlds*: it opens a site for and gathers in the presencing of the fourfold. World is not a thing or an object, but an opening and a clearing, a flash that discloses, an appropriation. Heidegger waxes poetic in his analysis:

> Each of the four[fold] mirrors in its own way the presence of the others. Each therewith reflects itself in its own way into its

> own, within the simpleness of the four. This mirroring does not portray a likeness. The mirroring, lightening each of the four, appropriates their own presencing into simple belonging to one another. Mirroring in this appropriating-lightening way, each of the four plays to each of the others. The appropriative mirroring sets each of the four free into its own, but it binds these free ones into the simplicity of their essential being toward one another.
>
> The mirroring that binds into freedom is the play that betroths each of the four to each through the enfolding clasp of their mutual appropriation. None of the four insists on its own separate particularity. Rather, each is expropriated, within their mutual appropriation, into its own being. The expropriative appropriating is the mirror-play of the fourfold.
>
> This appropriating mirror-play of the simple onefold of the earth and sky, divinities and mortals, we call the world. The world presences by worlding.[28]

Out of this mirror-play of the worlding world the thinging of the thing takes place as the thing stays—gathers and unites—the fourfold in its worlding. The thing things world.

Although it is unfair to Heidegger's thinking to employ any simple substitution of terms, we might nonetheless suggest that the relationship between the fourfold and world itself mirrors that between beings and Being as such. As the world grants nearness and presence to each of the four in their mutual relatedness, so Being grants the coming-to-presence, the presence-at-hand, of all beings in their interrelatedness. Neither world nor Being is itself a thing, although both are the essential context that the thing things. World and Being, that is, come at and to man *in the manner* of things, beings.[29] That Heidegger here resorts to the image of a mirror is noteworthy, for the thing-as-mirror reflects, fleetingly, something that is not itself. The light, in effect, that lightens the site of the mirror but which is not itself quite seen is Being as such. Revealed as present in the withdrawal of unconcealed-concealing, the world worlds the distant advent of the coming-to-pass of Being.[30]

If we think of this lightening-appropriating mirror-play as a world-moving showing we can gain entry into Heidegger's conception of language. The essential being of language is saying as showing. Saying, to Heidegger, is offering and extending world by lighting and proffering it. As world-granting saying, language is the disclosing relatedness of all relations, opening and holding open relatedness as such.[31] Like Being and world, however, language also conceals itself in the very process of showing. Heidegger offers a convenient instance of this revealing/concealing rhythm of language in his attempt to rethink what he calls his premature assertion, in the "Letter on Humanism," that language is the House of Being.[32] A house is a building in the domain or region of dwelling: we build in order to dwell and dwell, in fact, by building. Heidegger subjects this difference/sameness of terms to one of his infamous etymologies.[33] The German *Bauen*, "building," derives from the Old English and High German *baun*, "to dwell." As the verb *bauen* becomes the noun *Bauen* the real meaning of the human activity of dwelling conceals itself behind the objectified building. We might note in passing that this is the same hiding or withdrawal that conceals the thingness of the thing behind the usefulness of equipment or the Being of beings behind the objectivity of entities. But language lets us glimpse the very thing-Being that has been concealed, brings it into unconcealedness. Thus Heidegger finds—discovers—in the German word *Nachbar* (neighbor) a "trace" of the truth still preserved. The neighbor, in Old English, is *neahgebur*: *neah*, "near," and *gebur*, "dweller." The verbs *buri*, *buren*, *beuren*, and *beuron* all signify dwelling, both place and activity. Recognizing that we can still hear the echoes of *bauen*, *buan*, *bhu*, and *beo* in the modern verb *bin* (am), to be is thus to dwell. To hear language speak in this resonating, vibrating way, saying and showing the primordial truth of Being-as-dwelling, is to dwell properly, authentically, in the house of language. But—and this is crucial—the truth that language says always withdraws, conceals itself, or falls away from man as the objectifying nature of words increasingly assumes control and dominance over the existential activities they signify. And here we might begin to understand Heidegger's apparently idiosyncratic tendency of making verbs out of nouns. The thing things and the world worlds so that thing and world might be shown/heard to do the work that pertains to their being but which our conceptions of them as objective (standing over and apart from us) facts conceals.

Or, we might say, by bidding an essence (noun) into existence (verb), language summons us into the concealed region of Being itself. Again, region carries its full weight of relatedness: as spoken by language, Being is gathered into the openness of its own persisting in relation to all that persists by it. The word of language shows the thing lingering, abiding, in its capability of being-said.[34] It *represents* the thing by granting it as a site gathering Being, as a context of involvements for man-as-being, and it *presents* the thing as a thing by opening its mirror-play within the worlding world of the fourfold. If we then take the further step of emphasizing the *work* that the word of language frees the thing to do, then we can see why the work of art (whether poetry, as in Heidegger's use of Trakl and Hölderlin, or art, as in the example of Van Gogh) assumes an increasingly prominent place in Heidegger's thinking. The work of art frees being so that it might do its ontological work of remaining open to and preserving Being as such.

It is important to distinguish Heidegger's conception of language from the normative Western traditions of either a nominalistic identity of word and thing or a positivistic separation of word from thing. Heidegger shares with much modern philosophy the desire to free language from human control. Man does not speak language as much as language speaks man.[35] Similarly, language does not "express" inner thoughts or sensations, nor does it correspond to empirical realities. Rather, language *responds* to the relations between Being and beings: it says the complex of meanings (here signifying *aletheia*, the coming-to-sight of what is, the manner in which things let themselves be seen as such) into which the matter that is named by it unfolds throughout human history. Language thus shows something as abiding in the region of man's diachrony (the history of the word "building" is the best example).[36]

Heidegger tries to defend his own conception from misunderstanding by arguing that what is spoken in language is never at any time what is said.[37] This is because language itself, as the ontological ground which allows saying to take place, withdraws or conceals itself in the very process of that saying. Language grants being, calls or summons things into their thinging, and thus gathers, as we have said, the manner in which a thing persists into relation with all that persists by it. This calling Heidegger sees as an illumination, a bringing-to-light or a being-lit that renders the thing unconcealed. But the light that makes possible this illumination is not itself a being and it remains concealed behind the thing it brings into unconcealment. To this extent, we can see that language again shares important characteristics with Being. Being, says Heidegger, "contracts into the beings it makes manifest and hides by the very fact that it reveals."[38] Precisely the same point can be made about language. At the heart of both is a mysterious concealment that is inscribed in the very process of revealing.

That mystery can be clarified by returning to Heidegger's explication of equipment. In fabricating equipment, some matter must be used: stone, for example, is the matter of the ax. But insofar as the ax itself is used as equipment, the stone-matter is used up; it disappears into, withdraws behind, the usefulness of the ax-equipment. Both stone and ax come to presence as things only when we step back. This "step-back" is the crucial hermeneutic necessity of Heidegger's late work, the requisite "apartness" that allows nearness and being-a-part-of to be seen as such.[39] To step back from equipment is thus not to stand apart from it, but to bring it to stand before us as a thing that things in the worlding of world. Similarly, to understand the revealing/concealing nature of language, we must take the same step back, a step Heidegger names thinking/poetizing. Thought and poetry bring the concealedness of language into unconcealedness, into the gathering clearing where it can be glimpsed in its difference.

Thinking is attending on, being attentive to, Being. In Heidegger's system, thinking is always to be distinguished from inauthentic or improper thinking—the Cartesian split between subject and object in which what is thought is what is seen as either totally outside and other than the self or totally within and identical to the self. Such thinking Heidegger calls the calculating, accumulating, representing consumption of the Western system of subjective/objective dualism.[40] Such thinking thinks ideas, sensations, intentions, motives; it represents an extension of man's prideful will to power and overpower. And it neglects completely the Being of beings, is injuriously indifferent to both Being and beings. Such thinking is always blind to the elementary fact that Being and beings *need* man, for he is the only being that *can* think. And what man must think is the presence-at-hand of Being, how beings need him to lend his hand. Thinking is thus handcraft, proffering a care-taking hand to Being. Like language, authentic thinking frees Being from concealedness, bids it come into the openness or the clearing of unconcealedness. It is, in brief, a way of corresponding through which everything that is comes to stand in enlightened relation to everything else that is.

In order to clarify the handcraft of thinking and to prepare for its necessary correlation to poetizing, it will be helpful to follow a short detour through Heidegger's scattered notions of care. Although care is given a sustained interpretation only in *Being and Time*, Heidegger returns again and again to various implications of his claim there that "Dasein's Being reveals itself as care."[41] An initial sketch of the range of these implications can be drawn merely by noting the cognate terms Heidegger employs. Concern (*Besorgen*) and solicitude (*Fursorge*) are the most obvious because of their etymological link to care (*Sorge*); others are resoluteness, safekeeping, preserving, sparing, saving, and holding. Of these, perhaps, only holding is not transparently suggestive. When Heidegger argues, in *Poetry, Language, and Thought*, that Van Gogh's painting lets truth happen or sets truth free to work, he means that the revelation of the being of shoes is "brought into unconcealedness and held therein." And he immediately adds this observation: "To hold (*halten*) originally means to tend, keep, take care (*huten*)."[42] Behind all of Heidegger's correlative terms for caring lies the nostalgic notion of man as "the shepherd of Being": attending upon and tending Being's coming-to-presence in beings, man guards and keeps safe those essential sites (things, works, even words) in which Being can be seen to appear. Such shepherding of Being Heidegger calls authentic thinking.[43]

As developed in *Being and Time*, however, care is less nostalgic than structural. Being-in-the-world is characterized by concern and by a fascination for that world with which it is concerned. *Dasein*, that is, observes, concernfully, what is present at hand, looks explicitly at it, sets its sights toward and upon it, addresses itself to it. Concern, therefore, as care, is Being-*toward*. The entities or things toward which man turns are the objects of his solicitude. Solicitude, again as care, is Being-*with*. Both terms, or rather the two terms in relation to one another, attempt to describe what Heidegger calls

Dasein's facticity or thrownness. As Being-in-the-world, care "articulates the contexts of [*Dasein*'s] involvements" with all that is other. "Circumspective concern . . . that concern in which we tarry and look at something, uncovers entities within-the-world" and discloses our Being as "alongside" such entities and "already-in" such world.[44] Consequently, Heidegger argues, "if one were to construct the expression 'care for oneself,' . . . this would be a tautology. 'Care' cannot stand for some special attitude toward the Self."[45] Care, instead, is the structural formula for Being-already-in (a world) as Being-alongside (entities encountered within-the-world).

If this is the existential condition of man, then *Dasein*'s authentic dwelling-with both itself and others can be characterized as resoluteness: "Resoluteness, as *authentic Being-one's-Self*, does not detach Dasein from its world, nor does it isolate it so that it becomes a free-floating 'I'. And how should it, when resoluteness as authentic disclosedness, is *authentically* nothing else than *Being-in-the-world*? Resoluteness brings the Self right into its current concernful Being-alongside what is . . . and pushes it into solicitous Being with others."[46] Or again, "Dasein's resoluteness towards itself"—that is, its determination to act upon its "ownmost-potentialities-for-Being" *in*, *for*, *of*, and *with* world—"is what first makes it possible to let the Others who are with it 'be' in their ownmost potentiality-for-Being, and to co-disclose this potentiality in the solicitude which leaps forth and liberates."[47] Behind such statements we may already hear the intimations of care-ful shepherding: to free and preserve, to guard and keep safe that Being which needs both man and those things that are other than man. And it is because of that need, expressed in the phrase "potentiality-for-Being," that Heidegger is led to connect care with conscience, guilt, and anxiety. Conscience, as the "Call of Care," calls *Dasein* into consciousness: into a Being-guilty over and a Being-anxious about the fact that its ownmost potentiality for Being is always projected ahead of itself. Although Heidegger's full analysis of these two conditions is extremely complicated and not particularly relevant either to our concerns here or to his own subsequent developments of the notion of care, one aspect of his argument might be mentioned in passing, for it offers another perspective on the continuing problem of authentic versus inauthentic existence.

"Dasein's Being is care. It comprises in itself facticity [thrownness or Being-there], existence [projection or Being-ahead-of-itself], and falling."[48] Falling is Heidegger's designation of that kind or manner of being which belongs to everydayness: *Dasein* has fallen away from its concernful being-alongside the world and thus from its potential for Being. It loses itself in publicness, theyness, and idle talk. In effect, man becomes secure (*sine cura*, without care) when he submerges and conceals himself in the self-certainty and decidedness of the "they." In such a condition, or under such a way of being, man is lulled into accepting what "they" agree thinking is and what "they" say truth is. This condition is the danger from which being must be carefully guarded, protected, and freed, and it is what the later Heidegger has in mind when he defines the dialogue between thinking and poetizing as lending a care-taking hand to both man and Being.

With that, we may return to the principal terms by which Heidegger II, as Richardson calls him, tries to describe authentic, care-taking thinking. "If we think of the thing as thing, then we spare and protect the thing's presence in the region from which it presences."[49] Improper or inauthentic thinking refuses to respect the thing's being, refuses to acknowledge that that being needs to be cared for. In consequence, the thing's being is lost. In order to retrieve it, Heidegger argues, man himself must be reclaimed from the kind of public thinking that so thoughtlessly and indifferently neglects being. Heidegger calls, therefore, for a "conversion of consciousness" in which the immanence of things will be preserved in "the true interior of the heart's space."[50] To let the thing dwell in the innermost region of the heart, to provide a site in which to preserve and protect it as a thing, is to free both thing and man for authentic Being-with. "In saving the earth, in receiving the sky, in awaiting the divinities, in initiating mortals, dwelling occurs as the fourfold preservation of the fourfold. To spare and preserve means: to take under our care, to look after the fourfold in its presencing."[51] Such dwelling, sparing, preserving, and guarding are, moreover, not only the measures of man's moral obligation to Being, but are also the care-taking characteristics of genuine thinking. To think authentically, as we are capable of thinking, is to gather and preserve all that concerns us, all that we care for, and to grant Being to all that grants Being to us.

Thinking, consequently, is also a thanking; in authentic thinking, man thanks.[52] According to Richardson's analysis, thought (*Gedanc*) suggests not only *Denken* (to think), but also *Gedachtnis* (memory) and *Danken* (to thank). Memory, as re-collection, gathers together Being-thought-as-thanks and holds or preserves it caringly within the inmost center of man's being (the heart, *cor*, or *cordis*, as the clearing site of *re-cord*). In re-collecting the fleeting and scattered appearances of Being, thinking frees man from closure and isolation, from alienation and apartness, and draws him into the belonging-together that is authentic dwelling. To Heidegger, this means that Being's supreme gift to man is the very fact that it grants him thought. Man's acknowledgment of that fact is not so much a requiting of one grant with another as simply accepting the gift—assuming it, acquiescing in it, yielding to its demands. Acceptance, then, as thought itself, is the most original form of thanks and thanks-giving.[53]

Thinking, furthermore, reveals that man is a privileged listener to language and Being, that his relationship to both is responsibility, answer-ability, custodianship. It might be argued that it is precisely this notion of man as listener and respondent to the language of Being and the Being of language that leads Heidegger to draw thinking and poetizing into essential relatedness. Because thinking is thanking, it is also the gathering of saying into song.[54] Although thinking is never the same as poetizing, neither can it be separated from poetizing. The two belong together by virtue of that saying which has already responded to what is unspoken because it is thought as a thanks.[55]

As much as Heidegger speaks about poetizing in his later writing, it is clear that he never developed any comprehensive theory of poetry. To this extent, his thoughts on poetizing, like those on language or on thinking itself, must be characterized as "on the way toward."[56] What we can say is that Heidegger always begins by defining *poesis* as a bringing forth into presence. He relates it to the Greek *techne*, not in the sense of art or skill, but as *aletheia*, an "opening-up-as-a-revealing."[57] What poetry reveals is the unconcealedness of beings and Being as such. It bids all that is—world and things, earth and sky, divinities and mortals—to come, gathering, into the simple onefold of their intimate belonging-together.

He calls poetry, therefore, the topology of Being, showing man by saying the whereabouts of its actual presence.[58] To this extent, of course, poetizing is the same as thinking or language; all three grant being and Being. In the following statement, therefore, we could easily exchange the opening word with either thought or language: poetizing is a saying which, in preparing the sayable (being), simultaneously brings the unsayable as such (Being) into the world. But when Heidegger concludes that poetizing is a consecration, he has added a significant difference: poetry is "a consecration and a refuge in which the real [Being] bestows its long-hidden splendor upon man ever anew, that in such light he may see more purely and hear more clearly what addresses itself to his essence."[59]

Exactly what Heidegger's addition here means is not very clear. If "to consecrate" is taken to point toward a making or declaring sacred or holy, then poetizing might be interpreted as the originating grant of Being: the poet proffers Being to the thinker, who then devotes himself to such thanks as are due that gift. If "to consecrate" is taken as a veneration or a hallowing, then the poet points the thinker in his appropriate or authentic direction. What Heidegger seems to imply in either case is that poetry enacts and bespeaks a continual wonder at the mere fact of Being; it is the voice of surprise.

Although Heidegger insists again and again that "what is said poetically and what is said thoughtfully are never the same," he simultaneously asserts that "the one and the other say the same thing in different ways."[60] His attempts to clarify this difference/sameness are hardly revealing:

> What about the neighborhood of poetry and thinking? We stand confused between two wholly different kinds of saying. In the poet's song, the word appears as the mysterious wonder. Our thinking reflection of the relation between the "is" and the word that is no thing is faced with something memorable whose features fade into indefiniteness. In the song, wonder appears in a fulfilled, singing saying; in our reflection something memorable appears in a scarcely definable—but certainly not a singing—saying. How can this be a neighborhood, under which poetry and thinking live in close nearness? It would seem that the two diverge just as far as can be.[61]

Wonder, here, is "mysterious," but because it can be felt in the vibrating, resonating, echoing saying of language, it is heard as a harmony, a singing. What is memorable, capable of being recalled and remarked, is something indefinable. The difference, it seems, between poetizing and thinking lies not in the matter but in the manner of their sayings. What both seem to say is the same. If we recall that truth happens in the manner of a primordial relation between a clearing and a concealing, then the "neighborhood" (the near-dwelling and belonging-together) of poetizing and thinking is a necessary consequence of the way man is called to respond to language. To poetize is to bring that response thoughtfully to light, but in a way which is a wonder and a consecration, because what is brought is also guardedly, caringly, hidden.

Frank Lentricchia, speaking in the wake of a deconstruction already enacted by Lukacs, Marcuse, and Derrida, views Heidegger's enterprise as an archromantic mythology of unity and wholeness and thus not faithful or answerable to man's essential historicity.[62] If the measure of a thinker's importance is the extent to which he grounds us in the complex circumstances of our own historical moments, then Lentricchia's assessment may well be correct. But this does not seem to me the only level of inquiry upon which a given thinker might be engaged. To this extent, George Steiner's approach to Heidegger seems to me more fruitful, for it focuses on the Heidegger who poses necessary questions about the relations between Being and being. These are not the only questions, to be sure, but they are inescapable. In fact, at least one earlier poet has already asked them:

> Hast thou ever raised thy mind to the consideration of Existence, in and by itself, as the mere act of existing? Hast thou ever said to thyself, thoughtfully, IT IS! heedless in that moment, whether it were a man before thee, or a flower, or a grain of sand? Without reference, in short, to this or that particular mode or form of existence? If thou hast attained to this, thou wilt have felt the presence of a mystery, which must have fixed thy spirit in awe and wonder. The very words, There is nothing! or, There was a time, when there was nothing! are self-contradictory. There is that within us which repels the

> proposition with as full and instantaneous a light, as if it bore evidence against the fact in the right of its own eternity.[63]

Traherne, I believe, shares both the question of what existence is and the wonder at the fact that it is. By considering him in relation to Heidegger, it can be shown that he does not raise that question in any thoughtless way and that his wonder is very far from a purely idealistic mythologizing of man's condition.

II IN-DWELLING AND BEING

At the conclusion of the First Century of Meditations, Traherne ponders the "infinite Mystery" of the deity's dwelling in the human heart:

> An Object Seen, is in the Faculty seeing it, and by that in the Soul of the Seer, after the Best of Maners. Wheras there are eight maners of In-being, the In-being of an Object in a Faculty is the Best of all. Dead things are in a Room containing them in a vain maner; unless they are Objectivly in the Soul of a Seer. The Pleasure of an Enjoyer, is the very End why Things placed are in any Place. The Place and the Thing Placed in it, being both in the Understanding of a Spectator of them. Things Dead in Dead Place Effect nothing. . . . Since therfore all other ways of In-being would be utterly vain, were it not for this: And the Kingdom of God . . . is within you; let us ever think and Meditat on Him, that His conception, Nativity Life and Death may be always within us. Let Heaven and Earth Men and Angels, God and his Creatures be always within us. that is in our Sight, in our Sence, in our Lov and Esteem. (*CM*, I.100)

The initial difficulty with this crucial passage concerns the exact meaning of the poet's "eight maners of In-being." In the first printing of his edition, Margoliouth confesses simply that "This has defeated me"; in the 1965 reprint, he suggests an analogue in Aristotle's *Physics* IV.iii. In this chapter, Aristotle examines "the different senses in which one thing is said to be 'in' another":

1. the part is in the whole
2. the whole is in the part
3. the species is in the genus
4. the genus is in the species
5. the form is in the matter
6. the initiative is in the agent
7. the motive is in the perceived end
8. the thing is in a place.[64]

Although I agree in general with Douglas Jordan's interpretation of Traherne's eight manners as things either being "in" the three faculties (memory, understanding, and will), or "taken in" by one of five senses, Jordan is overhasty in dismissing Margoliouth's suggestion ("I fail to see how this has anything to do with Traherne's statement").[65] In fact, it could be argued that it is precisely Traherne's doubled concern with both "in" and "being" that assures the relevance of Aristotle's eight senses. And in that context it is helpful to note that Aristotle concludes his examination in this chapter by asking "whether a thing can be in itself or whether it must always be in something other than itself." His answer, that nothing could be without being in something else, is, as I hope to show, a position with which Traherne would have agreed entirely. To this extent, it seems to me extremely important to keep Aristotle's discussions of both "in" and "being" in mind as we read Traherne's various comments on either In-being or In-dwelling.

The passage I have just cited is Traherne's most extensive one on either In-being or In-dwelling, but it will be helpful to set it in the context of a few of his other statements. Four occur in *Meditations on the Six Days of Creation*:

> Thou, O my God, art the Temple of my Soul, and yet the Soul is the Temple of thee, my God; for we live in thee and thou in us. (p. 76)

> For the Truth is, by his entring in, he breathed in the Soul, that is, by manifesting himself within the Body; for by the in-dwelling of his Omnipresence do we conceive [sic: perceive?] him. Hence comes it to pass, that all Ages and Kingdoms,

> Heaven and Earth, Time and Eternity . . . are . . . in the Soul of Man. (pp. 80–81)
>
> Consider, in the Soul of Man, the divine Image, by these three Faculties, Understanding, Will, and Memory, which in the Soul are one, having thus an Impress of the Trinity within it. (p. 83)
>
> My Soul being like a noble Centre of thy divine Omnipresence, because it's filled with it, and indivisible, because wholly in the whole, and wholly in every part, as thou art. (p. 87)

The third of these citations supports Jordan's interpretation, but the other three obviously point toward the broader concerns of Aristotle. The second even draws upon Aristotle's subsequent "complication" of the ambiguities of "in" by subjecting the word to the continuums of time and space. And the fourth is clearly based upon the Aristotelian arguments over the relations between parts and wholes or between one cause and another. In the *Centuries* and *Christian Ethicks*, Traherne reiterates these positions:

> These Things [the blessedness of every creature and the services of the world] shall never be seen with your Bodily Eys, but in a more perfect maner. You shall be present with them in your Understanding. You shall be In them to the very centre and they in you . . . so shall you be with every Part and Excellency of them . . . (*CM*, II.76)
>
> A Perfect Indwelling of the Soul in GOD, and GOD in the Soul. So that as the fulness of the GODHEAD dwelleth in our Savior, it shall dwell in us; and the Church shall be the fulness of Him that filleth all in all. (*CM*, IV.100)
>
> For by the Indwelling of GOD all Objects are infused, and contained within. (*CE*, 73)

It is perfectly possible, of course, to read these passages in terms of a strictly metaphoric or figurative sense of in-being: creatures or objects are perceived by either the senses or the faculties and to that extent may be said to be "in." To do so, however, is to weaken the radical literalness of Traherne's assertions. By keeping the Aristotelian coordinates of *in* and *being* in mind, we enrich the resonance of Traherne's thought.

The importance of that resonance can be felt in a poem like "An Hymne upon St Bartholomew's Day." Here Traherne begins with the fairly innocuous assertion that "What Powerfull Spirit livs within!" The remainder of the poem is an extended play on various dimensions of that in-ness. The simple repetition of "In" (five times in thirty-five lines) and "Within" (seven times in thirty-five lines) suggests that Traherne is exploring something more than mere sensible perception, and this sense is heightened by the compounds Traherne accumulates within the same lines: in-habit, in-spires, In-ward, In-cludes, and In-ward again. The same conclusion can be drawn from the "Thanksgivings for God's Attributes." Traherne initially praises God for "Being infinitely present in every place . . . exquisitely so, and wholly there" (l. 105). As the poem continues, Traherne exposes again the various ways of In-being:

> Most really, O Lord, are [all beings] all within me,
> because thou art really dwelling there.
> Even thou my SUN, who with all thy Kingdom are dwelling there.
> Thou in me, and they in thee, for evermore.
> (ll. 133–37)

> In whom we live, and move, and have our Being.
> (l. 83)[66]

It is difficult to believe that Traherne means this In-dwelling in any strictly sensual or intellectual sense. "Most really," I would suggest, means exactly that. And it is precisely because he wants us to understand In-being in the broadest and most radical sense that Traherne can conclude: "all thine Eternity *after a manner incomprehensible*, / dwelleth within" (ll. 186–87; my italics).

Whatever interpretation we finally accept for Traherne's "eight maners of In-being,"[67] the manner he calls "best" is clear enough: proper In-being is to be an object, a thing, "actually present" in the faculties of another being. Being *is* insofar as being is *in*. Being is that which can "objectivly" be seen; in order to be seen as an object, being must be, appear, as a presence situated *in* some site. Let us, for the moment, simply bracket the exact identity of that site by observing that Traherne here calls it by several different names: soul, place, understanding, room, you, and us. By whatever name, the site proffers an in-sight: objective being is seen as present within a seer. The site, then, gathers both the presence of In-being and the seer's response, for being-in is Being enjoyed. In-being so enjoyed is Being esteemed. And esteem, as the final staging of site/sight, brings into unconcealment Traherne's version of the fourfold: heaven and earth, divinities and mortals.

These last two effects should be clarified. If we attend to the unsaid in Traherne's meditation, it seems to draw a careful distinction between enjoyment (to take pleasure in the simple presence of being) and esteem (to love and value being as a gift that has been granted). As we will learn from other contexts, this distinction is actually a necessary progress: the pleasure that a sight of being effects in a seer leads to the understanding that something or someone has "placed" that being in and before the faculties, and that, in turn, results in the seer's esteeming both the gift and the giver. We should also notice that the site and sight of the fourfold occurs only as we "ever think" on that Being that is within. In-being, therefore, can be identified as the thoughtful issue of the passage: how Being is present to and in beings; how beings are present to and in Being. And the terms by which this issue can be thought include Being's capacity to see and be seen as an object; its capacity to effect joy, thought, and esteem; and its capacity to be either a live thing in a sensible place or a dead thing in a dead place. This last potentiality, of course, also hints at far broader implications, for it supposes that even a live *In*-Being might be destroyed if the seer did not, or chose not to, see it. Within the horizon of that possibility, it is perhaps not accidental that the only two injunctions within the meditation are: let us ever think and let all that is be always *within* us. As we shall see, this connection is crucial to Traherne, for only what is within can become an object of thought and only that which is thought can be authentically within.

As we might expect, Traherne's meditations on In-being are grounded upon the apparently unquestioned and unquestionable fact that God is. *What* God is should therefore be the first logical question, although even that would seem to be contravened by

Being's own answer: I am that I am (Exodus 3:14). Not content, though, with that answer or even with the sheer facticity of God, Traherne tries to rethink both His essence and His existence. The Third Century states the ground of God-Being most precisely: "GOD is. For GOD is not a Being compounded of Body and Soul, or Substance and Accident, or Power or Act but is All Act, Pure Act, a Simple Being. Whose Essence is to be, Whose Being is to be Perfect, so that He is most Perfect towards all and in all. He is most Perfect for all and by all" (*CM*, III.63).[68] The divine Being is here offered as the measure of all being, not only in the whatness of its substance or essence, but also in the manner of its existence. And we might listen particularly to what Traherne's poetizing language tries to say by means of Being's prepositional relations. God's Being is *toward* beings (facing them, in an inclining regard or concern), *in* beings (amidst and within, engaged and situated inside them), *for* beings (for the purpose or use of them), and *by* beings (near or beside them, alongside them, by means of, on the authority of, or according to them). If we think of such prepositions as "placing before," they say both the whereabouts of Being and the manner in which Being dwells where it is. In-being-ness, then, how Being comes to be and to be seen in its pre-positional relatedness to being, might now be marked as a central concern of Traherne's text. "O What shall we be," he asks in the Second Century (*CM*, II.52), and that question ought properly to assume that if Being is *in*, so too is being. That Traherne does assume this inversion can be seen in a following Century, where he refers to the "Perfect Indwelling of the Soul in GOD, and GOD in the Soul" (*CM*, IV.100). What shall we be, therefore, means what shall we be in: where, in short, is the "whereabouts" of man's being? Whatever Traherne's answer, we can also assume that it will be developed in terms of the prior question of what/where we can be by virtue of the fact that and where God is. The poetic task, in consequence, can be redefined as the proper saying/situating of the belonging-together of Being (God) and beings (man).[69] And this means that Traherne, no less than Heidegger, must be committed to thinking both difference as difference and difference as sameness.[70]

When viewed from our privileged temporal distance, or heard within our accustomed frames of Christian reference, little that

Traherne says about the nature of God's Being is surprising. God is perfect, simple, undifferentiated. As such a being, however, God could not be thought, so Traherne must turn his attention toward the manners of God's being: to how Being is dependent upon its appearing—"He willed the Creation not only that He might Appear but be" (*CM*, I.53); "For not to *be*, and not to *appear*, are the same thing" (*CE*, 37)—to how Being must be present *in* in order to appear—"But present is, when it doth view / Being with the Being it doth note" ("My Spirit," ll. 20–21)—to how Being must regard being in order to be seen by or in being—"An Object seen, is in the Faculty Seeing it, and by that in the Soul of the Seer" (*CM*, I.100)—and to how Being needs beings in order to be at all —"[God is] despised and defied / Undeified almost if once denied" ("The Recovery," ll. 19–20). So consistent is Traherne in thinking such relations that God's essence becomes his existence: "IN GOD, to *Act* and to *Be*, are the same Thing. Upon the suspension of his act, his Essence would be gone. . . .And if his Act existeth, by Acting, his Righteousness is, and existeth of it self, and by itself compleateth its Essence forever" (*CE*, 76). God is, therefore, so that and because He may be in a certain way. The *way* or *ways* of Being, then, become the primary object of Traherne's thought.[71]

Assuming that, we may legitimately ask what are the definable ways of Being? Since Traherne never clarifies his notion of the "eight maners," we are left with the conception of In-Being-ness itself and the ways in which that condition is open to, or a potentiality for, both Being and beings, God and man. From a Heideggerian vantage, however, the very idea of Being-*in*-beings or beings-*in*-Being is a provocative instance of the reflective, echoing power of language itself to say originary truths, for that "in" functions principally as a mirror-image between the two beings. It brings them, so to speak, face to face in the site of their mutual appearing and proffers each to the other as its own image. Traherne's most startling illustration of this appropriation of Being by its image is his announcement that "I am what I am" (*CM*, I.67). Such linguistic mirroring, of course, however surprising in its boldness, merely says the "public" truth that man is the image of God. But insofar as that boldness seizes, with radical literalness, upon the implications of the language, we ought to be alert to its capacity to say more concealed truths, such as that God *is* only in the image of and the imaginings of man. By rethinking such implications of In-Being-ness, then, Traherne is able to re-present the question of Being as the necessary subject of man's thoughtful concern, of his surprise and his wonder.

The initial task of this portion of our chapter, therefore, is to provide a sketch of Traherne's sustained analysis of In-Being-ness. And while it is as difficult in Traherne as it is in Heidegger to keep the argumentative lines completely separate, I would suggest there are at least three different issues that structure this analysis. The first is Being-in-love, which seems to be the ground and origin of all In-Being. The second is Being-in-the-world, or the problem of how Being-in discloses world as the region of all existence. And the third is Being-in-things, how Being appears in or can be gathered by entities within that world. At stake in all three issues is a definition of God's In-Being-ness that will reveal the relation between His manners of Being-in and those of man himself. Once these manners are clarified, we can then approach the subsequent question of Traherne's notion of care as the nature of Being.

God is Love, Traherne states in *Christian Ethicks*, voicing a platitude so unquestionable that it scarcely can be thought. And yet Traherne tries very hard to think it, for his business, as he claims in each of his major works, is to make visible those truths which we know but have forgotten.[72] We have forgotten them because our entanglement in man's words, in the exploitive and self-serving ways man uses words, have rendered inaudible the originary saying of language itself. Much of Traherne's effort, then, is directed toward clearing language from "the Errors and the Wrongs / That *Mortal Words* convey," a clearing he frequently figures as unmetaphorizing in order to disclose "transparent Words."[73] Obviously, this does not mean never using metaphors; rather, it means that we must listen to what language itself says in the work (Heidegger's truth or *aletheia*) it sets words to do. "Love" is one such working word:

> [God] Loves, that he may Love, and begets that Love which is his Essence. . . . IT is GOD alone that Loves by his Essence, Angels and Men may Love by Inclination, but their Affection is Accidental to their nature, begins in time, may alter or cease. . . . In this it differs from the Love of God, but in many

> things there is a great Agreement and proportion between them. For GOD has made the love of Angels and men so like his own, by extending their Knowledge to all objects, that infinite Perfections are contained in their love. It is as GODLIKE as any Thing created is capable of being. (*CE*, 47)

Thus inscribed in difference, the relatedness of divine and human love says the sameness in which being belongs to, is open to and referred to by, Being as such. As a saying of language, love itself speaks this relatedness as Essence-and-Act, Self-and-Object, Origin-and-End in Godlike conjunction. Traherne continues his meditation on the word:

> For the better understanding of this Love, we will consider it in the power of Loving, in the inclination to Love, in its act and Perfection. It may seem a surprizing verity; but the Power of Loving is as necessary to Blessedness and Glory as life it selfe; an inclination to love as necessary as the Power; and the act of Love as necessary as the Inclination. The world is useless without Life, and Life without Love, the Body without the Soul, the Soul without the Power of Loving, the Power of Loving without the Inclination, the Inclination without the Act. (*CE*, 47)

Power, inclination, and act: a nominal essence, an infinitive desire, a verbal deed. The very conjugations of language say the relations Traherne wants us to hear: love is to love in loving and being loved.[74] The manner by which language says these conjugations, the originary logic and certitude of its grammatical relations, sings thoughtfully and astonishingly the gathering of Being and beings. God is love so that He may love, begets love that He may be what He is, is loving in order that He may be loved. These consequences, furthermore, are "necessary" insofar as existence is at all. Once the thought of necessity is brought to bear upon existence as such, it gives rise to the topic of world. Love, then, may be called, in Heideggerian fashion, a world-moving word: it summons Being and beings into the unconcealed presence of one another and thereby sets up and discloses the worlding of world as the relation of all relations (here life and love, body and soul, power and act).

It cannot be emphasized too much that Traherne is especially committed to hearing what conceals itself as unsaid in language. If it is fair to argue that the so-called metaphysical poets as a group are more attentive to and more committed to exploring this hidden side of language than the cavaliers, it is also fair to say that among them Traherne is the most attentive to what the "Naked" word itself may say. Many of the issues all critics have had to confront (or, more frequently, to explain away) in Traherne's poetry—reiterated rhyme schemes, literal repetitions and redundancies, paratactic lists and catalogues—involve his language. Paradoxically, however, criticism has never made that language the serious matter of Traherne's thought. More often than not, in fact, criticism has come to precisely the opposite conclusion: Traherne uses his own words thoughtlessly.[75] I do not think such a judgment will stand close scrutiny. Traherne's language is constantly exploring its own capacities to say the grounding truths of human existence and relatedness. Only by listening carefully to that language can we begin to hear the poet I have called "thoughtful" think at all. Merely to follow a few more of his grammatical and syntactical explorations of a word like "love" should be sufficient to dispel the notion that he writes "ecstatically," somehow beyond or outside the normative demands of a precise language.

In the First Century, we find this meditation on God-as-love:

> He was infinit LOV, and being Lovly in being so, Would prepare for Himself a Most Lovly Object. Having Studied from all Eternity, He saw, none more Lovly then the Image of His Lov, His own Similitude. . . . I see that I am infinitly Beloved. . . . GOD is LOV, and my Soul is Lovely! God is Loving, and His Image Amiable. O my Soul these are the Foundations of an Eternal Friendship between GOD and Thee. He is infinitly Prone to Lov, and Thou art Like Him. He is infinitly Lovly and Thou art Like Him. What can more Agree then that which is infinitly Lovly, and that which is infinitly Prone to lov! Where both are so Lovly, and so Prone to lov. (*CM*, I.67)

As the former passage displays love in its verbal conjugations (love, to love, loving), this one unfolds its adjectival consequences (love, lovely, beloved). If we hear in the meditation the answer of being to the summons God's infinite love issues, then the single word Be-loved describes the effect of In-Beingness itself: in love, both Being and beings become Be-loved. As Traherne will argue elsewhere, "All [being] is Love variously modified, according to the Circumstances wherein the Object is represented" (*CE*, 44). By playing out and playing with the various grammatical forms of "love," Traherne tries to reveal those modifications.

> For GOD is Lov. And by loving He begot His Lov. He is of Him self, and by Loving He is what He is *Infinit Lov*. GOD is not a Mixt and Compounded Being, so that His Lov is one thing and Himself another: but the most Pure and Simple of all Beings, All Act, and Pure Lov in the Abstract. (*CM*, II.39)

> In all Lov there is a Lov begetting, a Lov begotten, and a Lov Proceeding. Which tho they are one in Essence, subsist Nevertheless in Three Several Maners. (*CM*, II.40)[76]

> In all Lov there is some Producer, som Means, and som End: all these being Internal in the Thing it self. (*CM*, II.46)

> God is present by Lov alone. . . . By Lov alone He liveth and feeleth in other Persons. (*CM*, II.50)

> We are made to lov: both to satisfy the Necessity of our Activ Nature, and to answer the Beauties [i.e., the love-liness] in evry Creature. By Lov our souls are married and sodderd to the creatures. (*CM*, II.66)

Being-love, Being-lovely, Being-loved: these are the principal manners of Being-in-love, of In-Being-ness itself. Traherne attempts again and again to spell out these manners and to bring love itself into the open; but he discovers that, like Being, love always keeps itself somewhat concealed: "It seems that all Lov is so Mysterious, that there is somthing in it which needs Expression, and can never be understood by any Manifestation, (of it self, in it self). . . . there being still somthing infinit in it behind" (*CM*, IV.62). The mystery of love, the mysterious ways it summons both Being and beings into their mutual relatedness, is the necessity Traherne tries to think and say. And while these ways may not finally be expressible, they are essentially one in the subsisting facticity of their simple existence.

Two final citations will be sufficient to remind us that the "modifications" of Being-as-love involve not only the conjugations of love itself but also the prepositional and pronominal relations it is able to sustain. And these, we recall, identify love as a disclosing site of world: "As he himself is made Glorious and Delightful in the Eyes of all Angels and men *by* Love, so doth his whole Kingdom arise and Spring *from* Love" (*CE*, 50). "As"—that is, insofar as or in the process of—Being is *in* by being seen *by*, world arises *from* that relatedness Traherne names love loving. A slightly different dimension of world appears in Traherne's analysis of how we attend God's love and situate ourselves within that love: "Shall not all our Lov be where his is? Shall it not wholy follow and Attend Him? Yet shall it not forsake other Objects [i.e., beings]. but lov them all in Him, and Him in them, and them the more becaus of Him, and Him the more because of them. for by Him [Love] is redeemed to them. So that as God is omnipresent our Lov shall be at once with all: that is We" (*CM*, IV.68). Love loving is here once again a gathering site: Being, beings, and man, summoned by and summoning each other, articulate the "We" of world worlding In-being-ness as such.

If love is a saying that summons and gathers Being and beings into a mutual relatedness that discloses or is world, then world itself becomes the next logical object of Traherne's inquiry. World, of course, appears only insofar as it is world-as-love—the origin of love begetting, the product of love begotten, and the region of love proceeding. Traherne's most common figures for such a world are spring, fountain, and ocean. God, Being-love as such, Being-love as the ground or originating spring, overflows of His own accord and thereby becomes a fountain flooding all creation; so flooded, world appears as the ocean of God's overflowing, ever-flowing love. In Heidegger's terms, we might say that love loving is the world worlding:

> NOW if you enquire what Advantages accrue by this Love, to the Soul of the Lover, we are lost again in Oceans of infinite Abundance. The strength, and brightness, and glory of the Soul, all its Wisdom, Goodness and Pleasure are acquired by it, founded in it, derived and spring from it. . . . The solution of that one Question will open the mystery. . . . All that we

> gain by his Love amounts to the *Power* of Loving, the *Act* of Loving we gain by our own. . . . We gain our Souls and Bodies . . . all Ages and Kingdoms, Heaven and Earth, Angels and Men . . . because all these were without our care or power prepared by him, and his love alone. . . . He so loved the World . . . (*CE*, 265–66)

Because the Being of beings is love, loving must be the region, the dimension, of their being. That region is here named—beyond Being's inclination, power, and activity of loving—as the gathering of a fourfold that presences as world. "By being Lov GOD is the fountain of all Worlds" (*CM*, II.46); "Lov is the true Means by which the World is Enjoyed. . . . Lov in the Fountain, and Lov in the End is the Glory of the World" (*CM*, II.62). In the Fifth Century, Traherne defines the "Ocean" of Being's love as the "Spiritual Region [that] makes us infinitly present with God, Angels and Men in all Places" (*CM*, V.9). And here, once again, world, as the site that gathers the fourfold in their mutual loving, presents being as that which is only insofar as it is in: "by the Indwelling of GOD all [beings] are infused, and contained within" (*CE*, 73).[77] To turn the play of Traherne's language back upon its own unspoken resources, being becomes present, is brought to be, only when it is in-love. And it is this relationship between In-Being and In-Loving that Traherne's watery metaphors for world try to express. Spring, fountain, and ocean represent the rhythm, the flow and the flood, by which Being loves beings and beings love Being to the extent that either is *in* the region of the other.

To say merely that "The World it self was his next Theme" ("Adam," l. 25), however, does not reveal the extent to which world is an issue for Traherne. World *is*, of course, but no simple observation of entities around him would show man either *where* world is or what it *does* as the region of his existence. In the Second Century,[78] Traherne tries to consider the latter question: "The Services which the World doth you, are transcendent," he argues, "to all Imagination" (*CM*, II.1); but those services can be glimpsed in the activities world performs. Significantly, the activities are all verbs: world sustains, preserves, and comforts man; it "Discovers the Being of God" and opens or shows man his own being; it magnifies, serves, and entertains beings. As the site of love loving, world announces the potential manners by which love can be expressed and communicated, how it brings all that is into the relatedness of their mutual belonging: "we are all Knit together, and Delight in each others Happiness. For while evry one is Heir of all the World . . . all the World servs Him in Himself, and in them" (*CM*, I.35). "The Whole World [is] . . . the Theatre of your Lov. It sustains you and all [beings] that you may continu to lov them. Without which it were Better for you to hav no Being" (*CM*, II.65). Beings knit together in-love, sustaining and serving one another, articulate world as such. World, then, is not a physical entity, but a manner in which Being is. Since Traherne has already defined Being as Being-in, the location of world, its existential whereabouts, must be situated in the same place. The question, therefore, is whether "The World was more in me, then I in it" ("Silence," l. 81).

> We could easily shew that the Idea of Heaven and Earth in the Soul of Man, is more Precious with GOD then the Things them selvs. . . . What would Heaven and Earth be Worth, were there no Spectator, no Enjoyer? As much therfore as the End is better then the Means, the Thought of the World wherby it is Enjoyed is Better then the World. So is the Idea of it in the Soul of Man, better then the World in the Esteem of GOD: It being the End of the World, without which Heaven and Earth would be in vain. . . . The World within you is an offering returned. . . . the World in a Thought is more Excellent then the World . . . The Material World is Dead and feeleth Nothing. But this Spiritual World tho it be Invisible hath [and *is*] all Dimensions, and is a Divine and Living Being. (*CM*, II.90)

This meditation is strikingly similar to Traherne's definition of In-Being-ness. Being-in is Being seen, enjoyed, and esteemed, and it is only in the accepting and granting of such Being that World itself becomes a live thing in a living place rather than a dead thing in a dead place. World, as the exchange of love loving, thus grants all to Being and becomes the thoughtful dimension of that Being. "The World is," then, only as "it is the Beginning of Gifts" (*CM*, II.2). In a later meditation, World itself cries out to man, summons him to understand, that "We are all His Gifts: We are Tokens and Presents of His Lov" (*CM*, II.28). By returning to Being the grant (the present and the presence) of being that we ourselves are, we, as beings, come to be: "He giveth all the World to one, He giveth it to evry one, He giveth it to evry one in giving it to all, and Giveth it wholy to me in giving it to evry one for evry ones sake. . . . And I Comprehending His and theirs, am. . . . Here is Lov! Here is a Kingdom!" (*CM*, I.74). World worlding is the granting of love loving, the manner in which In-Being-ness gathers all that is into the mutual exchange of sustaining and preserving belonging-together. "All Things appear, / All Objects are / Alive" in the "World within" ("My Spirit," ll. 110–13). Giving life to being, disclosing it and magnifying it, observing it and sustaining it, man situates himself within In-Being-ness as such. That relation is Traherne's world.

Each one of Traherne's metaphors of spring, fountain, and ocean measures a different dimension of the region of love loving and its capacity to disclose world, but let us return to that of spring in order to reorient the progress within Traherne's thinking about world. If God is the origin or spring of the love that Being grants or extends to beings, and if the relationship in-love between Being and beings is reversible (as our earlier glance at the mirror-image implies), then being could conceivably be the source of God's own Being and the region of His existence. Traherne tries to tease out this thought:

> Am I a Glorious Spring
> Of Joys and Riches to my King?
> ("Amendment," ll. 29–30)

These lines from the Dobell manuscript signal a crucial turn in the progress of that sequence. Prior to them Traherne has been charting the process by which he comes to learn that God must exist and they are followed by this intriguing stanza:

> Thy Soul, O GOD, doth prize
> The Seas, the Earth, our Souls, the Skies,
> As we return the same to Thee;
> They more delight thine Eys,
> And sweeter be,
> As unto Thee we Offer up the same

Then as to us, from Thee at first they came.
("Amendment," ll. 36–42)

What has occurred, we might ask, in the poem's gap between lines 29 and 30 and the new subject announced here? To answer that question, we need to recollect the beginning of the sequence and Traherne's dawning consciousness of world and the fourfold:

From Dust I rise,
And out of Nothing now awake,
These Brighter Regions which salute mine Eys,
A Gift from GOD I take.
The Earth, the Seas, the Light, the Day, the Skies,
The Sun and Stars are mine; if those I prize.
("The Salutation," ll. 25–30)

What presences as an object to the eye is a present, a gift or grant from God. Traherne's wonder at such a gift is expressed in the important verb "prize." To prize is initially simply to take, but its "diachronic expressibility," as Heidegger phrases it, includes as well to accept as a gift and, finally, to value or esteem.[79] Because "these Brighter Regions" are taken, in the senses of both accepted and understood, as a gift, they are esteemed. (We will return in a moment to the conditional that operates here: the gift is mine only insofar as I prize it.)

Obviously, this stanza from "The Salutation" provides the occasion for that from "Amendment": in fact, the later poem merely reverses the present terms, for God must also "take" the world as a gift in order to prize it. Being-esteemed, we recall, is one of the manners by which In-Being-as-love is, so we may still hear behind the present lines on the gift a further unfolding of the prior question of Being as such. Here, though, Traherne is concentrating upon the fact that esteem is dependent on the grant. Whether it is offered originally or in return, the grant summons, calls upon and calls for, esteem—both for the gift itself and for the being that has given it, whether that be God or man. Within the reflexivity of that esteem, world appears as such. Earth and sky, divinities and mortals gather together in the exchange of esteem expressed as love.

Traherne lingers, astonished and wondering, over the sudden

flash of insight that God sees and esteems in the same way that man does:

> What can be more Incredible then this,
> Where may we find a more profound Abyss?
>
> And What then this can be more Plain and Clear
> What Truth then this more Evident appear!
> The GODHEAD cannot prize
> The Sun at all, nor yet the Skies,
> Or Air, or Earth, or Trees, or Seas,
> Or Stars, unless the Soul of Man they pleas.
>
> In {us} he sees, and feels, and Smels, and Lives.
> ("The Demonstration," ll. 31–32; 41–46; 71)

The "Abyss" that Traherne conceives here is the possibility that God exists—"lives," is or has Being—only as man himself sees, enjoys, and prizes the "Joys and Riches" God has given him. In Heidegger's terms, the Being that grants being to beings is itself *not*:[80] Being is only in relation to beings, to the manner in which anything that is comes to life in its being-present-to the "Brighter Regions" of its being-in-the-world. Traherne draws his conclusion in these terms:

> To see us but receiv, is such a Sight
> As makes his Treasures infinit!
> Because His Goodness doth possess
> In us, His own, and our own Blessedness.
> Yea more, His Love doth take Delight
> To make our Glory Infinite
> Our Blessedness to see
> Is even to the Deitie
> A Beatifick Vision! He attains
> His Ends while we enjoy. In us He reigns.
>
> For God enjoyd is all his End.
> Himself he then doth Comprehend.
> ("The Recovery," ll. 1–12)
>
> The End Compleat, the Means must needs be so.
> ("The Anticipation," l. 46)

"Only from human being," writes Heidegger, "from the manner in which man grants the word of response to the claim of Being, can a reflection of its dignity shine forth to Being."[81] Traherne's glimpse of this truth is spoken in the wit of God's own "Beatifick Vision."[82] The "response" of beings to Being, as that of Being to beings, Traherne names, at the conclusion of "The Recovery," as "One Voluntary Act of Love." And he does so in an interesting tautology:

> One Voluntary Act of Love
> Far more Delightfull to his Soul doth prove
> And is abov all these [effects] as far as Love.
> (ll. 68–70)

The tautology may return us to what we have already called the reflexivity at the heart of Traherne's thought. Love is the center and the sphere, means and end, essence and act, Being and beings. God loves in order to grant the power of loving, the inclination to love, and the act of love itself. Giving and receiving, making visible and thereby seeing, seeing and therefore prizing: God's love is our blessed end; God's loving is our means to that end. But man's love is simultaneously God's end, just as our loving is His means to achieve that end. "Both are the very same. / The End and Fountain differ but in Name" ("The Anticipation," ll. 35–36). If poetry names this difference, it also says that sameness. The Being within which beings are inscribed and upon which being is grounded is exactly this different-same of belonging-together in the mutual exchange of love which Traherne names world. And that, we may now predict, is the *circulation* (giving/receiving, taking/returning, calling/answering) of Being-in-beings and beings-in-Being: in short, In-Being-ness itself.

In Heidegger's analysis, like Traherne's, the world worlds the relation of all relatedness. But world as such appears to man only insofar as it presences as Being-seen. To be conceived as a thought within the soul, world must itself be a product of something that exists. Heidegger, we recall, argues that world arises out of things: the thing things world and the work that lets things be sets up and sustains the world which the thing grants. For Traherne, the site of world and the center of the reflexive circulation that defines world is the Eye of the soul, the soul's capacity for seeing that gathers all that is into the self-presencing of its own In-sight. Being-in is Being-seen-within.[83]

That a thing or object *is* means to Traherne that it appears to man, makes itself visible; that it is ready to hand, proffering itself for use by and in service to man; and that its presence-at-hand incites both esteem and praise. Each of these consequences becomes a discrete subject to Traherne's imagination, for it is not enough merely to perceive that the thing exists. Man must also understand how it exists, the manner by which it appears and presences. As with Being itself, the manner of appearance assumes marked priority over what a given thing is. For this reason, we rarely find in Traherne the kind of specific imagery typical of a Donne, or a Herbert, or an Edward Taylor.[84] All things thing in the same manner, and what the thing things is of more immediate and serious concern than what the thing itself is.

To some readers, this characteristic renders Traherne's poetry vague and abstract, but it is more accurate to say that Traherne thinks things in a particularly Heideggerian fashion: things are and appear, things gather and summons, things set forth and set up the specific regions of man's relatedness. This fact requires some critical adjustment, for what in most other seventeenth-century contexts we would applaud as the detailed imagery of concrete things is, in Traherne, merely the surface substance, the ontic matter concealing the thing's true phenomenological and ontological being. And in these terms, it is precisely that "clothing" of deceptive and concealing specificity that Traherne's poetry tries to remove. What must be emphasized is that this process does not result in abstraction. Traherne's things are specific *as things*. Thing itself, not ax or shoe or crown or bone, is the entity in question.[85]

Part of the relatedness that things set forth is measured in the simple fact that things are other than man. Indeed, they are both distant and concealed from the human eye that would behold them. Since things must "be absent somewhat" (*CM*, II.20) in order to appear at all, it is necessary to understand from the start the spatial and temporal difference within which things are grounded.[86] Traherne tells us again and again that his intention is to "Display the Thing"; but he can do so only "by taking all away"—by calling the thing forth out of its concealedness into the revealing, appearing light of unconcealed presence. The thing, in short, constantly hides itself in either the sheer fact of its common or "public" existence or in the verbal metaphors by which man tries to describe it. Like Herbert, but even more insistently, Traherne points directly at this avoidance of typical poetic imagery. Such imagery, he tells us, merely veils the "Naked Things" themselves:

> Their Worth they then do best reveal
> When we all Metaphores remove,
> For Metaphores conceal
> And only Vapours prove.
> ("The Person," ll. 23–26)

To think a thing, to think specifically the manner in which the thing appears or presents itself to the observing eye, is therefore also to undress or disrobe the thing. That implicit unclothing/reclothing metaphor runs throughout Traherne's writing, not only to mark the differences between thing and man and thing and word, but also to announce his basic intention to "Study of the most Obvious and Common Things" (*CM*, III.53).

Things *appear*. Traherne continually registers both his wonder at this fact and the elemental brilliance of the objects he sees. His first consciousness as a child, he tells us in the Third Century, was that "All Things were Spotles and Pure and Glorious" (*CM*, III.2); he later confesses in the same Century that that initial impression convinced him that "Evry thing in its Place is Admirable Deep and Glorious" (III.55). The issue of a thing's "place" will become increasingly central to Traherne's thought, but at the moment let us stay with the mere fact that "evry thing is present by its own Existence" (*CM*, V.10). The poems record most dramatically this appearing presentness of things:

> All Things appear,
> All Objects are . . .
> ("My Spirit," ll. 111–12)

> The usefull and the Precious Things
> Are in a Moment Known.
> Their very Glory does reveal their Worth,
> (And that doth set their Glory forth;)

As soon as I was Born, they all were Shewn.
("Speed," ll. 2–6)

Here I was seated to behold New Things.
("Nature," l. 81)

Those Things that are most Bright
Sun-like appear in their own Light.
And Nothing's truly seen that's Mean:
Be it a Sand, an Acorn, or a Bean.
("The Demonstration," ll. 23–26)

We might pause briefly to note the apparent inversion in the third line of the last citation. Given Traherne's emphasis on the thing's own light, we might expect him to conclude, "and nothing's truly mean that's seen" (even the rhyme would not be disrupted). But Traherne has reason to subvert our expectation, for he wants to enforce the point that the appearance of any object depends mutually upon its own brightness and upon the clarity of the eye that perceives it. Even though the thing's worth, as in "Speed," is immediately revealed, some eye must be equally present to receive, measure, and affirm that worth: "How Bright are all Things here! . . . / And evry Thing that I did see" ("Wonder," ll. 2, 7). To appear and to see, then, chart the essential and existential relatedness, the belonging-together, that binds things to man, man to things.

The privilege Traherne accords the eye can be noted also in the paradoxical fact that things appear and speak to him even before he is capable of language or of hearing:

All things did com
With Voices and Instructions.
("Dumnesse," ll. 66–67)

"The Things which in my Dumness did appear" ("Dumnesse," l. 80) "speak," we presume, those unsayable truths that the soul loves (that is, is attracted to and by) even without knowing them (*CM*, I.1). "The Naked Things," therefore, are not only "most Sublime, and Brightest Shew / When they alone are seen" ("The Person," ll. 18–19), but also when they are known and esteemed. "All things were made that they might be seen," Traherne argues in *Christian*

Ethicks (p. 72), but he extends the simple relation of seer and object to an assertion of authentic belonging-together: "the full exertion of perfect power . . . to all Objects whatsoever" is to see, know, and love even the least object, which implies, and therefore leads the understanding to recognize, "the Perfection of all . . . Objects" (*CE*, 20). "The Simple Reality of Things" is, then, the very ground of Traherne's belief and faith. Yet we have already said that the mere appearance of things serves only a preparatory function. What, in fact, appears in the thing and does the thing only appear? Both thoughts lead Traherne further into the manner of this appearing.

Although "Life without Objects is Sensible Emptiness," an object or thing that "stands still" is "dead and idle" (*CE*, 212). In appearing, the thing summons man into its presence; in observing things, man calls them into his presence. Only in this reciprocal interpresencing can thing and man be. While every thing may be "present by its own Existence," its manner of being and hence its relation to Being is dependent. "Understanding," Traherne argues in the Second Century, "permitteth all Objects to be" (*CM*, II.24). The paradox is exploited again in the Fourth Century: while things must be in order for the soul to gaze upon them, "Before she loves they are not, when she lovs they are. And so she givs them their Being" (*CM*, IV.85). At times Traherne stresses merely the visual paradox of this manner of appearing—"Had he [God] not made an *Ey* to be the Sphere / Of all Things, none of these would e're appear" ("The Improvement," ll. 23–24); "all objects appear in the interior Light of our *own* understanding (*CE*, 37)—but his more typical strategy is to inject motion into the relation between the presenting object and the perceiving eye. As each comes to and towards the other, the necessary reciprocity that governs the entire manner of appearance incites the living circulation of giving/receiving. Thus, in the present passages, the soul *gives* being and *receives* being insofar as it gives. The grant of things and the giving of things sketch that essential movement of love we have already witnessed several times:

> All Things to Circulations owe
> Themselvs; by which alone
> They do exist.
> ("The Circulation," ll. 29–31)

Before tracing this movement further, we need to think again about what appears in the thing's appearance. In Heideggerian terms, we need to ask what does the thing gather into the manner of its appearing and thereby bring into the open of unconcealedness? Traherne's answer is twofold, but it begins with an expected assumption about circulations: "all Things proceeded from God to Man, and [are] by Man returned to God" (*CM*, I.40). So the first thing that appears in the thing's appearing is Being itself: "a Sand Exhibiteth the Wisdom and Power of God" (*CM*, I.27); "nothing," in fact, "can be, but it exhibits a Deitie" (*CM*, II.24); "By Things that are seen the Invisible things of GOD are manifested" (*CM*, II.24). To make manifest, we recall, is a major portion of the poetic task Traherne sets for himself: to bring into the Open those things that have remained concealed. Things thing in a similar manner, gathering the concealed Being into the glory of its unconcealed appearing: "all things abided Eternaly as they were in their Proper Places. Eternity was Manifest in the Light of the Day, and som thing infinit Behind evry thing appeared" (*CM*, III.3). Traherne even puns on this paradox:

> All that is Great and Stable stood
> Before thy Purer Eys at first:
> All that in Visibles is Good.
> ("Instruction," ll. 9–11)

And that "Good," of course, is Being as such.

The second entity that appears in the thing's appearance is man himself. "You are to be present with Things," Traherne explains in the First Century (*CM*, I.45). The self-perception of self-presence is explained in the following one: "your Soul in its Rays and Powers is unknown: and no man would believ it present evry where, were there no Objects there to be discerned. Your Thoughts and Inclinations pass on and are unperceived. But by their Objects are discerned to be present: being illuminated by them" (*CM*, II.78). "Being," in this last phrase, is, of course, a pun. Thoughts too, as the passage suggests, can be seen only in the appearance of the thing, even as the thing appears present only as "represented to my View" in thought:

What were the Skie,
What were the Sun or Stars, did [Thoughts] not lie
In me! and represent them there
Where els they never could appear!
("Thoughts I," ll. 43–46)

And yet it is precisely in that reflexive appearing that thoughts themselves can be seen as "brisk, Divine and Living Things." In "Thoughts III," in fact, "A Thought / Is even the very Cream of all [God] wrought"; "the Things / That us affect"; "the highest Things" (ll. 18, 21–22, 27).[87]

Things are: present, visible, appearing. In that appearing, things bring both God and man to be in the unconcealedness of their mutual presencing. Indeed, *how* things appear to God and man is the crucial measure of all being. Having said that, of course, we come very close to opening the subject of the usefulness of things, but let us extend one step further the simple fact that things appear. The first observer of things was/is God; God's perception is Traherne's original and precedent. God initially values (prizes) objects simply by virtue of the fact that He chose to make them, to grant them being. Having done so, and having looked upon them, He affirmed their worthiness by having "pronounced concerning every Thing, that it *was exceeding Good*" (*CE*, 54).[88] Now insofar as God himself is an "object" that appears, is gathered into, the appearance of a given thing, then God's manner of observing that thing must also become visible. Man "is most like GOD," Traherne infers, when he "is sensible of evry Thing" (*CM*, I.45). This means that the things man perceives are less important (although now we are making extremely fine measurements of value) than "with what Eys we beh[o]ld them" (*CM*, III.68). "Tis not the Object," Traherne suggests in "The Preparative," "but the Light / That maketh Heaven; Tis a Purer Sight" (ll. 57–58). This "purer" sight is precisely to see things as God sees them: the "Infant" and hence innocent or authentic Eye

Things doth see
Ev'n like unto the Deity:
That is, it shineth in an hevenly Sence.
("An Infant-Ey," ll. 3–5)

Man's capacity to see "in an hevenly Sence," "ev'n like unto the Deity," is the principal instruction things offer by their sheer appearance. The thing gathers, we might say, the gazes of God and man into twofold relation; it becomes itself the site and sight of this manner of mutual seeing. The manner itself can be defined as being sensible of, present with, attentive to, and concerned in the Being of every being. So seen, the thing itself retires into its own concealedness, precisely so that the manner of its being seen may be brought into the open. Traherne tries to say this paradox in "My Spirit":

> It Acts not from a Centre to
>   Its Object as remote,
> But present is, when it doth view,
> Being with the Being it doth note.
>
> And evry Object in my Soul a Thought
> Begot, or was: I could not tell,
>   Whether the Things did there
>   Themselvs appear,
> Which in my Spirit *truly* seemd to dwell;
> Or whether my conforming Mind
> Were not alone even all that shind.
>
>   All Things appear,
>   All Objects are
> Alive in thee! Supersubstancial, Rare,
>   Abov them selvs, and nigh of Kin
>   To those pure Things we find
>   In His Great Mind
> Who made the World! thou now Ecclypsed by Sin.
>   There they are Usefull and Divine,
>   Exalted there they ought to Shine.
>
> (ll. 18–22, 45–51, 111–19)

The site of things, the sight by which things are seen, gathers God and man into mutual kinship, into that belonging-together that defines In-Being-ness as such. If the "place" of the thing becomes problematic at this point, that is only because it has been set in motion, in what Traherne calls the circulation to which all things owe themselves and "by which alone / They do exist."

A final passage can conclude this survey of how Traherne thinks about the manner in which things appear and open the question of how they are of use and to be used: "Evry Thing . . . is a Solid intire Object singly proposed . . . it Openeth the Riches of Gods Kingdom and the Natures of His Territories, Works and Creatures in a Wonderfull Maner, Clearing and preparing the Ey of the Enjoyer" (*CM*, III.44). It will, perhaps, seem somewhat perverse of Traherne to speak in one phrase of the thing "singly proposed," in the next of the entirety of God's creation, and in the third of the solitary eye of an individual observer. And yet Traherne is very precise here in trying to define the region or horizon of appearance, the "sphere" or world within which all beings are gathered into Being as such.

In order to characterize that region more fully, Traherne focuses on the use or service of things. Again we need to distinguish two strands of his thought: first, the mere fact that things are only insofar as they serve or are serviceable; second, the manner of that service. Traherne insists over and over that things serve man: "All Things were made to be yours" (*CM*, I.12); "Evry thing is ours that serves us in its Place" (*CM*, I.14); "all Things serv you Best" (*CM*, I.38); "I measured [all things] by their Serviceableness" (*CM*, III.53); "All Things are ours; All Things serv us and Minister to us, could we find the way: Nay they are ours, and serv us so perfectly" (*CM*, IV.16); "for things when they are usefull are most Glorious" (*CM*, IV.47); "The usefull and the Precious Things / Are in a Moment Known" ("Speed," ll. 2–3); "the Relation between the Use and Excellency of things is so near and intimate, that as nothing Useless can be at all excellent, so is every Excellence in every Being founded in its Usefulness" (*CE*, 38–39). Given this reiterated truth, it is somewhat surprising that Traherne only occasionally details the exact services things perform; but in the last citation we can see clearly the direction of his argument. Man, as a being himself, is obliged to be useful in order to be at all. Thus, the ways in which things serve man ought to disclose the ways in which man must be serviceable to Being itself.

Things serve man's needs. Fuller study of Traherne's conceptions of human needs and desires must await the following chapter, but this assumption, common though it may be, forms the ground upon which the service of things can be thought. By serving man, things are placed in a relation of means to an end; and the end, in general, is to promote man, to obligate him, and to render him glorious because full of treasures. God "hast made me," Traherne argues, "the End of all Things" (*CM*, I.69); therefore, I must "consider how much [I] need them. For thence they Derive their Value" (*CM*, I.46). The most basic need is established as a factor of Traherne's consistent focus on the relation between essence and act, or between the capacity of a being and its manner of exercising that capacity:

> All Objects are in God Eternal: which we by perfecting our faculties are made to Enjoy. Which then are turned into Act when they are exercised about their Objects. but without them are Desolat and Idle; or Discontented and forlorn. Wherby I perceived the Meaning of that Definition wherin Aristotle Describeth Felicity. when he saith Felicity is the Perfect Exercise of Perfect Virtu [here Traherne puns on the connotation of a *power* of the faculties] in a Perfect Life. for Life is perfect when it is perfectly Extended to all Objects, and perfectly sees them and perfectly Loves them: which is don by a perfect Exercise of Virtu about them. (*CM*, III.68)

To be "exercised about" a thing is, in turn, to let the thing serve us. We have already seen Traherne naming some of "the Services which the World doth you" at the beginning of the Second Century. Those services, we recall, were all verbs, to indicate that we are here dealing with existential activities, not essences. Thus, things sustain man's body, preserve his life, comfort his senses. They open God's nature, show us His wisdom, entertain us with objects, feed us with joys. They enflame our love and link us to God. A few meditations later Traherne derives this conclusion:

> The world servs you, as in serving those Cattle which you feed upon, so in serving those Men, that Build and Plow, and Plant, and Govern for you. It servs you in those that Pray and Adore and Prais for you, that fill the World with Beauty and vertue; that are made to lov. and Honor, to Please and Advance you with all the Services that the Art of man can devise. So

> that you are alone in the World, tho there are Millions in it beside. You are alone to Enjoy and rejoyce in all, being the Adequat Object of His Eternal Lov, and the End of all. Thus the World servs to promote and Advance you. (*CM*, II.15)

The meditation illustrates Traherne's continual privileging of the individual—he alone is the "Adequat Object" of God's love and the service of all things (note also how that totality, "all things," has here reverted to its proper name, "world": the thing things world). That service serves primarily to "promote and Advance" Being. How things accomplish this end is described in the Fourth Century: merely by being observed, by appearing to man's eye, things summon our being into Being as such:

> Objects are so far from Diminishing, that they magnify the faculties of the Soul beholding them. A sand in your conception conformeth your soul, and reduceth it to the Cize and Similtud of a sand. A Tree apprehended is a Tree in your mind, the whole Hemisphere and the Heavens magnifie your soul to the Wideness of the Heavens. All the Spaces abov the Heavens enlarg it Wider to their own Dimensions. And what is without Limit maketh your Conception illimited and Endless. (*CM*, IV.73).

We have come to call this aspect of Traherne's imagination the expanded voice—after Stewart—or the enlarged "I"—after Webber, but it is important to note that things provide the means to this end of promoting, advancing, magnifying the soul's innate capacities and faculties. Man's observation of things, therefore, is

> To see all Creatures tend
> To thy Advancement, and so sweetly close
> In thy Repose: To see them shine
> In Use in Worth in Service
> ("The Vision," ll. 34–37)

"The Circulation" offers another aspect of the same service:

> As fair Ideas [forms] from the Skie,
> Or Images of Things,
> Unto a Spotless Mirror flie,

> On unperceived Wings;
> And lodging there affect the Sence
>
> While being there, they richly Beautifie
> The Place they fill . . .
> (ll. 1–8)

Behind all these passages is the central notion that the Eye of the observer is transformed by what it sees, thereby taking in, making its own, all the glory that always appears in the appearance of the thing itself. The thing, that is, summons man into its own glory and sets his faculties to work upon that glory. "The value of the Objects, *imputes a Lustre and higher value*" to the Eye that beholds it (*CE*, 38). Traherne summarizes this service elsewhere in *Christian Ethicks*: "by Knowing all Things, as GOD Knoweth them, we transform our Souls into an Act of Knowledge, most Bright and Glorious: By Loving all Things as GOD Loveth them, we transform our Wills into an Act of Love, which is most Sweet and Blessed. We enrich and Beautify our selves with the Image of his Goodness, while we communicate our Souls (in our Powers) to all Objects" (*CE*, 70). Communication, as always in Traherne, is circulation —here of service itself: "All things serve you for serving them" (*CM*, I.20). Use and usefulness, therefore, are also obligatory, and the service of things consequently calls man into their attendance.

"All the Things in Heaven and Earth attend upon us, while we ought to Answer and Observ them, by upholding their Beauty within" (*CM*, II.89). The imperative things issue to man means that he "must of Necessity liv unto some Thing" (*CM*, I.71). To attend to things as they attend to us grants world its proper usefulness: "The World does serv you," not only as the site of your joys, but more essentially as "a Great Obligation laid upon all Mankind" (*CM*, II.93). Traherne defines this obligation in several ways, the most obvious of which is that man must recognize his own being is necessarily concerned with and in all other beings. To be acquainted with things, merely to observe

> Things is not only to know them, but by frequent Meditation to be familiar with them. The Effects of which are Admirable. for by this those things that at first seemed uncertain becom

> Evident [i.e., concealed things are gathered into unconcealment], those things which seemed Remote becom near [absence is gathered into and becomes presence], those things which appeared like shady clouds becom solid Realities [things come, that is, into Being]; finaly those Things which seemed impertinent to us, and of little concernment, appear to be our own. (*CM*, IV.96)

Concernment, then, is Traherne's description of how man appropriates the difference of things. By learning difference itself, man becomes concerned: he is called, by things, out of his blind In-difference.[89] In *Christian Ethicks* Traherne names this debt as man's righteousness or justice: "If we render to any Object less than it deserves, we are not *Just*" (*CE*, 21); "The office of *Righteousness* is to render to every Thing a Due esteem; And without this it is apparent that no Treasure can be to us . . . of any value" (*CE*, 30).

Rendering to all things their due esteem, man grants them their being as God's treasures, God's gifts to man-as-heir. This is what Traherne means by the "mystery" of "The Application of *Actives* to *Passives*" (*CE*, 72): unless man gives life and being to things, they remain dead in a dead place, and cannot do the work for which they were intended. At stake here would seem to be the Augustinian distinction between things that are to be used and those that are to be enjoyed. Augustine, we recall, argues that created objects are merely signs: they are not to be loved or enjoyed in and of themselves, but only insofar as they lead us to the realities of God. In short, created entities are to be useful.[90] Traherne follows Augustine's prescriptions, but he collapses the categories. Things are used *as* they are enjoyed. In order to enjoy them properly, however, with due esteem, man must understand the proper "place" of the thing. We recall that Traherne begins his thinking about the service of things with precisely that qualification: "every thing is ours that serves us in its Place" (*CM*, I.14).

Obviously, we have come around once more to what both Heidegger and Traherne call world. The thing things world and in so doing calls man into relatedness with world. "I was concerned in all the World," Traherne says in the Third Century (III.23), but the world appears, becomes present and visible, only in relation to thing: "So that every thing is best in its proper place. Were there no Sands or Atoms there would be no *Universe*: For the Earth, the Sea, the Skie, the Air, all Bodies consist of these, either united or divided. If they had been left unmade . . . there had been no visible World at all" (*CE*, 182). Earlier in the same work, Traherne had already made this point: "He Knoweth nothing as he ought to Know, who thinks he Knoweth any thing, without seeing its Place, and the Manner how it relateth to GOD, Angels and Men, and to all Creatures in Earth, Heaven, and Hell, Time and Eternity" (*CE*, 69). "The Place wherin the World standeth, were it all annihilated would still remain" (*CM*, V.3). World, in short, is not itself a place so much as a gathering site/sight: it is the mutual belonging-together of the fourfold.[91] Thus, while things thing world, world worlds In-Beingness: "it discovers the Being of God"; "it is the beginning of Gifts"; "it promotes and advances Being"; it opens the measure and obligation of relatedness. To "dwell upon" the object of the world ("The Vision," ll. 17–18) is to perceive "The Endless Ocean of Each Glorious Thing" ("The Circulation," l. 79) as it relates to every other thing.[92]

We will observe in a later chapter how Traherne exploits this world-relatedness, the world worlding, in terms of parts and wholes, one and all, but at the moment let us listen again to how world discloses relatedness as such:

> That any thing may be found to be an infinit Treasure, its Place must be found in Eternity, and in God's Esteem. For as there is a Time, so there is a Place for all Things. Evry Thing in its Place is Admirable Deep and Glorious: out of its Place like a Wandering Bird, is Desolat and Good for Nothing. How therfore it relateth to God and all Creatures must be seen before it can be Enjoyed. And this I found by many Instances. . . . Did it not relate to others it would not be Good. Divest it of these Operations, and Divide it from these Objects it is Useless and Good for nothing. And therfore Worthless, because Worthles and Useless go together. (*CM*, III.55)

To be of worth is to be useful; to be useful is to be in relation to every other being.[93] Traherne thus moves from the consideration of how things serve to how things are to be used by man in order to let world come into being. Rendering to all things their due esteem, man converts his treasures into God's pleasures, and himself into a proper thing in God's Eye. Prizing things, man lets them be, shows his concern for and his care to preserve them in their being, and offers them in turn to that Being by which both he and they are.

We have already noted that Traherne conceives of things as proceeding to man from God. As such, they are man's treasures, gifts of which he is heir and recipient, pleasures which he is to enjoy and esteem. Indeed, enjoyment is precisely the pleasure man accords his treasures and according to which they appear and exist as such: "the Objects which we lov are the Pleasing Objects, and Delightfull Things. And whatsoever is not pleasing and delightfull to us can be no Treasure. Nay it is Distasteful, and worse then Nothing, since we had rather it should hav no Being" (*CM*, II.65). If the thing does not please us, it *has* no being. Those things, therefore, that are the "Objects of our Joy" must simultaneously be "Objects of our Care, They are our true Treasures about whom we are wisely Employed" (*CM*, IV.39). "God would have / His Creatures Brave / And that . . . by their Continual Care" ("Thoughts II," ll. 16–18).

"Continual Care," or, as Traherne calls it in the *Meditations*, "my *habitual Care*" (p. 23), is the ethical dimension of the manner of authentic being. It is, therefore, an antidote to inauthentic existence, that Indifference by which we "contemn" God's works as we "careless pass them by."[94] Traherne's fullest statement of this condition and its consequences for Being occurs in "Another":

> We cold and Careless are, and scarcely think
> Upon the Glorious Spring wherat we Drink.
> Did he not lov us, we could be content.
> We Wretches are Indifferent!
>
> Tis Death my Soul to be Indifferent,
> Set forth thy self unto thy whole Extent.
>
> Thy Lov is Nothing by it self, and yet
> So infinit is his, that he doth set
> A Value infinit upon it. Oh!
> This, canst thou Careless be, and know!
>
> (ll. 9–12, 17–18, 33–36)

The obligation of care, then, is not only to retrieve our own being from the "death" of care-less-ness, but also to summon all beings into their authentic dwelling in Being as such. How will all beings love us, Traherne asks in *Christian Ethicks*, "when they find our Care / Brought them all thither where they *are*" (p. 204; my italics)—where, that is, they both already are and can ever and only *be*. Care taking, tending and safeguarding beings in relation to Being, man grants Being a site in which all may dwell.

As always in Traherne, man's essential actions arise in response to God's actions: being is as Being does. Thus, in the *Meditations*, Traherne focuses on "the Care [God] takes over [his creatures] to keep and defend them" (p. 68). In his subsequent analysis of the implications of such care Traherne discovers a clue to his own careful existence: "In those Words, *God created Man in his own Image*, we may understand that all his Care and Counsel was spent about the Creation of him; and not of many but of one, intimating that every one is so great, as if all the Care of God were about him alone" (pp. 72–73). A poem in Philip's Notebook records Traherne's application of the divine lesson:

> Who lives not full of care he lives noe King.
> The boundless glory of a King is such
> to sweeten care because his care is much.
> ("To bee a Monarch," ll. 2–4)

"Full of Care," we must assume, man cares for any thing *as if* all his care were "about" it alone. But since a thing *is* only in its relatedness to all, care is the authentic and full response of man to the World the thing things.

Like Heidegger, then, Traherne's sense of concern toward implies a caring for, rendering to things not only esteem but also the very being that they are due and preserving them there, in the site and sight of Being. "Things prized are Enjoyed"; "Prizing all things clearly with a due esteem" is to behold things with divine eyes, and in a heavenly sense. As Traherne meditates the morality of caretaking, prizing of things, he comes again to the same startling conclusion:

> His Wisdom, Goodness, Power, as they unite
> All Things in one, that they may be the *Treasures*

> Of one *Enjoy'r*; shine in the utmost Height
> They can attain; and are most Glorious *Pleasures*
> When all the Univers conjoyned in one.
> ("The Improvment," ll. 25–29)

"That so the End," which is man, "should be," in fact, "the very Spring" or means "of Evry Glorious Thing" ("The Anticipation," ll. 37–38). Traherne's circulation once more absolutely inverts man's role: instead of the end, the measure and recipient of all things, he has become instead the giver or bestower of all things. "All things do first receiv, that giv" ("The Circulation," l. 71), but all who receive must also give in order to be. God himself must "Benefit receiv from Things" ("The Anticipation," l. 8), but he can do so only insofar as they please and are prized by man:

> That all Things should be mine;
> This makes His Bounty most Divine.
> But that they all more Rich should be,
> And far more Brightly shine,
> As usd by Me:
> It ravisheth my Soul to see the End,
> To which this Work so Wonderfull doth tend.
> ("Amendment," ll. 1–7)

Traherne began his analysis of things with the simple wonder that they actually appear "bright in their own light." Now the circulation and the communication of that light brings man himself into unconcealment before God and God himself into caring presence with man. God, like man, needs and desires; and the things he most admires are the loving "thanksgivings" of man.[95]

"We must necessarily be acquainted with all Things in all Worlds, before we can thorowly and compleatly" love or be loved by God (*CE*, 140). To be acquainted with is to dwell caringly *in*, to be thankful for and to prize. Like Heidegger, Traherne is concerned here with both the fullness and the authenticity of our responsiveness toward things—the manner in which we take pleasure in and treasure them. Things, therefore, as we said before, are sites of relation between man and God, beings and Being as such. Conjoyning all to one and one to all, things summon Being into presence, gather the circulating joys, care, and concern in which all things exist. This In-being of things—things-in-man, man-in-God, things-in-God, God-in-things, God-in-man—is Being itself, the unsayable, concealed yet revealing thought that Traherne's poetry constantly tries to say.

CHAPTER THREE

Traherne and Lacan

The Structures of Desire

What happens in an analysis is that the subject is, strictly speaking, constituted through a discourse, to which the mere presence of the psychoanalyst brings, before any intervention, the dimension of dialogue.

The psychoanalytic experience has rediscovered in man the imperative of the *verbe* as the law which has formed him in its image. It manipulates the poetic function of Language to give to his desire its symbolic mediation.

Don't expect too much here, for since the psychoanalytic thing has become an accepted thing and its servants have their hands manicured, the arrangement they have come to can accommodate sacrifices to good form, which, as far as ideas, which psychoanalysts have never enough of, are concerned, is certainly convenient: cut-price ideas for all will make up the balance of what everyone needs. —JACQUES LACAN

We operate today within a certain network of significations marked by psychoanalytic theory, even if we do not master it and even if we are assured of never being able to master it perfectly. —JACQUES DERRIDA

I MIRRORS AND STAGINGS

It should not be surprising that the work of Jacques Lacan offers useful terms for interpreting a poet whose imagination constantly turns toward relations between the Eye and "I," between the glance in a mirror and the gaze that captivates the beholder of the mirror, between wants inscribed in various lacks and the insatiable desire such lacks occasion, or between a concept of self and the significant other with whom that self is irreducibly yoked. To turn our attention from the context of Heidegger to that of Lacan is also a logical critical gesture, for as much as the Lacanian project must be seen as a revision of the central texts of Freud, it is equally necessary to understand how thoroughly that revision is authorized and directed by Lacan's reinterpretation of Heidegger.[1]

That Heidegger profoundly influenced Lacan is incontestable, but for present purposes three aspects of that influence are important. First, like and following Heidegger, Lacan inscribes the human being in the saying-unsayable play of language itself. In one sense, of course, such an assertion is misleading, for it sidesteps the crucial figures of Saussure, Lévi-Strauss, and Jakobson; in a broader sense, however, it emphasizes Lacan's contribution to and continuation of the contemporary tradition of deriving the constitutive mechanisms of human thought and behavior from the linguistic system. Man does not speak language, Heidegger insists, language speaks him. And Lacan fully subscribes to this premise.[2] Thus, where Heidegger argues that authentic human being must attend and listen to the unspoken saying of Being as it comes into presence or reveals itself in language, Lacan argues that the aim of psychoanalysis is to provide the verbal pathways for the human subject to recognize and speak his unsayable desire.[3] I do not mean here to collapse Heidegger's Being into Lacan's Unconscious,[4] but the fact remains that both thinkers situate their subjects in a linguistic model, whether that be called language in systematic generality or discourse as a particular enactment of that system. In Lacan's terms, we could say that the philosophical enterprise of both authors is to call man out of his un-conscious captivation by the empty word (*la parole vide*) and into conscious relation with the full word (*la parole pleine*).[5] Language, for both, is the irreducible, primordial House of Being.

A second link between Heidegger and Lacan is a shared methodology. In the sense that we now accord the term (and withholding, for a moment, the negating gestures set in place by the subsequent "deconstruction"), both authors are fundamentally "structuralist." Regardless of the particular subjects each may address or question, their analytic strategies are grounded in dialectical structural relations. Both insist, moreover, that their brand of dialectics must be distinguished from Hegel's, that no reconciliation of whatever binary terms are employed is possible, and that the antinomies that structure human existence are more appropriately conceived as *un jeu de miroirs* constitutive of repeated and irreducible reversals. This methodology, of course, is a necessary consequence of a more basic agreement between Lacan and Heidegger that man, both ontically and ontologically, is a complex set of structural relations.[6] The interpretive gestures each makes attest to a faith that these relations can be uncovered by systematic analysis and that their functional mechanisms can be charted. In short, both authors deliberately set out to subvert the autonomous and transcendent Cartesian ego, that "I" of blissful independence.[7] Anthony Wilden calls attention to this convergence of presupposition and methodological intention when he explains Lacan's conception of the psychoanalytic subject by means of the philosopher's terms: "To employ Heideggerian language, the 'who' of Dasein is the unanswerable question, whereas the 'where' of Dasein is revealed in . . . every word he speaks: the 'who' of Dasein is the [linguistic] shifter 'I,' which is a locus not a person."[8]

Lacan's constant return to Freud's notorious and cryptic "*Wo Es war, soll Ich werden*" is an attempt to state the same thing: whether "Es" be read as ego, Being, the unconscious, the imaginary, or the *moi*, the human being is not a transcending individual ("I") but a constituted site, a network of structurally related signifiers. And

Lacan's own glosses on Freud's statement make explicit his reliance on Heidegger:

> There were it was just now, there where it was for a while, between an extinction that is still glowing and a birth that is retarded "I" can come into being and disappear from what I say. An enunciation that denounces itself, a statement that renounces itself.
>
> Being of non-being, that is how "I" as subject comes on to the scene, conjugated with the double aporia of a true survival that is abolished by knowledge of itself and by a discourse in which it is death that sustains existence.[9]

Heidegger's version is instructive:

> Drawn into what withdraws, drawing toward it and thus pointing into the withdrawal, man first *is* man. His essential nature lies in being such a pointer. Something which in itself, by its essential nature, is pointing, we call a sign. As he draws toward what withdraws, man is a sign. But since this sign points toward what draws *away*, it points, not so much at what draws away as into the withdrawal. The sign stays without interpretation.[10]

Or, perhaps, the sign stays only by virtue of a hermeneutic questioning that is itself distinct from any particular signification ultimately derived or imposed. The human locus is not a transcendental logos or meaning; it is a conceptual point upon which any number of signifying axes converge and which is itself sliding along a variety of signifying chains organized by the structural system.

The methodology by which this site or locus is analyzed continually employs, as we have said, a series of common binary terms. Presence and absence, self and other, Being and nonbeing, concealment and disclosure—these are some of the antinomies Lacan shares with Heidegger. It is not, however, my intention to attempt an intermapping of Heideggerian and Lacanian dialectics; the point is rather that Lacan's analytic method owes a great deal to and needs to be understood in terms of Heidegger's own strategies. Such cryptic grids as Heidegger's fourfold or Lacan's Schema R do not chart the same territories, but both derive from a common assumption that being *is* only insofar as it is structured, and that its structures are inevitably dialectical. Thus, Lacan clearly sees in Heidegger's ongoing attempts to describe the relations between Being and being a methodological model for his own analysis of the filiations entangling self and Other. Even so elementary a decision as to discriminate between others and Other(ness) is grounded upon the concepts of sameness and difference that Heidegger had already set in place.

Indeed, it might be argued that it is precisely this similarity between Heidegger and Lacan that urges Lacan's own peculiar analysis upon our present task. For if Traherne, as we have seen, is continually exploring the relations between Being as such and individual beings, he rarely does so without also invoking the coordinate structural relations between (a) self and (an) Other.[11] In both instances, Being and Other must be interpreted in a fully structural sense—not, that is, as existing in a domain that is separate from or accessible to man, but as the very context of the region in which man comes to be and to question what and where he is. No less than Heidegger or Lacan, Trahernean man, the "I" that so conspicuously dots his writings, is a structural locus, not a person.

Finally, we should note that Lacan, again like Heidegger, is aggressively committed to a highly idiosyncratic style—cryptic, repetitive, often impenetrable, sometimes poetic. It seems to me there are two different ways to account for this stylistic similarity. The first is clearly connected to subversive intentions: whether the normative style of discourse be taken as a general tradition of western metaphysics or the more narrow discipline of post-Freudian psychoanalysis, both Heidegger and Lacan are convinced that modern thought rarely attends to the implications of its own language, and both are committed to revitalizing discourse itself.[12] The second reason is an inevitable consequence of their notion that man is a locus of relations, for neither can countenance any arbitrary discrimination of the structures within which man is inscribed. When Lacan argues that the subject is caught in the sliding (*glissement*) of the signified under the signifier, or when he insists that each of his schemas be read in multiple dimensions simultaneously, he is voicing a fundamental agreement with Heidegger's insistence that any thoughtful entry into a particular relation between Being and being invariably opens all other relations.[13] Like Heidegger, Lacan returns again and again to the same set of terms, reinterpreting and revising, weaving and overweaving a complex verbal tapestry whose threads can never be completely disentangled. The styles of both authors, in short, are deliberate attempts to forestall premature answers and to privilege questioning itself.

It has long been acknowledged, of course, that Traherne's style is highly idiosyncratic, but this fact is usually explained as a consequence of either his fundamental mysticism or his failure as a serious poet. My own sense is that we need to rethink Traherne's stylistic decision not to write like Donne, or Herbert, or even Vaughan. If he shares a number of the conceptual concerns of our modern thinkers, it might be more rewarding to consider his stylistic choices as deliberate as theirs. In doing so, we may find a rather new Traherne: consciously shocking, subversive of normative discourse, intentionally committed to a more authentic relation to language itself. Although such an argument goes far beyond my own resources here and would ultimately require a more thorough investigation of Traherne's historical situation amidst the various literary and theological discourses available to him, we might at least reopen the question of his peculiar style to possibilities criticism has as yet not imagined.[14]

To return to Lacan, it is commonly acknowledged that he is primarily a rereader of Freud. The validity of his revision in psychoanalytic terms is not here the issue and we need not, therefore, follow the multi-leveled convolutions of Schemas L, R, or I or such cryptic formulae as $f(S \ldots S')S \cong S(-)s$ in order to understand the central components of his theory. Our own territory might better be staked out by noting that the psychoanalyst's distinctions between the subject as initiator of the dream or the session's discourse, as actor in and reporter of the dream, as speaker in an analytic situation, as consciousness of self, as mediator between inner and outer worlds, or as discriminator between fantasy and reality are not structurally different from the critic's problem of differentiating the various voices he hears in the literary text—the historical author, a fashioned or presented narrator, a literary ideal-ego, a submerged other-author, a particularized "I" or an abstracted "we," a "school" or a class.[15] The essential point is that whereas traditional "Freudian" criticism has most often focused on a valuable but restricted kind of symbol interpretation (what Lacan rather scornfully calls the dictionary approach), current psychoanalysis redirects critical attention to a wider assortment of structural systems and mechanisms. It shares, that is, with other modern methodologies a concern not for *what* the literary text says or means, but *how* it says or means. To this extent, it brings us into more direct confrontation with the implications of Saussurian linguistics in general and with more particular literary implications of structuralism.

We are interested, then, in those features of Lacan's thought that help us better understand Traherne's poetry. For this purpose, four of Lacan's notions seem to me especially fruitful: the *stade du miroir*, the triadic set of real-imaginary-symbolic, the concept of the Other, and the motivated structures of desire are, of course, directly involved in problems of self-recognition and the interplays of language,[16] and it will obviously distort Lacan's own intentions to treat the four as separable models. But our aim is practical criticism, not psychoanalytic coherence, and the application of Lacan to literature must inevitably risk an arbitrary privileging of some structural coordinates over others.

The *stade du miroir* is one of Lacan's earliest formulations. Derived in part from Freud himself and part from Henri Wallon,[17] its essential outline offers both a conceptual narrative of psychic development and a symbolic field within which Lacan can organize certain psychoanalytic facts. It is necessary, however, to introduce two cautions to this statement. First, all notions of psychic development ("stages" in normal psychological discourse) are suspect to Lacan. Thus we ought to be extremely wary of such schemes as are proposed by his interpreters—for example, the rather common assumption that pre-mirror, mirror, and post-mirror phases are indexes of maturation or that they can be equated with Lacan's real, imaginary, and symbolic.[18] The second caution emphasizes that despite the physiological evidence that Lacan brings to bear upon the *stade du miroir*, his mirror is purely symbolic (in our normal sense of that word), not literal:

> Lacan never intended to link the appearance of a human ego to a looking glass, nor even to the fact that—like Narcissus—an

> infant could see its reflection on the surface of a body of water. The scenario of the infant at the mirror is the index of something that has always occurred, with or without that apparatus: The mirror serves as a metaphor and a structural concept at the same time that it points [again metaphorically] to a crucial experience in psychic development.[19]

With these cautions in mind, we can sketch the imagined plot of the mirror stage, which, in Lacan's chronology, occurs somewhere between the ages of six and eight months and whose psychological repercussions govern the child's behavior until about eighteen months. The child's first sight of himself is as an object-image held by a parent, usually the mother,[20] in front of a mirror. As I interpret Lacan here, the child's attempts to seize the mirror-image(s) or to look for some body behind the mirror are evidence that he initially takes the reflection(s) to be real. That confusion,[21] however, does not become fully registered in the child's mind until a subsequent moment: apparently alone, though not necessarily so, and barely able to support or stand by himself, the child becomes captivated by his reflection. He poses in various ways before it; he jubilantly plays with it; he makes it appear and disappear. It is precisely this jubilation that Lacan seizes upon as the mark of the beginning of self-recognition. What is the power of the mirror-image, Lacan asks, that could account for such joy or incite such play? And his answer depends upon a conception of the premature birth of man: the child, still fully dependent upon and being fed by the mother, incapable of independent motor control, sees in the mirror-image an exemplary form of harmonious being. The image, in other words, offers the child an imaginary integration and unity that he himself, at this stage of his biological development, lacks. Assuming (that is, introjecting) and jubilating in the image, the child, as subject, is already being structured by alienation from himself, lack of wholeness, and nascent desire for reunification.

In Lacan's subsequent terminology, the child has been photographed, mapped by and inscribed within an irreducible split or bipartition of being which all later psychic development merely replicates.[22] Consciousness, knowledge or recognition of self, is from its inception grounded upon a specular confusion and a misconstruction: what the child sees is mistaken for what he is and imaginatively registered as what he knows (about himself). On one level, what is at stake here is nothing other than a narcissistic identification with something outside and other than himself, but Lacan tries, via the algorithmic structures of Schema L,[23] to demonstrate the full complexity of the child's dilemma:

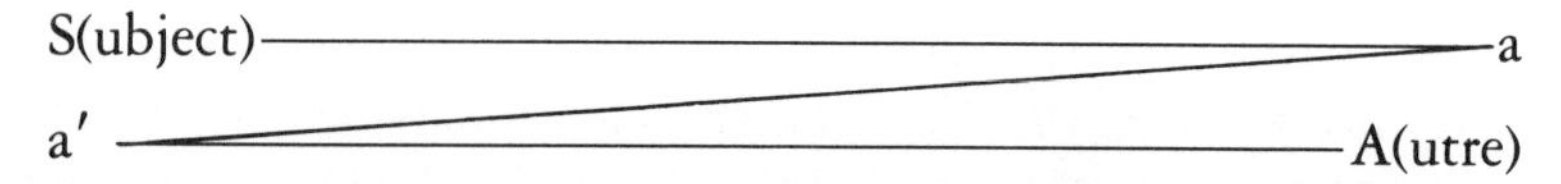

The schema attempts to chart what Lacan calls "the grammatical categories of childhood,"[24] the structural conditions according to which the subject is constituted by and within the reflections/deflections of an Other. At the level of the *stade du miroir*, *S* represents the child as subject, *A* the site (and sight) from which he first begins to be conscious of or to question himself as a person, as well as from which he begins to fashion an ideal-ego or *moi*; *a* represents the imagined objects of his need (the mother's breast, for example), and *a′* his developing *moi*.[25] Thus the "I" that will eventually name the subject as the individual being that he thinks he is is already a factor of specular re-presentation: I am what I offer to another's view; I am what another offers to me as an object that is viewed. Such an "I" is always screened, in effect, by two alienating relations: by those between the subject and the (m)Other and by those between the (o)bjects that satisfy my needs and the *me* (*o′*) to whom they are given or from whom they are withdrawn. Psychic existence, then, is ex-istence, a standing apart from and outside the self in order to see or know the self. At this stage, it does not really matter whether we name such existence as narcissistic or Oedipal, for the more crucial point is that consciousness requires a splitting of being: the primary structural categories of subject and object-image (Other) constitute the developing human child on the fundamental ground of self-alienation.[26]

As a narrative, of course, this sketch of the *stade du miroir* is misleading. For one thing, and as already mentioned, it is clear that the mirror stage is not an "event" that actually occurs as much as a structural interpretation of incipient self-consciousness as self-*méconnaissance*. Lacan himself contributes to the obscurity of his design by treating it from various developmental perspectives, some preverbal, others postverbal. What is clear, however, is Lacan's insistence that vision is the primary vehicle of initial self-consciousness,[27] that the subject always identifies with the object he perceives and thus distances himself from himself, and that that object always constitutes one dimension of the fundamental structural category of Other(ness) or difference.

To clarify and enforce these tenets, Lacan appropriates behavioral studies comparing a six- to eight-month-old chimpanzee with a human baby of the same age. The chimpanzee shows, at this age, a far greater problem-solving ability than the child, but he cannot assimilate his reflection in a mirror. After exploring the reflection, trying to seize it, and looking behind the mirror for some physical reality to substantiate it, the chimpanzee quickly loses interest in the image. Apparently he is unable to recognize himself in the reflection, and consequently the image serves no further function for him. The child, however, has a significant emotional reaction to his image, so that after going through the same explorations as the chimpanzee he becomes caught in what Lacan calls a *jouissance*, "a flutter of jubilant activity." Striking poses before the image, making it appear and disappear, the child obviously finds in the reflection something that answers to a need or a lack. Such captivation is understandable, Lacan argues, only on the basis of the child's organic insufficiency. Since the infant cannot walk, talk, or obtain its own food, its being is shaped only by gazing and hearing and by identification with those things it either sees or hears. The outside world thus assumes priority in structuring the child's identity and the child compensates for its own physiological prematurity by necessarily assimilating and integrating the world around it. The child's jubilant play before the mirror, then, represents both an imaginative mastery of and a compensation for an insufficiency of self and a simultaneous taking on or becoming the image that it perceives.

Lacan concludes that the *human* being, the being who can be conscious of himself, unable to escape this captivating play of and with his alter image, is immediately determined and distinguished by his relation to a specular form—so much so that Lacan calls the *stade du miroir* "the symbolic matrix in which the *I* is precipitated in a primordial form, before it is objectified in the dialectic of identification with the other, and before language restores to it . . . its function as subject."[28] Whatever his subsequent development —constituting the other as an object, constituted as an object by the other, constituting himself as an object posing before the other —the human subject is always caught in an infinite dialectic of images which governs the processes of objectification and identification. *Self*-consciousness cannot take place without that other image, and though the specular I may shortly be replaced by a social I (imaginary relations, in Lacan's terms, give way to symbolic ones), the structuring of the ego which appears in the mirror stage is merely repeated and replicated.[29]

In his seminar on *The Four Fundamental Concepts of Psychoanalysis*, Lacan extends his notions by citing a poem by Aragon entitled "*Contre-chant*":

> In vain your image comes to meet me
> And does not enter me where I am who only shows it
> Turning towards me you can find
> On the wall of my gaze only your dreamt-of-shadow
> I am that wretch comparable with mirrors
> That can reflect but cannot see
> Like them my eye is empty and like them inhabited
> By your absence which makes them blind.

The poem reminds Lacan of Merleau-Ponty and Sartre, both concerned with the conditions under which the human subject becomes object of another's sight.[30] Although Lacan does not analyze the poem itself, it is clear that both its subject and its terms are very close to the core of his own theories: the I that perceives itself as reflecting only the image of the Other's absence, the Other that demands in the eye's reflection the locale of its own imagined and unified ideal, the vain attempt by which self and Other strive to "meet" but can only "turn towards," and, above all, the gaze (*le regard*) that cannot itself be seen but whose presence structures the entire act of seeing and being seen. The gaze of Aragon's poem, in short, is equivalent to what Lacan elsewhere terms the barred subject, the split between need and demand, signifier and signified, self and Other. By distinguishing between the eye and this gaze, Lacan tries to reconstruct the structural mechanisms of the *stade du miroir*—or, since he does not himself connect the seminars on the eye and the gaze to this stage, perhaps it is better to say that he is constructing consequences of the mirror stage.

Insofar as the *stade du miroir* has already privileged (that is to say, posited as primordial) the sense of vision, Lacan seems to accept the phenomenological notion of man as a being "given-to-be-seen." There is no need, he argues, to suppose any Platonic or Christian universal seer in order for this to be so: it is the structural condition of our existence.[31] The real question is whether such notions as Valery's "seeing oneself seeing oneself" are accurate or distorted conceptions of self-consciousness as it emerges from the act of seeing. To Lacan, such conceptions are as false a view of the ego as the Cartesian *cogito*, and his discrimination between eye and gaze is another attempt to break down these idealistic monads in order to demonstrate that the ego is always already a factor of the structural split in being. As often the case with Lacan, his analysis is far from transparent, but its general features seem to be as follows. I, as a being who looks at things in the world and as a being looked at by the world, am both a subjective seer and an objective picture. What I see in the Other, moreover, is always screened by the objects and the needs of my own imaginings, just as the *moi*-as-picture is always my presentation of myself before the eye of the Other in response to the (imagined) demands of that Other. Lacan offers this diagram:[32]

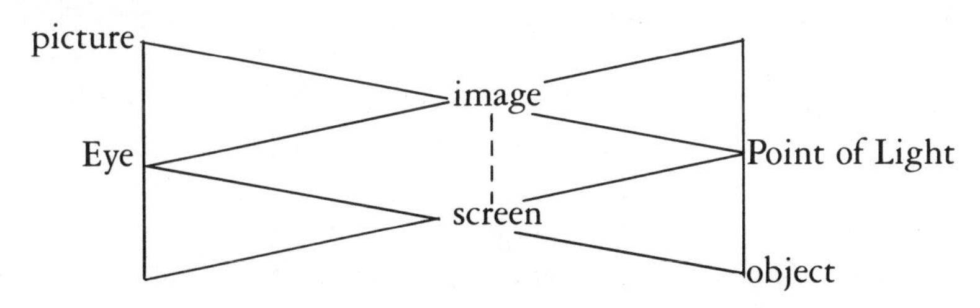

I have slightly redistributed Lacan's reference points in order to suggest an analogy between this diagram and the fuller Schema L:

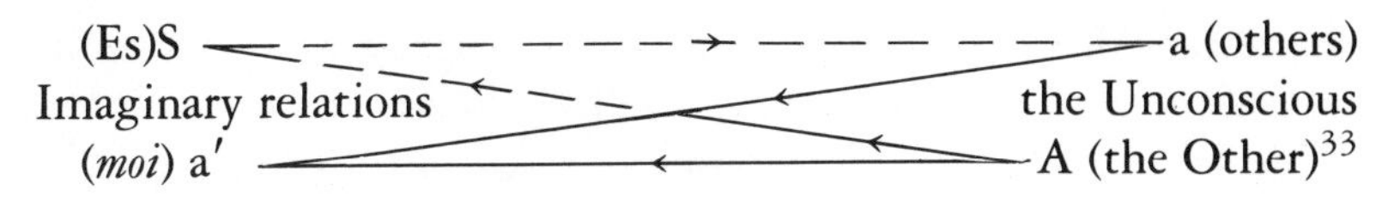

The image-screen through which both I and the object-Other look is the *a-a′* intermediation of the imaginary. What Lacan calls the gaze is precisely the structural ground upon which this seeing is enacted and which itself lies outside the field of vision as such. We might say that the gaze is the preexisting necessary lack or emptiness that the eye, through seeing, tries to fill. Just as in the *stade du miroir* the image satisfies a lack of motor coordination in the child, so the object-Other satisfies the full consciousness of self. The gaze is the structuring mechanism which constitutes both I and object within the field of vision as an other given-to-be-seen, probably even as a self-constructed-as-an-object-to-be-seen. Or, to map this field on that of the *stade du miroir*, just as the child is unknowingly captivated by and in his own *jouissance* before the mirror, so the I emerges into consciousness as eye only by a *trompe l'oeil* by which the desiring function of the gaze itself is concealed from sight. Lacan's strategy is thus reminiscent of Heidegger's: the gaze, like Being, withdraws into concealment the moment a given being (Lacan's other or an ego-ideal) is revealed, even though it is the necessary ground or condition of that revealing.[34]

Let us try to come at the distinction another way. The object-other that I look at is never exactly what I wish to see; conversely, the other that looks at me never sees me as I wish to be seen. On both sides of the visual field there is a lack. The gaze, *qua* gaze, is the desire that generates the manner in which I either see or am seen. Lacan thus extends Freud's explication of drive—*Beschauen und beschaut werden*—by calling attention only half-facetiously to the fact that we universally speak of an evil eye but nowhere of a good eye.[35] The evil eye is a metaphor for the subject's imagined condition of being subjected to the Other's gaze. The gaze makes the I desperate, suspicious, guilty, accountable. The gaze is heard as demand. And it judges in such a way as to transfer the scopic functions of the eye, the situating of the subject in imaginary object-relations, to the symbolic register of resubjectification under the law.

"I set out from the fact," writes Lacan, "that there is something that establishes a fracture, a bi-partition, a splitting of the being to which the being accommodates itself."[36] Whether that split be the subject-image dialectic of the *stade du miroir* or the eye-gaze dialectic of the scopic field, one consequence of split being is a reflexive interplay of subject-object, subjectification and objectification. We can chart some of the ways Lacan conceives this interplay by following two more notions he brings to bear on the *stade du miroir*—the phenomenon in children's behavior known as transitivism and Freud's famous anecdote of the *Fort! Da!* Both examples are central to Lacan because they represent an emergence out of the purely imaginary relations of the specular stage into the verbal region of the symbolic. They offer us, therefore, not only further reflections on the mirror stage itself, but some sense of Lacan's notion of psychological development.

In his cryptic explication of the mirror stage Lacan refers in passing to "the child who strikes another says that he has been struck; the child who sees another fall, cries."[37] Lacan finds such transitivism further proof of the confusion central to the *stade du miroir*, and he compares it to studies showing that the visual stimulation pigeons require to trigger ovulation can be accomplished merely with a mirror. This attempt to ground a psychoanalytic fact on a physiological basis, however, is not Lacan's real intention. Of far more importance in transitivism is the child's notorious inability correctly to use the pronouns that linguists (Benveniste in particular) call shifters.[38] The confusion of self and other, that is, precipitates the child into a system of linguistic signification in which the very centers of his consciousness—I and me—are already captivated in unstable and reflexive relations. Lacan concludes, in fact, that transitivism suggests that the pronominal "I" actually begins to be articulated in the site of this self-other confusion, that it can be only in relation to the other that the subject first lives and registers himself. Such a splitting of the ego between the subject who strikes and an object struck, between the I who sees and the me who is seen, invariably predicts again, now in verbal terms, the *meconnaissance* already registered in the *stade du miroir*.

Lacan does not argue that the child's confusion of the pronominal shifters is salutary, although he might have done so on the basis of analogy with the child who plays with his image in the mirror. For Freud, such play, particularly insofar as the child learns that he can control the absence or presence of the image, forms an integral part of the child's growing ability to master his environment. Prior to mirror play, the child is completely at the mercy of the mother, unable either to keep her from disappearing or to make her reappear. By means of his jubilant play with his own reflection in the mirror, however, the child begins to understand that presence and absence are functional coordinates and symbolic conditions he can control. For Lacan, this knowledge is the structural connection between the mirror stage and the *Fort! Da!*, but it would seem also to affect the significance of transitivism. The play with the pronoun shifters, that is, ought to be equivalent, structurally, to play with the mirror-image; and it ought, therefore, to map upon the child's Unconscious the truth that I and me are functions of purely structural relations.

Freud's scenario of the *Fort! Da!* begins, we recall, by his watching his nephew playing on his bed with a reel and a string. As the reel disappears over the side of the bed, the boy cries "o-o-o-o," which Freud interprets as *Fort* (gone). When the reel is pulled back into sight, the boy says *Da* (here). For Freud, this game replicates the educational lesson of the appearance/disappearance of the image in the mirror. For Lacan, it is rather the further capture of the child in the structural system of language: instead of mastering, he is himself mastered, becomes subjected to the primary binary phonemes registering absence/presence.[39] Again we can see that the structural effect is one of installing functional relatedness, that presence cannot be privileged or experienced outside its relationship to absence. Thus it is once more the condition of play itself that makes the *Fort! Da!* central to Lacan's interpretation. In the game with the reel, the child's needs (of the mother, for example) become split from his demand (that she return and recognize him) in such a way as to give rise to an unspecified desire. That is, desire, unlike need or demand, is purely symbolic, a constituent of the very system of transferring attention from the mother (real or imaginary) or an object directly associated with her to one of arbitrary signification (the reel). In Lacan's scenario, the reel gone incites the reel returned and vice versa: *Fort* can be articulated or imagined only in relation to its opposite *Da*. In one sense, then, the subject has now been inscribed within the dialectics of language in the same way that he was earlier inscribed within the dialectics of vision. But in a more crucial sense, he has made an important psychic step forward, for he has escaped from the primordial imaginary matrix of the ego and its image-mirages into the more fully human context of a variety of symbolic functions.[40] Lacan sees this in Freud's report that later when his nephew throws the reel over the edge of the bed, *Fort* is replaced by "Gone to the fwont." The boy's father, serving in the war, has now been added to the imaginary scene of the mother and has now become a full-fledged symbolic figure in the familial and social register that Freud names the Oedipus. The boy too, via the newly articulated game, is also fully registered within that symbolic field.

We have already shown that Lacan conceives the object-image in the mirror as body-as-unity; the child, however, is anatomically incomplete. Lacan relates this phenomenon—which he calls, after the embryologists, fetalization—to man's fascination with body parts, with "images of castration, mutilation, dismemberment, dislocation, evisceration, devouring, bursting open of the body."[41] Lacan inscribes these images of the fragmented body under the general Freudian notion of aggressivity, especially in children. Lacan's analysis of these images is not as convincing as his other glosses on the mirror phase,[42] but such images form an important link between Lacan's notions and Traherne's poetry. In fact, Traherne would seem to offer a more valid entry into the structural dialectic of body parts/whole than Lacan's own example of Hieronymus Bosch,[43] for Traherne deploys such imagery only in relation to his equivalent of the *stade du miroir*. And though it would be unfair to place too much emphasis on this relatively minor aspect of the mirror stage, it is, nonetheless, a compelling instance of how the modern psychoanalyst can help us interpret one imaginative center of the seventeenth-century poet.

Like most of his central conceptions, Lacan's explication of the triadic real-imaginary-symbolic is dense and difficult, but it is essential to his development of the structural subject of desire and the psychological function of the Other. The three terms appear to define dimensions of consciousness. The real is the irreducible region of organism and biological need. It is not "reality" in the normal sense, but what the subject takes as real and which remains always and forever beyond knowing consciousness, that which can never be articulated or expressed. The imaginary is the register of the ego and its images, the specular reflexivities Lacan demonstrates in the mirror stage. The symbolic is the region of the signifier, the field of speech and language, familial and cultural systems.[44] Of the three dimensions, the relations between the imaginary and the symbolic are the most important, for the subject who remains captivated in the imaginary fails primarily to understand the entire system of signification—fails, in essence, to recognize anything, including himself, as a signifier, as a function of an intersubjective system of communal relations.

Perhaps the easiest way to approach the three regions is through the child's relation to his parents, especially to the father. Biological dependence and organic need express the dimension of the real, and yet this dimension is unrealizable by the child. Insofar as he can conceive of his parents only in terms of fragmented parts (mother-breast, for example, and father-penis), he too is inscribed within the family structure as merely another bodily part. Here the lack of wholeness or of unalienated self-hood propels the child into imaginary identification: his specular assumption of the father's image reconstitutes the child in the position of the real father and thus in an untenable rivalry with him. This may occur at the level of the body part itself—the child wishes to be the phallus that he imagines the mother to desire—or on the level of the ego—the father is the ego-ideal of the child who is then unable to distinguish one "I" from another. In the symbolic register, the child takes over or on the *function* of the father by identifying not with the real father or the imaginary ideal, but with what Lacan calls the Name-of-the-Father, the linguistic term designating the child's entry into the consciousness of a system of intrafamilial exchange and cultural code—the register of the law. Only in the symbolic dimension is the child freed of specular identifications, for here he recognizes function as such, recognizes, that is, that he is a signifier in any number of structured systems.[45] The subject, Lacan argues, is resubjectified out of the various objectifications which govern and captivate him in the mirror phases of the imaginary. Entry into the symbolic thus allows not only a recognition (not *understanding*) in the subject of his own desire, but also a path out of the binding imaginary dialectic into a displacement of it at another level of signification (mother as love-object can now be replaced by another girl: [m]Other displaced by [an]other).

Lacan insists that the three registers do not represent developmental stages, that they coexist at all times, and that they describe only structural relations of the ego.[46] And yet, since the psychotic, for example, is precisely that subject who has not progressed beyond the imaginary, some notion of temporal development seems inevitable. Even if we simply take the imaginary as inscribing the specular region of the *stade du miroir* and the symbolic as the dimension of speech, the two realms would seem, on some level, to represent diachronic progression. Whether this is a justifiable reading of Lacan's remarks or not, it will serve us in treating Traherne, for I think the turns from real to imaginary and from imaginary to symbolic will offer a better explication than has yet been proposed for a text like the Dobell manuscript. To anticipate a later argument and to clarify the present one, the speaker of the Dobell poems is captivated throughout most of the sequence in an imaginary relation with the Other (God) that consistently fuses and confuses the identities of both the self and that Other. Only at the end of the sequence, when the signifying name-of-Christ is finally articulated, does the speaker escape the specular *meconnaissance* and gain entry into the full system of human and cultural interaction. As I understand that shift, the I that is caught in an imaginary configuration cannot distinguish between the others that he sees (Lacan's *a*) and the Other he can not see (Lacan's *A*). Only the symbolic register allows the subject to grasp the relations between *a* and *A* or to see that *a* (as well as *a'*) is a structural factor of *A*. Rather than reading the Dobell sequence as some version of mystic ascent or as an archetypal pattern of Christian birth-fall-redemption, I will try to use Lacan's notions of the imaginary and the symbolic to argue that the sequence charts instead a course of psychic development into fully human maturity.

"See how each one the other calls" ("On Christmas-Day"). Other men and the "significant Other," who is normally figured as God, are constantly being called by and calling upon Traherne. No less than Lacan, Traherne-as-subject finds himself situated in the locus of an Other and for that reason we may expect that Lacan's analysis of this locus can shed interpretive light on Traherne's poetic strategies.

"The *moi* of which we speak," Lacan writes in "Introduction au commentaire de Jean Hyppolite," "is absolutely impossible to distinguish from the insidious imaginary captures which constitute it from head to foot, in its genesis as in its status, in its function as in its actuality, by another and for another."[47] Such is the structural conclusion, as we have already seen, that Lacan draws from the *stade du miroir* as well as from his discrimination between the eye and the gaze. The *me* of the developing psyche is an *alter* ego: an alienating image or notion of self objectified in relation to the perceived (or misperceived) Other. The Other, for Lacan, is never a person; like mother, father, I, *moi*, and all other pronominal shifters, it is rather a function. Therefore, whether Lacan uses the term to designate the mother (the real dyadic relation between mother and child), the parent who holds the child for the first time before the mirror (the imaginary confusion of identity with the Other), or the father (who, as the symbolic other, wrenches apart the dyadic identification and forces the accommodation of a third term, thereby reconstituting the child in the family as a subject in his own right), the Other is a structural necessity for all human relations and for any consciousness of self. Or, in more elementary terms, all consciousness of self (here using "consciousness" in its most general sense and allowing for the coterminous fact of *meconnaissance* of self) is irreducibly grounded in the condition of recognizing and being recognized by some other. For Lacan, and unlike Hegel, no reconciliation of self and Other(ness) is possible, and to this extent, self and Other can be seen as analogous to Heidegger's being and Being. The split or separation of self and Other *is* the structural base of the human being. And that, in turn, gives rise to all Lacan will try to articulate under the general notion of desire.

There is a direct connection between Lacan's conception of the Other and his appropriation of Saussurian linguistics. As we have seen in the *Fort! Da!*, linguistic duality precedes unity: the phonemic couple or pair is anterior to either isolated element. Speech or discourse, in Saussurian terms, yields the same conclusion insofar as every term, every signifier, requires a complementary term in systematic relation to which it will be differentiated and for which it can be substituted.[48] At the level of self-recognition and articulation, that is, at the level of the child's entry into the system of linguistically shifting signifiers (I, me, she, he, it), where all terms name both the self and the Other, all signification is constituted by the intermapping relations between self and Other, subjectification and objectification. Whether the human being conceives of himself, or makes himself, a linguistic subject or a linguistic object, he is caught in this intersectional discourse between a self and an Other. Discourse—language, in fact—is precisely conditioned upon this necessity, for all speech calls for a reply in the same way that every *Fort* requires and incites a *Da*:

> What I seek in the Word is the response of the Other. What constitutes me as subject is my question [i.e., do you see me; do you love me?]. In order to be recognized by the other, I utter what was only in view of what will be. In order to find him, I call him by a name which he must assume or refuse in order to reply to me.
>
> I identify myself in Language, but only by losing myself in it like an object. What is realized in my history is not the past definite of what was, since it is no more, or even the present of what has been in what I am, but the future anterior of what I shall have been for what I am in the process of becoming.
>
> The subject as such is uncertain because he is divided by the effects of language. Through the effects of speech, the subject always realizes himself more in the Other, but he is already pursuing there more than half of himself. He will simply find his desire ever more divided, pulverized, in the circumscribable metonymy of speech. The effects of language are always mixed with the fact, which is the basis of the analytic experience, that the subject is subject only from being subjected to the field of the Other; the subject proceeds from his synchronic subjection in the field of the Other.[49]

Inscribed in his focus on the *stade du miroir*, the role of necessary alienation through "otherness" in the dialectical formation of human personality is Lacan's given. We can look again at Schema L:

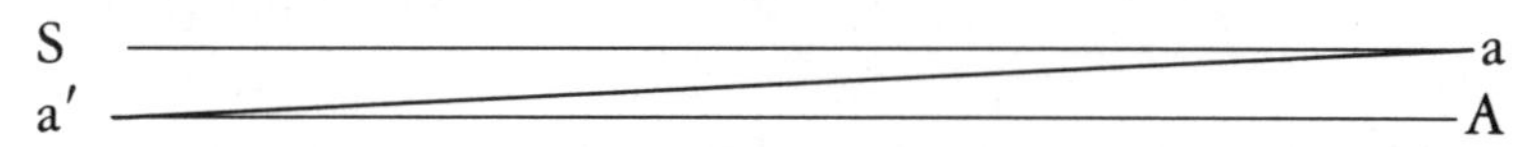

As Lacan says, the "schema signifies that the condition of the subject S is dependent on what is being unfolded in the Other O. What is being unfolded there is articulated like a discourse."[50] I take this to mean that the syntactic relation of *S-O* (*S-A* as given here) is articulated in the structural relations between an ideal ego (a') and what Lacan calls the *objet petit a* (the *autre* of l'Autre, the object the Other lacks, the lack of the Other which generates the ideal egos of the subject in order to satisfy the Other's desire, the others through which the subject tries to reach the Other).[51] We shall address Lacan's notion of desire as the intermapping of dual lacks in a moment, but what is crucial here is to distinguish between others-as-objects (*a*) and the symbolic field of Otherness as such (*A*). Others (small *a*) are never the Other, for the Other, as pure function, is itself empty, a lost object, an unnameable absence. Again, we can see that the relation between others and Other is analogous to Heidegger's discrimination between beings and Being. Neither Being nor Other is present as such: both are structural necessities upon which all self-recognition and other-recognition are inevitably dependent. Thus, for Lacan, the encounter between the subject and another (child and mother or father, for example) situates the living being in the "discourse of the Other." He or she is saying this to me, but what does he want or why is she telling me this? The child thus encounters, or imagines, a lack in the other which he is being called upon to satisfy at the same time as his own entry into language provides him with the power to articulate his own demand for the satisfaction of desires. That lack in the other becomes registered as Other, and it is now to that Other that the child's desire is directed.

Here Lacan's conception of the Other necessarily requires a fuller formulation of the mechanics of desire itself. As Jean Laplanche argues, Lacanian desire must be distinguished from need and demand. Need, for the child as for the adult, aims at a particular object (the breast, a home) and is satisfied with that. Demand puts another in question: it is an appeal to the other for love or recognition and it cannot be satisfied by any object (even love returned, or recognition granted). Another way of stating this distinction would be to argue that need is fundamentally biological whereas demand is strictly psychological. As Laplanche explains, then, it is precisely in this split between need and demand that desire as such is born. Desire

> is irreducible to need, because it is not in principle a relation to a real object which is independent of the subject, but a relation to a phantasy. It is irreducible to demand, insofar as it

> seeks to impose itself without taking language or the unconscious of the other into account, and requires to be recognized absolutely by him. Demand is thus *for* something, whether that something is desired or not, whereas desire, as an absolute, is fundamentally the Hegelian desire for recognition, in that the subject seeks recognition as a human subject by requiring the other to recognize his human desire; in this sense one desires what another desires.[52]

If we think again of the *Fort*! *Da*!, we could say that it stages all three of these drives. Insofar as the child lets the reel stand for the mother, his need to control her appearing and disappearing is answered in manipulation of the substitute object. The child's demand that the mother recognize him is not satisfied in the game with the reel, even though that game imaginatively articulates his demand and announces his absolute lack. Within the split, then, between a satisfiable need and an unsatisfiable demand, desire arises on a totally different level of psychic registration. The reel is thrown over the edge of the bed for the sole purpose of drawing it back; the reel is returned precisely in order to make it disappear again. What the child effects in the game is the production of desire itself, desire that is, in effect, neither necessary to the object in play nor recognized at all by the child who is playing.

Desire, Lacan reiterates in his favorite formula, is the desire of the Other, meaning that "it is a question of a sort of desire *on the part of* the Other, at the end of which is a showing," that is, a *donner-a-voir*, a giving-of-self-to-be-seen, objectifying the self before the Other's gaze, as Lacan articulates it in the *stade du miroir*. "How could this showing satisfy something," Lacan continues, "if there is not some appetite of the eye on the part of the person looking?"[53] This means, I think, that desire is always situated in both a dependence upon demand and an imagined relation to need. That is, the subject must perceive a lack in the Other as the necessary precondition of the Other's desire. The appetite of the gaze, of the Other's eye, needs an object to see. So the subject responds to that appetite by objectifying himself in relation to a supposed lack. But the subject also recognizes, perhaps unconsciously, that the self he gives to be seen is not the self he wishes the Other to see. Indeed, demand is for the

Other to see him as he really is, subjectively, not objectively. This wish, or demand, thus articulates a lack in the subject himself which the Other is then called upon to satisfy. Self and Other are irretrievably caught in what Lacan calls a want-to-be, and desire as such is born from the discovery of a *difference* (between subject/object, presence/absence, self/Other, etc.) which situates all beings in that *manque d'être*, that lack of being.[54] Neither the Other nor the subject is capable of satisfying this desire: I cannot be loved for what I am; I can only be loved as a signifier of what you lack. If, then, I am a metonymy of your desire, you are a metonymy of my want-to-be.

> One lack is superimposed upon the other. The dialectic of the objects of desire, insofar as it creates the link between the desire of the subject [as he perceives a lack in the Other, he wishes to *be* what is lacking—Lacan's favorite example is the child who identifies himself with the imaginary object of the mother's desire insofar as the mother herself symbolizes it in the phallus which she lacks] and the desire of the Other. . . . this dialectic now passes through the fact that desire is not replied to directly. It is a lack engendered from the previous time that serves to reply to the lack raised by the following time.[55]

The desire of the Other, moreover, is precisely the inexpressible and irreducible enigma to which the subject's desire is inevitably subjected:

> A lack is encountered by the subject in the Other, in the very intimation that the Other makes to him by his discourse. In the intervals of the discourse of the Other, there emerges in the experience of the child something that is radically mappable, namely, *He is saying this to me, but what does he want?*
>
> It is there that what we call desire crawls, slips, escapes, like the ferret. The desire of the Other is apprehended by the subject in that which does not work, in the lacks of the discourse of the Other, and all the child's *whys* reveal not so much an avidity for the reasons of things, as a testing of the adult, a *Why are you telling me this?* ever-resuscitated from its base, which is the enigma of the adult's desire.[56]

Out of this superimposition of lacks and desires comes man's entry into the symbolic register of language itself, of the systematic interplay of sliding signifieds whose signifiers always elude definitive capture or expression. The symbolic, in short, is the law of the signifier, the subject's acceptance of the fact that he *is* only insofar as he becomes object and subject in the binary interplay of the discourse of the Other.

"Man's desire is desire of the Other." Man desires to *be* the desire of the Other and desires insofar as he *is* Other. No mediation of this split in being is possible for man, much as he may try to segregate himself from others, desire from demand, or ego from image. His gaze, like his language, traps him in the continual exchange of signifying functions and specular confusions. And his desire, constantly regenerating itself out of this exchange or those confusions, remains ever unsatisfied and even, finally, inexpressible. For Lacan as much as for Derrida, man becomes man only insofar as he is inscribed within the trace-structures of a primordially empty language. The full word is merely the return to what Lacan calls the psychoanalytic and poetic function of language itself: to give man's desire its necessary symbolic function and register.

II THE EYE AND I

There are a number of ways Lacan's theories are applicable and interpretively useful to Traherne's poetry, and we might begin with some general observations. Insofar as the *Centuries of Meditation* and the Dobell manuscript represent Traherne's attempt to fashion a *verbe* or *epos* by which he re-collects in the present the origins and historical development of his own person, it is curious that no one has remarked on the structural necessity of the "friends" to whom both works are addressed. I do not mean here the general "reader" about whom Stanley Stewart speculates or a particular Susanna Hopton, but the "significant Other" in terms of which the narratives could not proceed at all. Neither do I mean the "Som Great Thing" that is addressed as Christ early in the First Century and as God throughout the Dobell poems. Both of these "others" are necessary to Traherne's project and both serve structural functions that we can and will chart. But the unnamed Other, whose desire Traherne seeks to incite and address, who incites and is made answerable to Traherne's own desire, is the ground upon which the entire *epos* of linguistic re-creation is begun. From the first meditation to the last, as from "The Author to the Critical Peruser" to "Goodness,"[57] the symbolic register of the pronominal shifters—I, you, we, me, us, them, Him—could not be articulated without the present absence of this Other. This means, I think, that even prior to the particular themes Traherne will treat or the particular language he adopts in treating them, his entire poetic is predicated upon a specular objectification, a fashioning of a self-to-be-seen for the Other who is conceived of having a desire to see.[58] The specular or scopic register, therefore, inscribes not only the narrative structures of Eye and I, image and object, man and God, but the entire speech act as such: enacting and staging an ideal-ego before the gaze of the desiring Other. To conceive Traherne's poetic in this way allows us to deflect attention away from the more common focus on the insistent "I" and toward the structural mechanisms that inevitably bind that recollected self to a recollecting Other.

The same kind of shift in focus emerges once we begin to look closely at Traherne as preeminently a poet of desire. Most criticism has concentrated on a Traherne who, unlike Donne or Herbert or even Vaughan, rarely suffers from any sense of sin or alienation or despair. The frequency with which he resorts to such terms as bliss, joy, glory, felicity, happiness, pleasure, and so forth lends authority to this view. And yet the portrait of a comfortable and innocently blissful Traherne is very wrong. Whether, to adopt his own favorite categories, we begin with poetic causes or ethical ends, desire is Traherne's constant concern: man's desire, God's desire, his own private desires, his reader's desires, all become subject to Traherne's thoughtful poetizing.[59] As he says himself in the First Century, "Desire imports somthing absent: and a Need of what is Absent" (*CM*, I.43). To this extent, viewing Traherne as a poet of desire will again allow us to reconsider the structuring mechanisms of his thought. This is not to say that Traherne, like Lacan, is primarily concerned with the psychic structures of desire, but rather to argue that such structures are precisely what his poetry constantly articulates and displays. It is also to urge that we understand in a far more radical sense the significance of Traherne's plea in *Meditations on the*

Six Days that God "give me *Perfection* in my Desires at least" (p. 23).

The most interesting, and most surprising, application of Lacan to Traherne concerns the Dobell manuscript, and before we attempt to chart the fuller implications of Lacanian theory for Traherne's text it might be helpful to have a general sense of the end toward which this chapter is heading. So I offer the following plot as a tentative *epos* of the Dobell narrative.

Childhood, to Traherne no less than Lacan, is a stage of specular confusions. The child's first impressions are of fragmentation —separate body parts, disconnected sensations, discrete objects. Through a dramatic scene of imaginary and narcissistic reflection, the child is captivated by a specular image of himself, an ideal-ego which serves as a cohesive *imago* to re-collect the scattered fragments. At approximately the same time, the significant Other in relation to whom this image of self is perceived—and whom Lacan normally designates as the mother—is imagined as lacking something. The child, then, trying both to incite and to fulfill the demand of this Other, imaginatively identifies with the object that s/he lacks, indeed makes himself into that object. In Lacan's terms, the child who imagines the mother as lacking the phallus fantasizes that he *is* the phallus, objectifies himself in relation to her imagined need/demand, in order to satisfy her and his own desires. For Traherne, the specular capture of the mirror phase means that the I of the poems must constitute God in the structural position of the mother—must, that is, imagine God-as-(m)Other as an entity suffering from a primordial *manque d'être* which he, by becoming the lost object Being lacks, can fulfill. In short, the mirror stage of Traherne's manuscript predicts a doubled imaginative re-creation: of God as incomplete; of man as that being that God needs and desires in order to complete Himself.

Seen in this way, Traherne's otherwise astonishing (at least for the Christian reader) suppression of the preeminent figure of Christ until the penultimate poem of the narrative takes on important meaning. For it is Christ, not God, who functions in the sequence as the Lacanian Name-of-the-Father. Only the now symbolic recognition of Christ frees the child from the objectifying and fantasizing alienations of the mirror stage and allows him entry into some full functional subjectivity of a human signifier. And it is only at this point—which Lacan calls the fulfillment of the Oedipal relations—that the human subject can recognize and respond to others authentically and realistically: that is to say, as symbolic functions of intersubjective relationships and not merely as objects of his own specular fantasy or narcissistic ego-ideals.

It will be recognized at once that such a psychic plot for the Dobell poems reverses more normal interpretive assumptions. God-Mother and Christ-Father radically subvert both man's own son-of-God *imago* and the Son of God Himself. That subversion, however, is not my primary focus; rather, I wish only to argue that Lacanian theory offers a key point of entry into the significant structural mechanisms of Traherne's imagination. Thus, rather than viewing the Dobell poems as sketching stages of mystical ascent or Bonaventuran meditation, I want to argue that what Traherne presents here is nothing less than an *epos* of Christian maturation, from un-knowing and confused childhood to authentic and responsible adulthood.

In order to prepare for this argument, let us return to the larger Trahernean text and the principal Lacanian notions of the *stade du miroir*, the Other, and desire. As with Lacan himself, it is difficult, if not impossible, fully to separate Traherne's thoughts on any one of these topics from their implications on and for the others. But let us try to focus for a moment on desire itself.

"Man's desire is desire of the Other," desire of being recognized by the Other, of being the Other's desire, of being desirable to the Other, of desiring the Other. In Traherne's version of these dialectical and irreducible structures, the principal actors are man and God. Both are treated in the same terms. Indeed, it is fair to say that it is precisely upon the coterminous structures of desire inscribing both God and man that Traherne's entire conception of the mirror stage is based. We can begin with God, recognizing, however, that God Himself is conceived only as an object of man's desire, not, here, as a separate or even prior being.

God desires and desires infinitely. Although Traherne is careful not to limit God's self-sufficiency or His perfection, his thoughts on the Deity continually return to questions of desire: *what* does God desire, *how* does He desire, and *why* does He desire. Insofar as God is perfect, he does not need anything; but insofar as He is God, He demands all. Like Lacan, Traherne situates God's desire in this gap between need and demand, a gap that is defined most often as a lack, an absence, a want, and a loss. "God," Traherne writes in the First Century "is from Eternity full of Want: Or els He would not be full of Treasure": "Infinit Want is the very Ground and Caus of infinit Treasure. It is Incridible, yet very Plain: Want is the Fountain of all His Fulness. . . . For had there been no Need He would not hav Created the World, nor Made us, nor Manifested his Wisdom, nor Exercised his Power, nor Beautified Eternity, nor prepared the Joys of Heaven. But He Wanted Angels and Men, Images, Companions" (*CM* I.42).

Although Traherne immediately adds "And these He had from all Eternity," that caution does not weaken the paradoxes he himself finds "very Strange": empty *and* full, needs *and* treasures, presence *and* absence. The following meditation extends those paradoxes: "Infinit Wants Satisfied Produce infinit Joys. And, in the Possession of those Joys are infinit Joys themselvs. *The Desire Satisfied is a Tree of Life*. Desire imports som thing absent: And a Need of what is Absent. GOD was never without this Tree of Life. He did Desire infinitly. yet He was never without the Fruits of this Tree, which are the Joys it produced. I must lead you out of this [paradox]" (*CM* I.43). "The Anticipation" tries to do so:

> From Everlasting he these Joys did Need,
> And all these Joys proceed
> From Him Eternaly.
>
> Wants are the Fountains of Felicitie
> No Joy could ever be
> Were there no Want. No Bliss
> No Sweetness Perfect were it not for this.
> Want is the Greatest Pleasure
> Becaus it makes all Treasure.
> O what a Wonderfull Profound Abyss
> Is God! In whom Eternal Wants and Treasures
> Are more Delightfull caus they both are Pleasures.
>
> He infinitly wanteth all his Joys;
> (No Want the Soul ore cloys.)

> And All those Wanted Pleasures
> He infinitly Hath.
> (ll. 19–21, 64–76)

Like Lacan, Traherne is exploiting the double sense of "want" as both verb (to desire, wish for) and noun (something lacking, absent). But if God is fullness, what could he desire or lack? Traherne begins to raise this question when, in "The Approach," he wonders why God persists in visiting him, why He forbears "tho Sleighted many a yeer." And his answer, recorded in the *Centuries*, is a provocative revisioning of the Fall in terms of God's desire for a lost object (the other that Lacan terms *objet petite a*):

> By how much the greater His Lov was, by so much the Greater may his Sorrow be at the Loss of His Object: and by so much the Greater His Desire also of its Restauration. (*CM*, II.31)

> All the Desire wherwith He longs after a Returning Sinner, makes Him to esteem a Broken Heart. . . . The Falling out of Lovers is the Beginning of Lov: the renewing, the repairing . . . of it. (*CM*, III.83)

> He [that is, I] thought that men were more to be Beloved now than before. And which is a strange Paradox, the Worse they are the more they were to be beloved. The worse they are the more they were to be Pittied and Tendered and Desired. (*CM*, IV.26)

God desires all souls to love Him and is, in Traherne's terms, "infinitly" displeased when they choose not to do so. But such a fall away from God is fortunate. God's "loss of their Lov [may be] an Evil past Imagination"—because "it is a Removal of the End of Heaven and Earth" (*CM*, IV.86) and because "nothing can supply the absence or denial of that Love" (*CE*, 251)—but it also increases God's desire. The Fall, in short, ensures that the love and desire of man is the "Sovereign object" of God's own desire.

Having inscribed God in relation to desire for a lost object, an absence and a lack, Traherne tries to rewrite God's desire as precisely "the desire of the Other." The question, in other words, has become not so much *why* God desires—although this is still of central concern—as *what* He desires. Traherne's answers are not surprising: God desires esteem, love, admiration, glory, and desire as such. But while some of these "objects" appear relatively uncomplicated—like the assertion in *Centuries* I.10 that a soul which enjoys all it has been given "doth accomplish the End of His Desire"—most reveal a Traherne who is extremely sensitive to the kind of dialectic Lacan describes as the irreducible structure of desire. In the Second Century, for example, Traherne argues that God's love "endlessly desireth to Delight it self, and its Delight is to Magnify its Beloved" (II.25); it is also "Right Wise unto it self, in satisfying it self in its infinit Desire of becoming Delightfull to its Object" and "in making you [man] that Object" (*CM*, II.25). God's love is "Righteous to its self . . . in requiring that [it] be infinitly Esteemed, of which it is infinitly Desirous" (*CM*, II.28).

Later in the same Century, Traherne collapses any distinction between desire as such and Being itself: to be is to desire, even for God: "For this End therfore did He desire to Lov, that He might be LOV. Infinitly Delightfull to all Objects, infinitly Delighted in all, and infinitly Pleased in Himself, for being infinitly Delightfull to all, and Delighted in all. . . . And thus you see how GOD is the End of Himself. He doth [desire] what He doth, that He may be what He is" (*CM*, II.47). We may hear behind this passage a submerged echo of a more primordial lack: that *manque d'être* which Lacan situates at the very center of all desire. And in these terms we might suggest that Traherne's "infinitly" may best be understood as "eternally" or "irreducibly": desire is exactly that which can never be satisfied and which must therefore seek always to replicate or heighten itself by requiring/desiring ever more desire on the part of the Other. "Becaus therfore God is Lov and his Measure infinit: He infinitly desires to be Admired and Beloved" (*CM*, III.82); the insatiable nature of that desire must, as a consequence, inspire an equally insatiable desire in the object of its desire.

The lack of being that gives rise to desire may also be heard in the Fourth Century: "He could never Enjoy Himself, but as He was enjoyed of others, and that above all Delights in all Worlds, he desired to be a Joy and Blessing to others" (*CM*, IV.32). If we have seemed here to move the issue of desire closer to the necessity of the Other for recognition of the self, that is only because Traherne himself structures desire on these terms. "For abov all Things in all Worlds," he writes in *Centuries* IV.62, God's love "desires to be Magnified, and taketh Pleasure in being Glorified before its Object. for which caus also it does all those Things, which magnify its object and increase its Happiness." "Magnify" here carries a residue of specular capture: in order to be seen by the Other as glorious, the self must invest the Other with the capacity of glory. Thus, while God may "desire Glory as his Soveraign End" (*CM*, IV.64), he must equally "desire som one, that might Weigh and reason, lov the Beauty, and admire" that glory in order that He himself might see it (*CM*, IV.75).

In chapter one we defined glory as synonymous in Traherne's mind with that giving/receiving motion of love he calls circulation or communication. We can bring this motion to bear upon God's desire by examining a longer passage from *Christian Ethicks*:

> GOD does desire Love from us, because his *Wisdom* very well knows, that without Love the World would be in vain, and the End of the Creation frustrated: his *Goodness* is diffusive and infinitly desires to communicate it self, which it cannot do, unless it be Beloved. . . . His *Blessedness* consisteth in the pleasure he taketh in the Felicity of others, and brancheth it self out into two Parts, the Pleasure of communicating all to others, and the pleasure of receiving all from others . . . His *Glory* desires to be seen, and delighted in: To be esteemed and beloved: to be honored and admired, is natural to *Glory*, the Brightness of whose splendor is more Sensibly Pleasant in the Reflection of its face, and in the Joy that it makes in anothers Soul. . . . There is an *Objective fitness* and Excellency in Love . . . It is one of the first and immediate Properties of Love to desire to be beloved, to make its object most Amiable and Beautiful, as well as Blessed; to be united to it, to have its own Goodness acknowledged, its Essence approved, its excellency desired, admired and delighted in; to see all its Actions, Appearances, Gifts and Tokens esteemed; and to feel its own Efficacy, in the Grateful Acceptance it finds, in the Raptures it occasions, in the flames it enkindles in anothers Soul. (*CE*, 56)

The desire of God needs (because it lacks), requires (because it demands), and obligates (because it calls forth and sanctions) the desire of man. Like the Lacanian subject, God's desire is the desire of the Other. Traherne works constantly to express this dialectic, here using the terms of communication, reflection, and objective fitness. Each term tries to spell out further implications of God's desire. Communication grounds desire in the giving/receiving pattern of language—as Lacan reminds us, every word always already contains its own reply. Reflection focuses on the specular capture within which both the self and the Other generate ideal-egos answerable to imagined desires. And objective fitness directs us to the energies that reshape subjectivity into a scopic object for and of the Other. Each of these terms, moreover, suggests that the principal task of desire is to fashion not only the self, but also an object that is adequate to the desired desires of that self. And the adequation of any object of desire is, in turn, measured by its possibility of being lost or withheld and the impossibility of its being fully possessed. Only on the twin poles of that dialectic can desire continually generate itself out of itself. Desire desires desire! Traherne's consciousness of this replicating structure can be seen in his analysis of man's desire.

"Man's desire is desire of the Other." Traherne's versions of this Lacanian proverb immediately situate God in the structural position of the Other: "Is not His Desire yours" (*CM*, I.53); man "desires all that GOD desires" (*CE*, 285). This congruence of desire, however, is not the most telling fact, for we must ask what occasions it. Is Traherne's engagement with his own and every man's desire an inevitable consequence of his conception of a desiring God and his effort to demonstrate how man is created in imitation, as a specular image, of that God? Or is his conception of God itself a consequence of the originary fact of man's desire? Given Traherne's emphasis on childhood, on a developing consciousness of being, it seems more likely that God is Himself an object fashioned by an already insatiable desire. As such, God, like man himself, is captivated in a specular exchange—that is, Traherne's God is imaginatively recreated in the image of man—and fully inscribed within the dialectical structuring of desire itself.

"There is an instinct," Traherne suggests in *Christian Ethicks*, "that carries us to the beginning of our Lives" (*CE*, 212). That beginning he frequently defines in terms that are fraught with meaning for immanent desire. In the Dobell poems, it is a silence "Beneath the Dust . . . in a Chaos," an abyss; man himself was "Nothing from Eternitie" and he arises "out of Nothing." In *Christian Ethicks*, "our Original" is again "that eternal abyss of Idleness and Vacuity out of which we were taken . . . made of Nothing" (*CE*, 213). In Lacanian terms, man's originary condition is a *manque d'être* which gives rise to a desire that, in its persistent replication, seeks ever to fill that lack.[60] The creature that was Nothing from eternity desires subsequently to be All. We will see later how this dialectic of empty/full structures much of Traherne's thought, but at the moment we might simply note that the imagined end of desire—"it is the desire of the soul to be filled with all the fulness of GOD" (*CE*, 227)—is firmly grounded in the original want, lack, and absence. Such a ground predicates, of course, an equally absent satisfaction: desire must imagine *more*, must continually posit higher, more unattainable, objects, and validates itself only to the extent that it can remain insatiable.[61]

It is in this sense that man's Fall becomes more central to Traherne's imaginative endeavor than most criticism has recognized, for the Fall opens man's loss—his wants and his lacks—to the desiring urgencies of restoration, recollection, recovery. The *epos* thus already mapped for man is precisely that diachronic process Lacan calls the "temporal pulsation" within which consciousness and the Unconscious strive: "What is realized in my history is not the past definite of what was, since it is no more, or even the present perfect of what has been in what I am, but the future anterior of what I shall have been for what I am in the process of becoming."[62] And it also poses the crucial questions of man's being on the grid of an eternal absence which desire continually seeks to fool itself into perceiving as a presence.

Perhaps the best place to observe this generation of desire is in the Third Century, where Traherne tries to record his first childhood impressions and to define his nascent desires. As early as the second meditation Traherne's description of the new, strange, innumerable joys of childhood is grounded upon loss and absence: "I knew by Intuition those things which since my Apostasie, I Collected again";

"I knew Nothing of Sickness or Death, or Exaction, in the Absence of these I was entertained like an Angel" (*CM*, III.2). In the third meditation, as if in unconscious preparation for the Fall he records at its close, Traherne writes that "som thing infinit Behind evry thing appeared: which talked with my Expectation and moved my Desire" (*CM*, III, 3). Though all was his, and he "the only Spectator and Enjoyer of it," even before he is corrupted there is lack, the "som thing" that is wanting (behind, hidden, inaccessible) and thus inciting desire. Meditation seven suggests that this desire, rather than leading Traherne to imagine God, instead led him away from the sovereign object: "I was weak, and easily guided by [all men's] Example: Ambitious also, and Desirous to approve my self unto them" (*CM*, III.7). It is precisely in the context of this new desire, of installing men as the objects of his desire, that Traherne finds "the first Light which shined in my Infancy in its Primitive and Innocent Clarity was totaly ecclypsed" (*CM*, III.7). From this point on in the Century, desire is irretrievably embedded in loss and lack. It is also, of course, irreducibly bound to the Other, for "I was quickly tainted and fell by others" (*CM*, III.8). What may seem here—and throughout Traherne—an ungenerous and even un-Christian deferral of his own culpability onto another is perhaps best understood as a necessary cancellation of man-as-the-object-of-desire in order to reinstall God as the only fully adequate object of that desire. That installation, in fact, is what the remainder of the Century portrays.

The tenth meditation begins by suggesting how the divine object was originally displaced: "My Soul was only Apt and Disposed [i.e., desirous of] to Great Things; But Souls to Souls are like Apples to Apples, one being rotten rots another. When I began to speak . . . Nothing began to be present to me, but what was present in [men's] Thoughts. Nor was any thing present to me any other way, then it was so to them. The Glass of Imagination was the only Mirror, wherin any thing was represented or appeared to me. All Things wer Absent which they talkt not of" (*CM*, III.10). *Nothing* is present; *All* is absent. The specular capture of the Other, of other men and especially of their language, inscribes the original loss. The world Traherne now sees is described as a "Miserable Gulph of idle talk," empty, vain, forlorn (*CM*, III.14). "All [was] lost, and Absent from me" (*CM*, III.16). Only by "forgetting" this world can Traherne begin to ask the crucial questions of Being: why the world is, what was before, what and where man is, why is he not Other? "I mightily desired to Know." And that thirst to know, the aspiration to knowledge, is once again grounded in desire and lack: "I was som times . . . visited and inspired with New and more vigorous Desires after that Bliss which Nature Whispered and Suggested to me" (*CM*, III.22). Desire here, we might note, is at a second degree: it presupposes the unsatisfied desire of the Other that has occasioned the Fall. Traherne asks, therefore, "What Secret Force movd my Desire," and he answers, "I Thirsted Absent Bliss" (*CM*, III.26). On these grounds, desire generates or recollects presence: whatever is "Absent to my Ey" becomes "present to my Understanding." Understanding, in this context, must be interpreted as imagination, for it is only objects of desire that the self is now driven to conceive or construct in order to satisfy itself. And satisfaction here does not mean fulfillment of desire, but rather the generation and replication of more desire.

Desire, argues Lacan, is concurrent with man's initial questioning of Being;[63] indeed, all questions about his being are spoken from and within the discourse of desire. Traherne, in his own terms, would agree: it is precisely because Being is situated within desire that Traherne is able to image God as the only adequate object of being's desire. The stages of this imaginative movement from self to Other and man to God are sketched in the middle of the Third Century. In questioning the Being of humanity, Traherne argues,

> we search into the Powers and Faculties of the Soul, enquire into the Excellencies of Humane Nature, consider its Wants, Survey its Inclination Propensities and Desires. . . . Wherby we com to know what Man is in this World. . . . by discerning [his] real Wants and Soveraign desires. (*CM*, III.42)

Sovereign desires, of course, require sovereign objects. Traherne identifies two: "Felicitie is a Glorious tho [i.e., because?] an unknown Thing. And certainly it was the infinit Wisdom of God, that did implant by Instinct so strong a desire of felicity in the Soul. . . . That there is a Felicity we all know by the Desires after, that there is a most Glorious felicity we know by the Strength and vehemence of those Desires" (*CM*, III.56). What is interesting about this statement is that felicity is obviously only an imagined object: it has sprung from the internal discourse of desire as such, a desire which legitimizes itself by its own fantasizing urgencies. Desire, grounded upon lack, furnishes the fancy with an unattainable object in order to generate further desire. This structure proceeds to its highest geometrical power[64] in the following meditations: "My Desires [were] so August and Insatiable that nothing less then a Deity could satisfy them" (*CM*, III.59).[65] Because God must "satisfy" an "insatiable" desire, "we so Ardently and infinitly desire His Absolut Perfection" (*CM*, II.63). An interesting transference has occurred in this sentence, for the typical adjective by which God's own desire is defined has suddenly been applied to man himself. Thus, if God "infinitly desires to be Admired and Beloved," that is because we infinitely desire to be admired and loved. For both man and God, desire is the desire of the Other. And each must imagine that Other as infinitely desirous if he is to be an adequate object of its own desire. At the very end of the *Centuries*, Traherne brings this dialectic of desire full circle: that the human soul "is Distinct from [God's], is manifest becaus it is the Return or Recompense of it. The only thing which for and abov all Worlds he infinitly Desires" (*CM*, V.85). On the ground of distinction, separation and alienation, an absence and a loss, desire infinitely desires an infinite desire. What, therefore, "Man is in this World" can now be answered: a being that insatiably desires the return or recompense of another's insatiable desire.[66]

Obviously at this point we need to turn our attention away from Traherne's treatment of desire as such and toward his notion of the Other. Fortunately, Traherne himself offers a convenient transition: "the pleasure we take in any Object is the root of that Desire, which we call Love . . . All is Love variously modified according to the Circumstances wherin the Object is represented" (*CE*, 44). If we are attentive to the specular resonances in the verb represented, we may begin to understand the ocular ground upon which all relations between the self and its desired/desiring Other are "modified." The terms of modification are hinted in Traherne's very language: the self is either an object to the Other, objectifies itself for the Other, or makes the Other its object. Here, by the way, is one illustration of Lacan's thesis concerning the problematics of desire. The subject makes or fashions himself into the object he imagines the Other wishes to see, but he also knows that he is not an object and wishes the Other would see him as he really is, that is, as a subject. At the same time, the Other is made over into an object too. Yet the Other's desire, in order to be adequately desirable, needs to be conceived as coming from the Other-as-subject. Here the specular capture by which self and Other variously modify one another as objects of a desiring gaze continually screens or bars the full entry of both into the register of significant and signifying subjectivity. Both are caught in an objective declension which can only give rise to ever more, and more unsatisfied, desire.

As with Lacan, therefore, it is not possible fully to separate Traherne's treatment of the dialectic of self and Other from the specular confusions of the *stade du miroir*. All we can do is observe the primary levels (Lacan would call them powers or stages)[67] upon which the structures of desire are mapped and photo-graphed. The first charts man as object of and to other men; the second is man as object of and to God.

"We need Spectators," Traherne says in the Second Century,

> and other Diversities of Friends and Lovers, in whose Souls we might likewise Dwell, and with whose Beauties we might be Crowned and entertained. In all whom we can dwell exactly: and be present with them fully. Lest therfore the other Depths and Faculties of our Souls, should be Desolat and Idle, they also are Created to entertain us. And as in many Mirrors we are so many other selvs, so are we Spiritually Multiplied when we meet our selvs more Sweetly, and liv again in other Persons. (*CM*, II.70)

Here the specular capture within the gaze of the Other reconstitutes the self in defense against its own absence and lack. Dwelling in the Other's gaze, the self can meet or see itself, come to life in full and appropriated presence.

This desire for presence—"recovered" from originary absence—also structures the seventy-eighth meditation: "The Rays of the Sun carry Light in them as they Pass through the Air, but go on in vain till they meet an Object: and there they are Expresst" (*CM*, II.78). "Ex-press," we might note in passing, perfectly catches the

Lacanian sense of the self alienated from itself, a bipartite being that can conceive itself only outside and beyond itself. Traherne's meditation continues:

> They Illuminat a Mirror, and are Illuminated by it. . . . Even so your Soul in its Rays and Powers is unknown: and no man would believ it present evry where, were there no Objects to be Discerned. Your Thoughts and Inclinations pass on and are unperceived. But by their Objects are discerned to be present: being illuminated by them. for they are Present with them and Activ about them. They recover and feel them selvs, and by those Objects live in Employment. Being turned into the figure and Idea of them. For as Light varieth upon all objects whither it cometh, and returneth with the Form and figure of them: so is the Soul Transformed into the Being of its Object. (*CM*, II.78)

Here again the specular capture objectifies the self, "variously modifies" it according to the circumstances within which it is perceived. And until man is so objectified, he is himself absent and unknown. The specular transformation that takes place before the gaze of the Other is thus the "recovery" and "return" of the self to itself. To "turn into" the idea of the Other is, in fact, to be the Other. Traherne would seem very close here to Lacan's point that man is himself the Other that he desires.

In *Christian Ethicks*, the objectification of the self before the gaze of the Other is extended to a fascination with the image-object the self thus forms: "Our Life upon Earth, being so diversified like a Sphere of Beauty, so variously adorned with all sorts of Excellent Actions, shall wholly and at once be seen as an intire Object, rarely and curiously wrought; a Lively Mirror of the Nature of the Soul, and all the Elements of which it is compounded, all the Parts that conspire in its Symetry, all the Qualities, Operations, and Perfections that contribute to its Glory, shall afford wonder and pleasure to all Spectators" (*CE*, 164). The real "Spectator" here is the self, rapt in narcissistic pleasure of its own *imago* in the mirror, and imagining in that ideal *moi* a wholeness that compensates for its various parts and elements. What Lacan describes as the jubilation with which the child engages his mirror-image is here duplicated by

Traherne in the joyful sense of how "rarely and curiously wrought" the mirror object seems. If we recall how Traherne, in the Dobell poems, defines the Eye of the child as a sphere subsuming all, then we might see here the consequences of that specular capture: the Eye that gazes upon itself adorns the I as an entire world, whole and eternally present to some imagined external spectator, by confusing the subjective I with the objective *moi*.[68] This kind of specular display controls even Traherne's sense of Christian ethics: "All kind of Vertues must concur to Compleat [the] Perfection" of a "Vertuous man": to "joyn all kind of Vertues together" is to "make their owner Venerable in the Eys of the World" (*CE*, 156–57).

We might pay particular attention to the plural "Eys" in this last citation, for it will help to correct two potential misconceptions about Traherne's understanding of the mechanics of desire. One is that given his insistence on the comprehensiveness of the individual Eye, the self needs no Other; the second is that a single other will suffice. At times, Traherne seems to license this latter conclusion:

> The Natural End of Goodness is to be Enjoyed: it Desireth to be anothers Happiness. Which Goodness . . . is so deeply implanted in our Natures, that we never Enjoy our selvs but when we are the Joy of others: of all our Desires the Strongest is to be Good to others. (*CM*, II.57)

> For the End of Riches is that we may be Beloved: we receiv Power to see our selvs Amiable in anothers Soul, and to Delight and Pleas another Person. (*CM*, II.59)

> Lov studieth to be Pleasing Magnificent and Noble, and would in all Things be Glorious and Divine unto its Object. Its whole Being is to its Object, and its whole Felicity in its Object. And it hath no other thing to take care for. It doth Good to its own Soul while it doth Good to another. (*CM*, IV.59)

In each of these passages, Traherne recognizes that the self "is apt to transform it self into all shapes, that the necessity of its Object requires" (*CE*, 103), and that man's very knowledge of Being is absolutely dependent upon that Other. Without seeing himself as the object of another's love, man cannot see himself at all.

And yet, since Traherne has already determined that the only "adequate Object" of man's love is God, and since he so frequently focuses upon the solitary I as the only adequate object of God's love, what necessitates the existence or the sight of other men? In Lacan's terms, we might suggest that desire—even desire of and for God—must invariably seek to raise itself to a higher, or second level of, power. "Had [God] Determined to Creat no more [but one man]: there had been no Witnesses of thy Glory. No spectators of thy Communion with GOD" (*CM*, I.68).

In *Christian Ethicks*, Traherne makes this argument in more dramatic terms: "Every man Loves to have many Eys fixt on his Beauty, and to have many Delighted Objects and Transactions for his own. Be the Theatre never so Magnificent, the Actions and Actors are more Delightful to the Spectators [and the spectators to the actors] than the Gildings, and Dead Engravings. Were all other men removed out of the World to make room for one, the empty Theatre would remain, but the Spectacle would be lost" (*CE*, 59). Here the conventional Renaissance trope of the world as the theater of God's judgment is radically inverted: for the "Spectacle" of even that judgment would still require others. "We need Spectators" of every sort, at every conceivable level, and as many as the imagination can desire. Traherne's specular avarice knows no bounds; like desire itself, the Eye is insatiable in its demands upon and for an infinity of gazes. Regardless of how the structural relation between a self and an Other is imagined, desire always generates a third other (Lacan's Father, Traherne's Christ, other men) that must validate that relation only by virtue of the fact that it can be perceived as an object.[69]

This tendency of desire to duplicate or replicate itself upon the structural relations between self and Other effects a final twist in this passage from the concluding pages of *Christian Ethicks*: "For we have an inclination to delight in the Joyes, of which we are the Authors, and by a kind of Eccho, or reflection, find the Pleasure doubled which we take, and which is taken in the communication of our Bounties. And in this there is founded a certain sympathy of Delight, which carries us to feel and be affected with anothers Joy, and makes *it* an Object, and a Cause of ours, nay almost the very Form and Essence of ours, when we are the Authors of it" (*CE*, 271). Here specular confusion and capture reaches a level that is clearly describable as Lacanian: man's desire is the desire of the Other; the Other's desire is an object of the self's desire; and the self *is* the Other that it desires. The reflexivities of image and spectator, desire and object, author and auditor, self and Other all collapse into the complex dialectical structuring of the mirror or the echo.

Thus far we have been mapping Traherne's notions of the Other and mirror as they are deployed to explicate man's desire for other men. How that desire in turn generates desire for God and how image and Other are deployed in regard to Him can be suggested by two transitional passages. I should caution, however, that the narrative my order of topics thus imposes upon Traherne is clearly false to his complexities. That is to say, in some respects it is the failure of desire to find an adequate object of desire among other men that necessitates imaginative objectification of God-as-Other. But it is equally true that the inability of desire to be satisfied even with an other that is God necessitates the demands upon other men. Traherne's desire, in short, is always caught upon and sustained by this dialectical interchange and it is therefore always moving, like a shuttle, back and forth between its polar objects to weave the self-sustaining texture of its own replication.

In the Second Century Traherne ponders the "infinite" capacity of the individual soul:

> But that which of all Wonders is the most Deep is, that a Soul, wheras one would think it could Measure but one soul, which is as large as it: can exceed that, and Measure all Souls, wholy and fully. This is an infinit Wonder indeed. for Admit that the Powers of one Soul were fathomles and infinit: are not the Powers so also of another? One would think therfore, that one Soul should be lost in another: And that two Souls should be exactly Adequate. yet my Soul . . . [is] prepared to see innumerable Millions. (*CM*, II.71)

Because his soul is capable of all souls, Traherne argues in the next meditation, it subsumes "All Souls with all their Objects in evry Soul" by making them adequate objects of itself. And yet the Soul's capacity exceeds even that power, for it is indeed "infinitly infinit" (*CM*, II.72). At this point, another level of power is required —another level of desire, another structural level yoking the self and the Other, another dimension of specular capture. At this heightened level, the infinite soul becomes itself an object of higher desire: "while [God] seeth us to live in all [others], we are a more Great and Glorious Object unto Him; the more we are Beloved of all, the more we are Admired by Him; the more we are the Joy of all, the more Blessed we are to Him (*CM*, II.61). Seeing others see us, God comes to desire us more as adequate objects of His own desire. Not only the individual man, it seems, but even God, requires the gaze of others in order to perceive or recognize his own object of desire. And man, desiring the desire of others, hopes thereby to incite the desire of God, to transform himself into or to adorn himself with the gaze of others so as to fashion himself into the object that God desires. Here mirror-image, Other, and desire all converge to chart the human subject on what Lacan calls a second degree of registration.

From our earlier sketch of Traherne's assertions about God's desire, we already have some idea of how the correlative notions of mirror-image and Other are brought to bear on Him. But since both of these notions assume rather startling proportion in Traherne's imaginings of God, we might pursue them a bit further. As we have seen, desire is grounded upon loss, lack, and absence. As much as man desires to compensate for these imagined lacks by becoming present to and magnified in the gaze of another, the originary loss remains. In Traherne's narrative of his own history, the entire human dialectic with the Other occurs as the result of the Fall. It is ultimately the full recognition of that that forces the imagination to conceive God as an object that will compensate for such a loss. "What [man] hath lost in himself is regained in the perfection and Goodness of his Object. THAT GOD is the sovereign Object of Love I scarcely need to mention" (*CE*, 134). The Other that is God, then, is the ontological image of wholeness equivalent to the image of bodily perfection and control that Lacan's child sees in the *stade du miroir*. And the dialectical reflexivity that structures all subsequent relations between the child and that imagined ideal-I also structures Traherne's thoughts of man's relationship to God.

If, then, God-as-object is conceived as an adequate Other for man's desire, this can be so only insofar as God Himself needs and desires the Other that is man. Like man himself, God is imaginatively inscribed in lack, in the same *manque d'être* that is the irreducible ground of man's existence: "By Love alone [God] is Pleasing to Him self. . . . By Love alone attain[s] another Self. By Love alone live[s] in others" (*CM*, II.50). God's recognition of Himself is, as man's, absolutely dependent upon a reflected vision, upon seeing Himself in the gaze of the Other. By his love, God "is multiplied and magnified in every Soul, as the same Object is in several Mirrors, being intirely represented in every living Temple of his Eternal essence" (*CE*, 81). Present to Himself only as represented in the glass, God's lack requires Him to become an object of man's desire. Self-love and love of the Other are thus the necessary circuit upon which all presence and all vision must be founded. God "loves himself becaus he is infinit and Eternal Lov to others. . . . His Lov unto Himself is his Lov unto them. And his Lov unto them is Lov unto Him self. They are individualy one" (*CM*, IV.65). As in Lacan, however, that "one" is subsequent to the originary twoness that binds self and Other in irreducible dialectical relation.

"We need Spectators," and so too does God. Likewise, God, as man, "is apt to transform [Himself] into all shapes, that the necessity of [his] Object requires." Man, God's object of desire, desires an image of his desire. God offers himself as that object in order to become such an image. Both Being and beings are revealed as such in the specular capture on the surface of the mirror: "I had never known the Dignity of my Nature, hadst not Thou [Christ] esteemed it: I had never seen, nor Understood its Glory, hadst not Thou Assumed it" (*CM*, I.78). By transforming Himself into an ideal image of man's desire, God inscribes man as the image of His desire. Traherne thus turns the conventional definition of man—made in the image of God—to very literal specular capture. The image is always that which can be seen, that which reflects the Other's gaze, that which answers to the Other's demand.

"O Let me so long Eye Thee, till I be turned into Thee, and look upon me till Thou art formed in me, that I may be a Mirror of thy Brightness, an Habitation of thy Lov and a Temple of thy Glory" (*CM*, I.87). In the dialectical transfer of the gaze, man and God become present objects to one another and images of each other's desire. Inhabiting a mirror, both offer themselves as objects to be admired. Neither can see himself unless so seen in the gaze of the Other as reflected on the surface of this mirror. "Man is made in the

Image of GOD, and therfore is Mirror and Representativ of Him" (*CM*, II.23): not only *of*, but also *for* Him. Presenting a re-presentation to the Other, man and God see themselves *as* the Other. Once again the specular capture inscribes the Other as an irreducible absence of the self to itself. Man is the Other as God is the Other. Ultimately, of course, such specular confusions license desire's grandest ambition and identification: man *is* God. "[God's] Essence . . . is the Sight of Things. For He is all Ey and all Ear. Being therfore Perfect, and the Mirror of all Perfection, He hath Commanded us to be perfect as He is Perfect: And we are to Grow up into Him till we are filled with the Fulness of His GODhead. We are to be Conformed to the Image of His Glory, till we becom the Resemblance of His Great Exemplar" (*CM*, II.84). Within the reflexivities of the mirror, the gaze itself escapes specular capture. As the mirror reflects another mirror, the Eye sees another Eye. In the confusion that results, the desire of one becomes the desire of the Other. Man is God seeing man as the image of Himself.[70]

Such a con-formation of gazes structures all of Traherne's mirror imagery and licenses the specular transfers that invariably occur in the *jeu de miroirs*. Within that play, self and Other, object and image lose their discreteness; so too do origin and end, cause and effect, what is given and what is received. And so too do the grounds of desire and desire's object, for the specular interchanges played out and upon the glass of the imaginative mirror define precisely the infinite progress of any and all desire. Traherne, as much as Lacan, understands the reflexive structure of these mechanisms, knows, as clearly as the modern psychoanalyst, that desire can only replicate and duplicate itself upon itself.

This means, of course, that while the mirror-image initially serves to define and validate the structures of Traherne's desire, it also poses significant problems in terms of the self's sense of its own being. We might watch, therefore, as Traherne struggles with this problem in two remaining passages. The first concerns the idea of gratitude, which Traherne describes as a virtue wherein self-love and love of the Other are indissoluably interwoven:

> And if GOD dwelleth in the soul as the Sun in a Mirror, while it looketh upon him, the love of GOD must needs issue from

> that Soul, for GOD *is Love*, and his love is in it. The impression of all his Beauty swallows up the Being of the Soul, and changes it wholly into another Nature. The Eye is far more sensible of the Day, and of the beauty of the Universe, than it is of its self, and is more affected with that light it beholds, than with its own essence. Even so the Soul when it sees GOD is sensible only of the glory of that Eternal Object: All it sees is GOD, it is unmindful of it self. It infinitely feels him, but forgets it self in the Rapture of Pleasure. (*CE*, 264)

We can hear in such a passage Lacan's notion of the barred subject, the self that must try to see itself in the image of the Other, only invariably to lose itself in the rapt pleasure it takes in the object in the mirror.[71] Forgetting itself and thus eternally lost to itself, the self is thus inscribed in that *manque d'être* which desire must always seek to fill or supply. Being, in these terms, is exactly what is "swallowed up," forgotten and lost. *Un jeu de miroirs*, the dialectical structuring of desire, is all that remains. And this, Lacan argues, is what being human is. Traherne, at one level at least, would seem to agree.

Yet this conclusion also seems unacceptable to Traherne, for desire is ever seeking validation of its own source. Traherne is led, therefore, at the end of the Fourth Century, to retract the very metaphor upon which so much of his thought is structured:

> as a Mirror returneth the very self-same Beams it receiveth from the Sun, so the Soul returneth those Beams of Lov that shine upon it from God. For as a Looking Glass is nothing in comparison of the World, yet containeth all the World in it, and seems a real fountain [i.e., origin] of those Beams which flow from it so the Soul is Nothing in respect of God, yet all Eternity is contained in it, and it is the real fountain of that Lov that proceedeth from it. They are the Sun Beams which the Glass returneth: yet they flow from the Glass and from the Sun within it. The Mirror is the Well-Spring of them, becaus they shine from the Sun within the Mirror. Which is as deep within the Glass as it is high within the Heavens. And this sheweth the Exceeding Richness and preciousness of Lov, It is the Lov of God shining upon, and Dwelling in the Soul. for

> the Beams that Shine upon it reflect upon others and shine from it. (*CM*, IV.84)

Within this mirror-play, the self is God reflecting love upon Himself in the glass of the Other. Source and object, the sun without and the sun within, are constantly exchanging identities. But desire—as desire of and for the Other—cannot be content with such exchange, and it thus tries to extricate itself from the specular capture within which it is trapped: "That the Soul shineth of it self is equaly manifest. for it can lov with a lov distinct from GODs. It can lov irregularly. And no irregular Lov is the Lov of GOD. It can forbear to lov while God loveth. It can lov while GOD forbeareth. . . . This shews plainly that it can lov regularly, with a Lov that is not meerly the Reflexion of Gods. for which caus it is not called a Mirror, but esteemed more, a real fountain" (*CM*, IV.85). Posing before itself its own irregularity, its own distinctive failure to conceive itself as an adequate object of God's love, man's love imagines itself as thereby "esteemed more."

This "more," and the urgencies of a desire that must constantly demand more, will occupy us in the next chapter. Here we may simply note the lengths to which desire drives the self to corrupt itself in order to elicit the further desire of the Other: "And were [Souls] Mirrors only that return his Lov, one would think it impossible, while he shines upon them, to forbear to shine. but they are like the Ey, Mirrors with Lids, and the Lid of Ignorance of Inconsideration interposing, they are often times Ecclypsed, or shine only through som Cranies" (*CM*, IV.86). The self "ruines it self," "forfeit[s] all its Interest in Heaven and Earth," in order to recover itself as the lost object of God's desire. The Eye eclipsed, the mirror with a lid, the gaze peering through some cranny—here is Traherne's attempt to restructure desire at a second, or third, degree of power. At this level we might be reminded of Lacan's treatment of the evil eye, the eye that registers judgment, the gaze that fixes the law. Only by distinguishing man's eye from God's can man assure himself that God does indeed look upon him. Behind this moment, perhaps, we might understand Traherne's final step into the Lacanian field of the symbolic, the region within which the subject is restructured not in terms of its own specular and imaginative confusions, but in terms of the Eye of Judgment which charts man's communal condition under the Name-of-the-Father, which defines him, therefore, as a function of others and the Other.

III THE *EPOS* OF DOBELL

In the final section of this chapter I will violate my own principle of not treating Traherne's texts in isolation. I do so now because I think Lacan's theories offer a better way of understanding what Traherne is about in that sequence of poems we have come to call the Dobell manuscript. The most sustained scholarship on this manuscript has concerned its overall structure, for which several models have been proposed. A schematic table of contents will reveal both the range of models and a basic agreement about narrative stages.

The Dobell Manuscript: Poems and Structures

1. The Salutation
2. Wonder
3. Eden
4. Innocence

5. The Preparative
6. The Instruction
7. The Vision
8. The Rapture
9. The Improvment
10. The Approach
11. Dumnesse
12. Silence

13. My Spirit
14. The Apprehension
15. Fullness
16. Nature
17. Ease
18. Speed
19. The Designe
20. The Person
21. The Estate

22. The Enquirie
23. The Circulation
24. Amendment
25. The Demonstration
26. The Anticipation
27. Recovery
28. Another
29. Love

30. Thoughts I
31. Blisse
32. Thoughts II
33. Ye hidden nectars
34. Thoughts III
35. Desire
36. Thoughts IV
37. Goodnesse

This division of the sequence corresponds to the structures suggested by four traditional analyses: (1) Bonaventura's stages in the *Itinerarium mentis ad Deum* (a preparatory "bestirring of the self"; polishing the mirror of the sensible world; polishing the mirror of the self; the essential attributes of God; intellectual retreat and spiritual repose);[72] (2) the conventional stages of medieval Christian mysticism (preparation, purification, illumination, perfection);[73] (3) Loyola's stages of preparatory meditation (composition of place, premeditation, memory, understanding, and will);[74] and (4) the general pattern of the Christian progress of the soul (innocence, fall, and redemption).[75]

Each of these structures enables us to see a different feature of the Dobell poems, but none, I think, reveals the central imaginative urgency that holds the sequence together or shapes its internal development. For this reason, I would like to propose another approach to the text as a whole—not one that depends upon external stages of progress, but one that seeks in the imaginative movement from poem to poem a more dramatic psychic narrative. Earlier I called this *epos* the maturation of an adult Christian; here I will try to refine that generalization by focusing on the particular mechanisms of desire that propel Traherne from his origins to his end, from a myopic and narcissistic view of childhood to a more realistic and symbolic understanding of adulthood. In order to do that I will be forced to re-imagine each of Traherne's poems in Lacanian terms. Such a procedure brings into clear view a critical strategy we more often strive to disguise, but I trust that the preceding pages have offered sufficient demonstration that Traherne and Lacan are, despite their different terminologies, concerned with charting similar psychic relations.[76]

I begin, then, with "The Salutation," even though Philip Traherne's manuscript is prefixed by "The Author to the Critical Peruser" and even though that poem might remind us of Lacan's distinction between *la parole plein* and *la parole vide*. For Traherne, of course, this dialectic is always deployed for its rhetorical paradox: the empty, plain word is the fullest; the word given its full figurative flourish is always empty. We will return to this dialectic at a later point. "The Salutation" opens a more central Lacanian vein: it poses the originary question of *where* being is or was and it grounds that question upon a primordial lack-of-being:

Where have ye been? Behind
What Curtain were ye from me hid so long!
Where was? in what Abyss, my Speaking Tongue?
(ll. 4–6)

The being that "Was Nothing from Eternitie," that "Beneath the Dust did in a Chaos lie," now perceives a "Glorious Store," "Wide and Bright." But the self that the poem displays is hardly a unified I as much as a sequence of fragmented body parts ("These Little Limmes, / These Eys and Hands . . . / These rosie Cheeks") and discrete senses.[77] To this extent, the ego has not yet been formed: the subject-speaker exists only as a "Stranger" in the world, alienated not only from the "Strange Things" that both surround and comprise him, but also from the fleeting ideal conception of himself as "Son and Heir."

"Wonder" tries to subdue this sense of estrangement by supposing a passive unity of the senses: all that is seen is enjoyed in wonder and amazement. The body fragments of the opening poem here dissolve into the more fanciful wholeness of a "SPIRIT" that knows no limits, no bounds, no divisions. What is most interesting about the poem, however, is that even this imagined unity of sensory impression is grounded upon lack:

Harsh ragged Objects were conceald,
Oppressions Tears and Cries,
Sins, Griefs, Complaints, Dissentions, Weeping Eys,
Were hid . . .
(ll. 25–28)

Cursd and Devisd Proprieties,
With Envy, Avarice
And Fraud, those Feinds that Spoyl even Paradice,
Fled from the Splendor of mine Eys.
And so did Hedges, Ditches, Limits, Bounds . . .
(ll. 49–53)

Such "lacks," of course, are themselves disturbing or distressing objects; but the point is that the re-collection and re-presentation of a sensory wholeness depends upon a "forgetting" of subsequent difference. "I nothing in the World did know, / But 'twas Divine."

Not quite, the poem seems to say, for the very knowledge or acknowledgment of the "Divine" occurs only when the "human" is openly excluded. Whether we read this bipartition of being as a further estrangement of the self from itself or merely the disparity between the unknowing wonder of the child and the too knowing wonder of the adult striving to recollect childhood, the fact remains that the I is here straining against itself, that what *we* hear in the poem is the difference between the conscious I and the fantasized Eye. Out of this difference, I think, comes all of Traherne's later attempts to collapse these two homonyms, to rewrite them as the same.

"Eden" continues this desire to bracket or exclude the alienating differences only to reinstall them at the center of the speaker's consciousness of self:

> A learned and a Happy Ignorance
> Divided me,
> From all the Vanitie,
> From all the Sloth Care Pain and Sorrow that advance,
> The madness and the Miserie
> Of Men.
> (ll. 1–6)

The me divided, separated from other men, and from all the human woes that they suffer: only on these grounds does the I discover an ideal-ego, another self that supplies the kind of unity that he himself lacks. Here that ideal is named Adam, who, in his "Original Simplicitie," sees only "The Glorious Wonders of the DEITIE" (ll. 35, 49). This identification founded on alienation seems to me an important key to Traherne's entire sequence. The self must draw "away my Infant feet / Quite from the Works of Men" in order to recognize itself and restructure itself in terms of an idealized Other (whether the ego-ideals of Adam or God or the ideal-ego of an all-inclusive, self-sufficient "Ey"). The paradox at work here is clear enough: the self must differentiate itself in order to know itself, but it desires a sense of self that presupposes sameness and unity. Ironically, the very urgency to define the self as other than others still requires an Other in terms of which it can present itself.

"Innocence" again defines Adam—here obviously a fragmented

Adam, an Adam prior to the Fall that makes him an accessible Other—as the ideal-ego: "I was an Adam there, / A little Adam in a Sphere / Of Joys!" (ll. 51–53). But once more that imaginative identification is secured by exclusion and lack. The I, in short, must first conceive what it is *not*—not stained, not dark, not taken in with "Outward" objects, not proud or polluted, not guilty—in order to announce/pronounce what it *is*. Like the preceding poems, "Innocence" is bound to the past tense, grounded, therefore, in the initial question of *where* being originally was. And, like them, it must also presuppose as a condition of self-consciousness an alienation from all things human. If we suppose that each of these poems is spoken by the fallen adult looking backward on his life, then our sense of his desire might be sharpened.[78] Insofar as he is a man, the speaker is all that these poems have sought so hard to exclude. The child, the ostensibly unalienated, unsplit being he would become again, is but the Other of his desire. The adult I, we might say, lacks the child that he was; should he "becom a Child again," he would lack the adult he has become. "I have been this only in order to become what I can be." Lacan calls this the permanent fulcrum of the subject's assumption of his own mirages, his own failures to see that he is the Other he desires or that each step of his temporal progress reinscribes the irreducible fracture of being within which he is situated.

"The Preparative" is Traherne's initial attempt to act upon the injunction to "becom a Child again." Significantly, it is also the first poem in the sequence to raise the central image of the mirror. At this recollected stage of development, the psyche knows only one sense—that of sight—and one organ—the Eye:

> Then was my Soul my only All to me,
> A Living Endless Ey,
> Far wider then the Skie
> Whose Power, whose Act, whose Essence was to see.
> (ll. 11–14)

The final infinitive marks the convergence of Being and Seeing: I see therefore I am. It is important, however, to understand that this is but a "preparatory" condition, that it presupposes no consciousness of self:

My Body being Dead, my Lims unknown;
Before I skild to prize
Those living Stars mine Eys,
Before my Tongue or Cheeks were to me shewn,
Before I knew my Hands were mine,
Or that my Sinews did my Members joyn,
When neither Nostril, Foot, nor Ear,
As yet was seen, or felt, or did appear;
I was within
A House I knew not, newly clothd with Skin.
(ll. 1–10)

Even the Eye is not perceived as an organ distinct from its operations or its capacities. The Eye, like the self, is simply the act of seeing. As the remainder of the poem tries to describe the consequences of this condition, it identifies the specular capture within which the seeing Eye is immediately caught:

Pure Empty Powers that did nothing loath,
Did like the fairest Glass,
Or Spotless polisht Brass,
Themselvs soon in their Objects Image cloath.
Divine Impressions when they came,
Did quickly enter and my Soul inflame.
(ll. 51–56)

Two crucial events are recorded here. First, the faculty of seeing, the ability to see, is itself lost or withdraws behind what is seen. Adorning itself with the image-reflection of the Other, the Eye can only then recognize itself as it withdraws ("Tis not the Object, but the Light / . . . Tis a Purer Sight"). Second, although Traherne tells us that

I then no Thirst nor Hunger did conceiv,
No dull Necessity,
No Want was Known to me,
(ll. 21–23)

desire arises as soon as the self reflects upon itself through the images of what it sees. As objects "impress" themselves upon the "Empty

Powers," the Eye is "inflamed" for more—for a *purer* sight, for *all*. It is tempting to argue that it is precisely the presence, in Traherne's recollection, of the mirror that generates this desire and that structures its urges on the binary terms of empty and full. Indeed, as we shall see, however various Traherne's uses of the mirror-image, each carries with it the sometimes open, sometimes screened correlatives of empty/full, the lost or hidden gaze, and desire as such.

A word should be added here about the "Soul," here identified with the Eye, shortly to be associated with the I. Traherne's soul is perhaps best understood as a power or as the whole of the individual's manifold powers. In Heideggerian terms, it might be analogous to the Being that lets the self be. As such, it is not recoverable in conscious terms or describable in speech. At best, it is a signifier of the lost object the self desires in order to free itself of desire, at least so long as desire thinks it can be "satisfied." When the self learns, or recognizes, that desire always is only desire, then the soul can come to signify desire itself and can offer the self an entry into the symbolic field within which it must serve a function in relation to others and the Other. At this point in the sequence, however, no functional or signifying value can be assigned to soul or recognized by the speaker in the soul.

"The Instruction" repeats the self-alienating separation of the opening movement of the sequence and suggests how complete the specular capture of the preceding poem has been. Convinced that the childlike Eye and its "Purer Sight" offer an undefiled, unpartitioned existence, the adult speaker tries to purge himself of those subsequent desires that have bound him to other men. What the poem really betrays, of course, is the fear of transience. The imaginary recollection of origin sharpens the desire for oneness, stability, purity. And in order to privilege those desires, others have now to be excluded or erased. As often happens in Traherne, unwanted desires are excised by imagining they are not self-generated: "all Men on Earth conspire" to sully the individual with false desires. Despite that bit of wishful fantasy, it is clear that in either recollected or present terms, *all* desire is grounded in the Other, whether one calls that Other "thy God" or "all Men." The speaker, however, cannot yet understand that structural necessity.

I would push this argument a step further by suggesting that once the subject's desire has arisen, he is then caught in an imaginative necessity of legitimizing that desire by differentiating it from others he perceives: my desire is *not* other men's desires. Such a structuring of the self's desire is, of course, an attempt to raise desire itself to a second power, but it also places a Christian poet like Traherne in an absolutely untenable position of making the human other merely the lost and accurst.[79] Only the imagined desire of God for such an other will reinscribe him as an adequate object of the self's desire. Yet even that reinscription is dependent upon the recognition and acceptance that the self *is* the Other—not subsequently ("Spue out thy filth, thy flesh abjure"), but originally and irreducibly. But this is to press too far too quickly; at the end of "The Instruction," the speaker has not progressed to this knowledge.

"The Vision" returns to the specular field and its structural consequences. The scopic gaze adorns the world with order so that what initially appears as "Ten thousand Heaps of vain confused Treasure" can be seen as "The very Life and Form and Caus of Pleasure" (ll. 13, 11). To see the world as pleasure is to convert it into an object and to "dwell" upon that object. Such a display, however, is preparatory to a more important stage—to convert the self into an object of and for the world:

> To see all Creatures tend
> To thy Advancement, and so sweetly close
> In thy Repose: To see them shine
> In Use in Worth in Service, and even Foes
> Among the rest made thine.
> To see all these unite at once in Thee
> Is to behold Felicitie.
> (ll. 34–40)

To see all things tend to and unite in thee is to make the self the object of the sight of all things, to objectify the self as a coherent, unified, and desirable whole. Obviously, this is a very different reading of Traherne's notion of felicity than criticism normally assumes.[80] The imagined unitary object is the focus of the final stanza, but once again the dialectic of self and Other surfaces in predictable but unacknowledged ways:

From One, to One, in one to see *All Things*
To see the King of Kings
At once in two; to see his Endless Treasures
Made all mine own, my self the End
Of all his Labors! Tis the Life of Pleasures!
To see my self His friend!
Who all things finds conjoynd in Him alone,
Sees and Enjoys the Holy one.
(ll. 49–56)

The Eye here seems initially to perceive the twoness that precedes oneness, but the specular confusion of identities allows the self to conceive itself *as* the Other it sees—as, in fact, "conjoynd" to the Him who "alone" is the "Holy one." This confusion of identities is apparent in the text itself, for, as Ridler notes, the capital *H* in line 55 is "misleading." She argues that it refers to the child himself, not to God; but surely the more appropriate point to make is that it is precisely such a confusion that allows the originary twoness to be reimaged as oneness.[81] Again we might observe that the specular objectification of the self requires a simultaneous restructuring of other men: "Mens Woes shall be but foyls unto thy Bliss"; "Their Ignorance shall make thee Bright"; "Their Faults shall keep thee right" (ll. 25, 28, 30). What Lacan defines as the intermapping of the desire of the Other with those of the self has here once more become the self against the other(s) in order to be with an Other. To me, this alignment of identifications smacks of an earlier Oedipal phase in which the child wishes to supplant the father as rival for the mother's desire. In Traherne's family scene, the son-child wants to exclude other men from God's sight so that he alone is the object God desires. God, then, here functions as the structural equivalent of the mother (He even supplies those things that the child needs and treasures); other men are the structural equivalents of the rival father who must be displaced in the mother's affections.

"The Rapture" represents the stage Lacan describes as the child's fascination with his own image reflected in the mirror. The *imago* supplies the child with the unified form that he himself now lacks, magnifies himself in his own eyes. Traherne registers this jubilant captivation in "How Great am I," "O how Divine / Am I!" (ll. 4,

16–17). But as soon as the jubilation is recorded, the questions of origin and Other reassert themselves:

> Who raisd? Who mine
> Did make the same? What Hand Divine!
> (ll. 19–20)

The source of self becomes the Other that the self originally desires. And that Other, of course, must now be imagined as desiring the self into order to bring it into existence. Traherne's first attempt at so refashioning the Other is "The Improvment."

At the center of "The Improvment" is a necessary distinction between God-as-subject and God-as-object. The subjective aspect of God, God as creator, is thus refashioned as God-the-recollector or arranger who makes Himself into an object given to be seen, and hence known, by presenting His Wisdom, Goodness, and Power to the gazing Eye:

> Had he not made an *Ey* to be the Sphere
> Of all Things, none of these would e're appear.
> (ll. 23–24)

Presenting Himself to man's Eye, God thereby becomes "present here." At the heart of Traherne's analysis, then, is an imaginary lack on God's part—a want-to-be-seen that is the precondition of His existence. And His desire is equally grounded in objective reflexivity: His bliss is to be a delight to the Eye of the Other who is man:

> For Man he Endless Pleasures doth *Provide*,
> And shews that *Happiness* is his *Delight*,
> His Creatures Happiness as well as His:
> For that in Truth he seeks, and thats *his Bliss*.
> (ll. 51–54)

The pronominal shifters in lines 52 and 54 signal the crucial confusion the poem charts, for in order to imagine a God who will serve as an adequate Other before whom man can offer himself as being-to-be-seen, God himself must be conceived as a being who gives Himself to be seen. The gaze that binds both man and God to the structural locus of the Other's desire is the condition that gives rise to the first conception of *moi*:

But neither Goodness, Wisdom, Power, nor Love,
Nor Happiness it self in things could be,
Did not they all *in one fair Order* move,
And joyntly by their Service End in *me*.
(ll. 19–22)

This *me*, this imagined Other in terms of which "I" must be structured, follows the Lacanian model of Schema L:

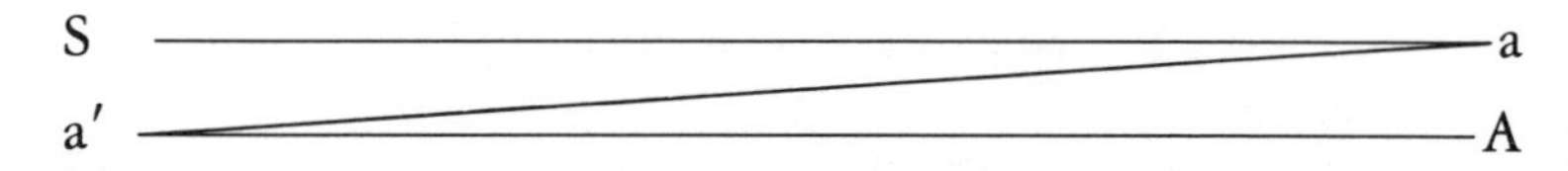

If *S* is the developing "I" and *A* is God, *a′* is the *moi* which I imagine God to desire, and *a* is the being I imagine I was when God originally created me. Any relation between God and the child is irreducibly captivated by the screened relation between the objects each desires and the objectifications each presents in order to become visible and present to the imagined Eye of the Other. What is unrecognized at this point is the extent to which the child's entire conception of self is being formed by the specular *meconnaissance* that confuses the pronominal signifiers. For the fact is that it is not God who is the recollection of this poem, but man himself, fashioning the Other as fashioning him and thereby fashioning himself in the reflexivity of the enacted double gaze. The I that at this stage of its development is "unperceivd" must first recollect a *me* that is the object of an Other's Eye in order to become re-collected as the "I" before whom the Other can offer himself as object-to-be-seen. Sliding beneath these recollections is the unseen and thus unrecognized structurings of a *manque d'être* and the desire those double lacks occasion.

Indirectly, or by misdirection, "The Approach" turns Traherne's attention away from the imagined Other of God and back to the developing consciousness of self. Again, however, desire can be seen as the structural mechanism by which such consciousness first arises.

O Lord I wonder at thy Love,
Which did my Infancy so Early move:
But more at that which did forbear,
And move so long, tho Sleighted many a yeer:

> But most of all, at last that Thou
> Thyself shouldst me convert I scarce know how.
>
> Thy Gracious Motions oft in vain
> Assaulted me: My Heart did Hard remain
> Long time: I sent my God away,
> Grievd much that he could not impart his Joy.
> I careless was, nor did regard
> The End for which he all these Thoughts prepard.
> (ll. 13–24)[82]

But now, Traherne confesses, "with New and Open Eys" he sees that God did continually "Approach" and "me did Woo." In short, he conceives himself—his *moi*—as object of God's desire. Interestingly, the submerged issue of desire allows Traherne to speak the original lack which that desire seeks to counteract:

> From Nothing taken first I was,
> What Wondrous Things his Glory brought to pass!
> Now in this World I him behold,
> And me enveloped in more then Gold;
> In deep Abysses of Delights,
> In present Hidden Precious Benefits.
> (ll. 31–36)

The I sees the Other now because it imagines the *me* the Other desires to see. As an object of the Other's desire, that me is adorned with value. Yet the conversion of the "Nothing" the self was to the "all" it would become has merely replaced one want with another, for the originary *manque d'être* is here reinscribed in the hidden abyss of desire itself. The wonder Traherne registers at several points in the poem is perhaps his acknowledgment that the true complexity and reflexivity of this desire has not yet been fully recognized even though his captivation by it has been felt.

"Dumnesse" and "Silence" bring this initial stage of Traherne's narrative to a close by glancing both forward and backward along its temporal sequence. Both are spoken primarily by the adult consciousness attempting to recollect his childhood perceptions. What we hear, therefore, is one level of lack and its correlative desire superimposed upon another. In Lacan's terms, we can see desire itself being raised to a higher power or registered in a secondary key. Both poems, therefore, deal with the Fall, and it is only in terms of that subsequent loss that the preceding desire can be recognized as such. In their paired relation, moreover, the two poems represent a crucial stage in the Christian's conception of himself as a human subject, for they confront, for the first obvious time in the sequence, the key notions of word and work. Traditional Christianity, of course, sees man's work as the necessary and expected reply to God's word,[83] but Traherne is more interested in the oppositions resident in both work and word as these come to structure the child's developing ego. This explains, perhaps, why word and work are initially conceived in negative terms.

Language, like good works, signifies plurality, whether that be the elementary split between speaker and auditor or the more encompassing separation between the self and other men. To the child, Traherne seems to suggest, words and works threaten the imaginary identification he has formed with the Other and coerce him into the alienating structure of difference. The consequent twoness he now perceives must be reimagined as a fall away from wholeness in order not to elicit a debilitating sense of fractured or split being. Although Lacan does not specifically focus on these kinds of self-defensive maneuvers, they are logical corollaries of the specular captivation of the mirror phase. Whether the "I" and the "me" are conceived within the imaginary or the symbolic fields, the *meconnaissance* that determines either conception is inevitably an unconscious attempt to rewrite the originary bipartition of being into a desired oneness. In the Dobell poems, then, it is revealing that immediately upon fashioning the imaginary identification of the self with God and God with man, the original difference between them reasserts itself on another level—here, paradoxically, the level of man himself.

We could come at the issue of this stage of Traherne's narrative from another angle. If the preceding poems have established the relationship between man and God in the Lacanian terms of self and Other, then they must also imply the reflexivity of that dialectic. Because the self finds itself presented as the other of the Other,[84] it must also be on the verge of recognizing that self *is* Other. Again, the sense of a being split from himself is the necessary origin and end of the self-Other dialectic. Through his analysis of good versus bad words or prefallen versus postfallen works, Traherne tries to articulate this truth of fractured being.

"Dumnesse" rethinks the self in terms of language. "Speechless made at first," man's only work was "in himself [to be] profoundly Busied": to see and admire "with a Steddy and immediat Sence" all things (ll. 5, 6, 45). In recollection, this childhood stage seems overwhelmingly one of wholeness and oneness even though, paradoxically, it must be posed on the ground of difference: "Then did I dwell within a World of Light, / Distinct and Seperat from all Mens Sight" (ll. 31–32). Still, the principal conception of the self is *one*:

> There I saw all the World Enjoyd by one;
> There I was in the World my Self alone;
> No Business Serious seemd but one; No Work
> But one was found; and that did in me lurk.
> (ll. 35–38)

Such misconceptions[85] of unity are immediately shattered by the child's entry into language: "I *then my Bliss did, when my Silence, break*." "Sin and Death, / Are most infused by accursed Breath," by the breath that first speaks "*Mortal Words*" (ll. 20, 13–14). Although the adult can fantasize that his "Non-Intelligence of Human Words" defined his earlier bliss, his two dramatic adjectives reveal far more than he imagines. Words are "mortal" and "human," and they thus propel the self into its very nature, not out of or away from that nature. Man, as the being he is, is what language speaks him. If he conceives this fact in terms of being "depravd with Tongues" or "Injurd by the Errors and the Wrongs" that speech conveys, that conception only reinscribes the irreducible split which fractures his being from the start. The Fall, that symbolic "Wound" that rends the human soul, is merely the real bipartition of being reimaged on a second (or third) level. Indeed, Traherne cannot imagine a speechless state; even when he is dumb, "(Nothing besides was dum;) All things did com / With Voices and Instructions" (ll. 66–67). Similarly, those things speak "Words" that are, despite the self's despoiled coasts, still heard. What the "noise" of mortal words conveys, then, is nothing other than *human* being as such, and the fragmentation that structures that being. Although Traherne does not yet see the functional value of this perception, he here adumbrates the psychological progress from a condition of imaginative specular confusion to a symbolic register.

"Silence" continues to focus on the effects of the Fall on the condition of being human by distinguishing between the "Inward Work" of preverbal childhood and the "outward Busy Acts" coterminous with man's entry into language. As in "Innocence," Adam represents the child's ego-ideal, and only those acts that he performed are deemed excellent. The specular confusion that structures this identification also licenses a collapse of the distinction between the self and God. "Present with the King of kings," the soul conceives itself in divine terms:

> He was an Ocean of Delights from Whom
> The Living Springs and Golden Streams did com:
> My Bosom was an Ocean into which
> They all did run.
>
> . . . .
>
> For so my Spirit was an Endless Sphere,
> Like God himself, and Heaven and Earth was there.
> (ll. 71–74, 85–86)

Such fantasized wholeness and unity are much like those in "Dumnesse" and love appears as "the High and only Work" the child has to do.

But while the poem recollects this mirror phase, it also registers its loss, that lack or want which gives rise to unspecified and absolute desire. Ironically, what is "occasiond by the Fall" is not only, or even primarily, ignorance, poverty, and sickness, but such "meaner Matters" as:

> Building of Churches, giving to the Poor,
> In Dust and Ashes lying on the floor,
> Administring of Justice, Preaching Peace,
> Ploughing and Toyling for a forc't Increas,
> With visiting the Sick, or Governing
> The rude and Ignorant.
> (ll. 11–16)

Missing, that is, are all those activities that measure man's relationship to his fellow men, that work that inscribes him in functional and communal terms. The poem tries to protect the child's *imago* from the "pollut[ion]" and "Contagion" of such work by imagining it as a fallen version of the interior activity of the self-satisfied and undesiring soul. As in "Dumnesse," the soul tries to console itself with the fantasy of "The Satisfaction of all True Desire," apparently unaware that it is precisely because desire cannot be satisfied that this recollection is undertaken. The poem thus betrays its own assertions, for, as we have seen, the questioning of where being was is always already grounded in the sense of lack and loss. The Fall merely rewrites that originary condition onto another level; it does not alter the nature of the "Interior Work" in which the imagination has from the start been engaged—the fashioning of an I and a me in relation to the significant Other whose word articulates and entangles the self's desire.

Traherne ends "Silence" on the specular relation with that Other, now conceived as God:

> There nothing was by I, and all my Treasures.
> In that fair World one only was the Friend,
> One Golden Stream, one Spring, one only End.
>
> . . . .
>
> The Union was so Strait between them two,
> That all was eithers which my Soul could view.
> His Gifts, and my Possessions, both our Treasures;
> He mine, and I the Ocean of his Pleasures.
>
> . . . .
>
> And to Himself in me he always gave,
> All that he takes Delight to see me have.
> (ll. 62–65, 67–70, 83–84)

Treasures and pleasures, giving and receiving, He and I, his and mine: the reflexivity of the relation between self and Other is an appropriate close to the initial stage of the Dobell narrative. The next stage attempts to build upon the recollected specular scene a revised version of the essential self.

If the first stage of the narrative (that is, "The Preparative" through "Silence") seeks to define *where* being originally was, the second stage ("My Spirit" through "The Estate") asks *what* being was. Both install the self within a scopic field, but where the first tends to focus on the child as specular object of another's gaze, the second focuses on the speculating gaze of the subject himself. In slightly broader terms, we might say that the initial narrative moment establishes the essential *stade du miroir* which binds man and God to the structural conditions of reflexive vision. The present moment describes the imaginative enactment of the self that has been structured by that vision. The third narrative moment (from "The Enquirie" through "Love") describes the Other (God) with which the self has visually identified and reenacts the dialectic that structures their relation. Only when the full scope of the specular field has been charted can Traherne, in the final poems of the sequence, move beyond the imaginary confusions of the mirror phase to a more symbolic conception of man as a functional, signifying self.

"My Spirit" immediately announces both the scopic field in which the self is constituted and the specular ego that is its consequence:

> My Naked Simple Life was I.
> That Act so Strongly Shind
> Upon the Earth, the Sea, the Skie,
> It was the Substance of My Mind.
> The Sence it self was I.
> (ll. 1–5)

Traherne relies here upon the echoed pun already established in "The Preparative" and "The Vision": "Then was my Soul my only All to me / A Living Endless Ey"; "I / . . . was all Sight, or Ey"; "Tis all that Ey can see." Eye, then, was the sense; the sense itself was I. Initially, we might be misled into thinking Traherne is describing Valery's condition of "seeing myself seeing myself." In fact, neither the Eye nor the I is actually seen: like Lacan's gaze, both withdraw behind the activity of seeing itself. As Traherne explains, "My Essence was Capacitie" and that ability or power to see does not recognize the organ that makes sight possible:

> It hath no other Wings
> To Spread abroad, nor Eys to see,

Nor Hands Distinct to feel,
Nor Knees to Kneel.
(ll. 11–14)

Similarly, the I that the Eye registers in the mirror is also unseen. This is the conclusion of Traherne's elliptical imagery of orb and sphere throughout the poem, for what initially appears as an extended "Sphere of Joy" is immediately rewritten as "A Strange Mysterious Sphere! / A Deep Abyss," "an Indivisible" and "Invisible" "Centre." "Thou which within me art, yet Me!" (ll. 75–76, 92, 102, 108). Neither Eye nor I appears as such, although both are captivated by the scopic reflections. Rather, what appears to be seen is the *moi* confused for both: the line I have just cited continues, "Thou which within me art, yet Me! Thou Ey."

Also seen is the "flutter of jubilation" the self experiences in the sudden consciousness of a seemingly unbounded "Power":

O Act, O Power infinit;
O Subtile, and unbounded Air!
O Living Orb of Sight!
(ll. 105–7)

Such jubilation not only overwhelms all other consciousness, but so thoroughly screens all distinction as to effect an imaginary wholeness and self-sufficiency. Thus, the initial astonishment over unbounded capacity dwells totally and narcissistically upon itself:

My Essence was Capacitie.
That felt all Things,
The Thought that Springs
Therfrom's it self . . .
(ll. 8–11)

"Simple like the Deitie / In its own Centre is a Sphere" (ll. 15–16). The act of seeing knows, in short, neither center nor sphere, neither self nor Other:

It Acts not from a Centre to
Its Object as remote,
But present is, when it doth view,

Being with the Being it doth note.
(ll. 18–21)

The imaginary confusions multiply throughout the poem. The "Spirit" is "more Voluble then Light: / Which can put on ten thousand Forms / Being clothd with what it self adorns" (ll. 32–34).

And evry Object in my Soul a Thought
Begot, or was; I could not tell,
Whether the Things did there
Themselvs appear,
Which in my Spirit *truly* seemd to dwell;
Or whether my conforming Mind
Were not alone even all that shind.
(ll. 45–51)

Of course, from Lacan, we can understand that there is no either/or disjuncture to such dialectics. Self and Other, Eye and object are each "conforming" to the invisible gaze to which both are bound and from which both are screened. Screened, at this moment, not only from the specular function of the gaze itself, but also from each other. The subject/object confusion is nothing other than the result of the scopic jubilation that here photo-graphs or maps the self within the specular field.

"Fullnesse" represents the next step in the mirror phase, as the self identifies totally with the power or capacity of sight:

My Power exerted, or my Perfect Being,
If not Enjoying, yet an Act of Seeing.
(ll. 9–10)

The identification that tries to collide Being with Seeing seems simultaneously to recognize a lack—here hinted in "if not Enjoying." Perhaps that lack is what Traherne is referring to in the cryptic fragment "The Apprehension," but whether that is true or not there is no question that out of this sense of want arises a conception of duty (demand in excess of need) and consequently a desire:

A little Spark
That shining in the Dark,
Makes, and encourages my Soul to rise.
(ll. 25–28)

In other words, Traherne's jubilant captivation by his own capacities to see has, by the end of "Fullnesse," incited an undefinable and insatiable desire for *more*. To see the self seeing is not to see the self, but to raise the desire to see itself to a secondary level. The fullness of the poem's title, I think, points directly to that mechanism of desire: a self grounded in lack, or want, or emptiness, which constantly desires to be filled. The generation of this further desire is confirmed in the following poem, "Nature":

> The very Day my Spirit did inspire,
> The Worlds fair Beauty set my Soul on fire.
> My Senses were Informers to my Heart,
> The Conduits of his Glory Power and Art.
> His Greatness Wisdom Goodness I did see,
> His Glorious Lov, and his Eternitie
>
> . . . .
>
> I was by Nature prone and apt to love
> All Light and Beauty, both in Heaven above,
> And Earth beneath, prone even to Admire,
> Adore and Prais as well as to Desire.
> My Inclinations raisd me up on high,
> And guided me to all Infinitie.
> (ll. 5–10, 13–18)

With the raising of desire, the self is fully inscribed in the dialectic of the Other, here registered as God, subsequently called "A Secret self I had enclosd within, / That was not bounded with my Clothes or Skin, / Or terminated with my Sight" (ll. 19–21). Indeed, it is precisely because the self *is* the Other that it is continually "Dispersing and Dilating evry Way." Likewise, that dilation, because it can know no bounds, can find no limit, structures as well the generation of yet more desire:

> Vast unaffected Wonderfull Desires,
> Like Inward, Nativ, uncausd, hidden fires,
> Sprang up with Expectations very strange,
> Which into New Desires did quickly change.
> (ll. 39–42)

Here we are on the ground of more traditional Traherne scholarship. The beauty of the world leads the imagination to desire to see the beauty of heaven and to know the source of the beauty of both:

> But yet there were new Rooms, and Spaces more,
> Beyond all these, Wide Regions ore and ore,
> And into them my pent-up-Soul like fire
> Did break, Surmounting all I here admire.
> The Spaces fild were like a Cabinet
> Of Joys before me most Distinctly set:
> The Empty, like to large and Vacant Room
> For Fancy to enlarge in, and presume
> A Space for more.
> (ll. 71–79)

Such aspiration, such insatiable desire ever to seek out and to fill all spaces is the reflexive other of the demand that *all* be brought to fill an otherwise empty self. The consciousness that was originally an "Abyss" and "Nothing" must now imagine "I am made the End." In the context of "Nature," this means the self reenacts itself as the object of the very thing it desires. Desiring to see all beauty of all space, it imagines all beauty reflects only that it might be seen by him alone.

"Ease," "Speed," and "Designe" offer further analyses of such desire by reimagining nature's beauty in terms of possession. The *moi* that consciousness fashions here is a consequence, that is, of the *mine* the specular confusions allow. "All we see is ours"; "evry One / Possessor of the whole"; "each by all possest": what the self sees, the self owns.[86] The Eye, like desire, is an insatiable appetite, voracious and unbounded. The ideal-ego that is also being formed in these poems is quickly expanded to divine proportions:

> I was as High and Great
> As Kings are in their Seat.
> All other Things were mine.
> The World my House, the Creatures were my Goods,
> Fields, Mountains, Valleys, Woods,
> Floods, Cities, Churches, Men, for me did shine.
> ("Speed," ll. 13–18)

> New all! New Burnisht Joys;
>
> . . . .

New all and mine.
Great Truth so Sacred seemd for this to me,
Becaus the Things which I did see
Were such, my State I knew to be Divine.
(ll. 25–30)

As Lacan's notions of the *stade du miroir* predict, however, the subject who possesses is also caught in the necessary dialectical consequence of being possessed. Therefore, while "Ease" and "Speed" enact an I-Eye that sees and thus owns all others, "The Designe" enacts the correlative *moi*, a me that becomes the object of another's sight and thus his ownership. Interestingly, from a Lacanian perspective, the Other that "preposses[es]" man, shines upon him so that he "might likewise Shine" and thus be "soon . . . of all possest" as Truth. Although Traherne is not very precise about his conception of truth, it seems to function as his equivalent to Lacan's mirror. "When first Eternity Stoopd down to Nought / And in the Earth its Likeness sought" ("The Designe," ll. 1–2), it took special "Care" about its daughter, Truth. The Truth that is God's "Likeness" is man's "Likeness" to God.

In the reflexivity of that glass, man and God both affirm their own divinities and confirm the divinity of the Other:

That being Truth, and Fair and Easy too,
While it on all doth Shine,
We might by it becom Divine
Being led to Woo
The Thing we view,
And as chast Virgins Early with it joyn,
That with it we might likewise Shine.
(ll. 39–45)

Specular identification here not only licenses the transferral of attributes between self and Other, but also incites the desire by which both are led "to Woo" each other in reflexive attempts at possession.

It is in the context provided by "Designe" that "The Person" must be interpreted. Ostensibly a parody of the Elizabethan-Jacobean blazon, "The Person" offers to redress the human body by stripping away all the false ornaments with which it is usually clothed. At issue is what "Thing" Traherne here wishes to "Display" and how his derogating remarks about "Metaphores" function toward that end. Metaphors, we are told in the second stanza, "conceal" the most sublime and brightest things; so Traherne casts aside the glories by which man normally fashions himself as an object to "Bewitch the Ey" in order to praise "My Tongue, My Eys, / My cheeks, my Lips, my Ears, my Hands, my Feet" (ll. 60–61). Significantly, however, these "ornaments" are themselves metaphors: "Their Harmony is far more Sweet; / Their Beauty true" (ll. 62–63). The truth to which both Beauty and Harmony point is the divine "Likeness" of the preceding poem, the conventional but reimagined fact that man is made *in the image* of God. "The Person" thus serves as a culmination of the self's self-inquiry and affirms the specular identification with the *imago* God himself offers. Having so objectified the self, Traherne can turn, in the final poem of this narrative stage, to the desire of the Other before whom such a self must be "Display[ed]."

"The Estate" injects a new urgency into the sequence by acknowledging a self subjected to potential death and waste. The sense of death seems to give rise to a newer form of desire, desire now more openly to be the desire of the Other. Desire for the Other, in short, has given rise to a need to respond to the Other's demand; hence the new urgency of duty and obligation (which, I think, is also a budding consciousness of the law):

> My Palate ought to be a Stone
> To trie thy Joys upon:
> And evry Member ought to be
> A Tongue, to Sing to Thee.
> There's not an Ey thats framd by Thee,
> But ought thy Life and Lov, to see.
> Nor is there, Lord, upon mine Head an Ear,
> But that the Musick of thy Works should hear.
> Each Toe, each Finger framed by thy Skill,
> Ought Oyntments to Distill.
> (ll. 15–24)

In a sense, Traherne is here re-dressing the body parts that were stripped bare in "The Person," readorning them with the love they should express to God as the Other. But the imaginative core of the poem falls in the third and fourth stanzas, where the human organs become "the Pipes, / And Conduits" of God's praise and man's love for the express purpose of intensifying the dialectic of desire. In stanza three, the rays of light with which Traherne always announces a specular relation are suddenly transformed into water:

> They Drink in Nectars, and Disburs again
> In Purer Beams, those Streams,
> Those Nectars which are causd by Joys.
> And as the spacious Main
> Doth all the Rivers, which it Drinks, return,
> Thy Love receivd doth make the Soul to burn.
> (ll. 37–42)

In these lines it is not God's love that gives rise to man's desire, but the fact that man's love of God is *returned* in a circulating motion. The soul burns in the desire to receive its own love back again. Such desire is analogous to that Lacan defines in the *Fort! Da!* If the originary desire is simply to have the absent reel present again, the replication of the disappearance/reappearance of the reel is desire of another order—desire to throw the reel over the bed *in order to* bring it back *in order to* throw it over, and so forth. In Traherne's terms, man loves God so that God will desire him *more*; desiring man more, God's love becomes more desirable. This reflexivity, which I have elsewhere identified by the more normative Trahernean term circulation, plays out its consequences for God-as-Other in the fourth stanza:

> Our Love he more doth prize:
> Our Gratitude is in his Eys,
> Far richer then the Skies.
> And those Affections which we do return,
> Are like the Lov which in Himself doth burn.
> (ll. 52–56)

Both the soul and God "burn" in desire for the desire of the Other, and the field wherein that desire photo-graphs each is "in his Eys." In this dialectic, the "Devouring fire" of God's desire "Doth feed and Quicken Mans Desire" only to the extent that man's desire feeds and quickens God's desire. To be the sole and adequate object of the

Other's desire is, to this point, the only objective of both man and God.

I have said that this third section of the Dobell sequence is primarily concerned with the developing consciousness of the self as an object in the Eye of another. By "The Estate," however, that enacted objectification is complete and desire as such becomes the central issue. The fourth stage of Traherne's narrative, "The Enquirie" through "Love," focuses less upon the self than upon the Other to which it is bound. I do not mean that the self's consciousness-of-self ceases to be of major concern, but rather that the realization of the dialectic structuring relations between self and Other must also heighten the sense of difference between them, the self's own sense of alienation from the Other. Here, then, the self must refashion the Other as it has already reimagined itself. As a consequence, a different question begins to emerge in this phase of the sequence: what must God lack that he needs me? Perceiving the Other's desire to be motivated by want, the self must now seek to become the object the Other lacks. And that, in turn, means that the self must turn its attention more squarely upon the Other, unaware, perhaps, that the lack it seeks in the Other replicates the lack that generates its own desire for the Other.

"The Enquirie" opens this stage of the narrative by seeming to renounce the two immediately preceding poems:

> Men may delighted be with Springs,
> While Trees and Herbs their Senses pleas,
> And taste even living Nectar in the Seas:
> May think their Members things
> Of Earthly Worth at least, if not Divine,
> And Sing becaus the Earth for them doth Shine.
> (ll. 1–6)

The self-deprecating tone serves functionally to incite the "enquirie" that governs much of the next seven poems:

> But can the Angels take Delight,
> To see such Faces here beneath?
> Or can Perfumes indeed from Dunghils breath?
> Or is the World a Sight

Worthy of them?
(ll. 7–11)

In short, can I really be the object of delight and desire that I imagine myself to be? The dramatic importance of this question lies in the fact that for the first time in the sequence others (the plural is now essential to emphasize) intrude upon the heretofore closed specular relation between the solitary self and the single Other. I take the question, therefore, to signal a critical turn away from the narcissistic capture of the earlier poems and toward the mature social functions of the later ones. At the moment, however, it is enough to observe how Traherne deals with the question. Angels may indeed be delighted in man, and may feed and please their "Appetites" (desires) here on earth because they conceive in man their own ego-ideals. That is possible because man is the mirror of "The Wonders which our God hath done, / The Glories of his Attributes" ("The Enquirie," ll. 25–26). Those wonders and attributes become "Angelick Joys" only as they become man's joys: "The Angels hav them only for our sake!" (l. 33). Like all beings, angels need an Other by which their own bliss may be conceived and apprehended.

If we pause here for a moment, we can see that Traherne has radically altered the condition of man. Prior to this he (and the self he fashions) has been the sole end of all the Other-God desires. Now he is a mediating screen through which another sees God's desire. Man serves, in short, a signifying function, becomes, in Lacan's vocabulary, himself a signifier. In one sense, the remainder of the Dobell manuscript explores the various ways in which man functions as this signifier—for angels, for God himself, for other men. Initially, in poems like "Amendment" and "The Anticipation," Traherne seems merely to invert the subject/object relation of the preceding poems by making man the Other of God's self. But his intentions are considerably more radical than this (although this is radical enough to border on something that savors of heresy), for both man and God are gradually being rewritten in what Lacan might call the mode of symbolic discourse. Each will eventually be seen as performing the systematic functions of the Saussurean and Levi-Straussian signifier. How that shift occurs is the central subject of the remainder of this chapter.

"The Circulation" offers an initial step by reconceiving the mirror imagery that has sporadically appeared in the preceding poems:

> As fair Ideas from the Skie,
> Or Images of Things,
> Unto a Spotless Mirror flie,
> On unperceived Wings;
> And lodging there affect the Sence,
> As if at first they came from thence;
> While being there, they richly Beautifie
> The Place they fill, and yet communicat
> Themselvs, reflecting to the Seers Ey,
> Just such is our Estate.
> (ll. 1–10)

The original confusion of identities that marks the *stade du miroir* is here openly acknowledged, and yet it is also carefully subscribed. The image does *communicate* and it reflects *to*, not *in*, the seer's Eye. The self, in short, is changed in the specular exchange: an emptiness or lack is filled. Traherne uses this notion of reflection to ponder circulation itself:

> All Things to Circulations owe
> Themselvs; by which alone
> They do exist: They cannot shew
> A Sigh, a Word, a Groan,
> A Colour, or a Glimps of Light,
> The Sparcle of a Precious Stone,
> A virtue, or a Smell; a lovly Sight,
> A Fruit, a Beam, an Influence, a Tear;
> But they anothers Livery must Wear:
> And borrow Matter first,
> Before they can communicat.
> Whatever's empty is accurst.
> (ll. 29–40)

It would not be too distorting to see in these lines merely a reconfirmation of the self's need of the Other, but in fact Traherne goes further. Now the issue is not *what* is seen, but what is exchanged and expressed from one to the other. Thus Traherne revises his own terms: reflection becomes circulation becomes communication. At issue here is the same relation we have already seen in "Dumnesse" and "Silence," that between word and work, between essence and act. Communication is, to Traherne, a structural relation which binds speech and reply, image and Eye, subject and object, self and Other into mutually fulfilling terms.[87] Each gives to and receives from the Other. Only God is exempted from such a structural system, for he, Traherne argues in the poem's concluding stanza, "in himself doth live." And yet the final lines hint that even the apparent exception reinscribes the rule:

> He is the Primitive Eternal Spring
> The Endless Ocean of each Glorious Thing.
> The Soul a Vessel is
> A Spacious Bosom to Contain
> All the fair Treasures of his Bliss
> Which run like Rivers from, into the Main,
> And all it doth receiv returns again.
> (ll. 78–84)

If man were to refuse to express what he originally has drunk in, he would dam up the circulating flow of this "Endless Ocean." The soul, which begins in line 80 as a minute vessel, grows by the next line into a "Spacious Bosom" capable of receiving all the treasures God can give, giving all back to God, and receiving all again from God. If "whatever's empty is accurst," this circulation of communication can be nothing less than the obligation to fill any vessel until it in turn overflows. Traherne is extremely close here to arguing that as man is fulfilled by God, so God must be fulfilled by man.

Once that assertion is made, of course, the dialectic between self and Other has been opened to absolute exchange, in effect, to what Lacan only half-facetiously calls *un jeu du miroirs*. "The Amendment" takes some tentative steps in this direction by extending the ideal of circulation: that all things appear "far more Brightly" in God's Eye as they are used and prized by man.

> Thy Soul, O GOD, doth prize
> The Seas, the Earth, our Souls, the Skies,
> As we return the same to Thee;

They more delight thine Eys,
And sweeter be,
As unto Thee we Offer up the same,
Then as to us, from Thee at first they came.
(ll. 36–42)

Traherne wonders, therefore, whether he isn't "a Glorious Spring" and "Mirror" to God as God had earlier been to him. "The Demonstration" moves ever closer to an answer that Traherne, already sensing its implications, can call only "Incredible" and a "profound Abyss":

And what then this can be more Plain and Clear
What Truth then this more Evident appear!
The GODHEAD cannot prize
The Sun at all, nor yet the Skies,
Or Air, or Earth, or Trees, or Seas,
Or Stars, unless the Soul of Man they pleas.
He neither sees with Humane Eys
Nor needs Himself Seas Skies
Or Earth, or any thing: He draws
No Breath, nor Eats or Drinks by Natures Laws.

The Joy and Pleasure which his Soul doth take
In all his Works, is for his Creatures sake.
So Great a Certainty
We in this Holy Doctrine see
That there could be no Worth at all
In any Thing Material Great or Small
Were not som Creature more Alive,
Whence it might Worth Derive.
GOD is the Spring whence Things come forth
Souls are the fountains of their Real Worth.
(ll. 41–60)

Traherne works awfully hard here to keep his imaginative reconstruction of God within the bounds of acceptable dogma, but once he has defined a lack in God (he wants "Humane Eys") other needs must inevitably follow. Although Traherne denies that God needs anything and is not bound by "Natures Law," He is bound by what

Traherne himself has been defining as the scopic law. Without "som Creature *more* Alive," some Other according to whom the "Real Worth" of anything could be judged, God "cannot prize" at all.

Traherne has so inverted the specular relation here that he feels compelled, in the poem's final stanza, to step back from the apparent conclusion towards which he is driving. Ironically, that stanza only furthers its progress:

> In [man God] sees, and feels, and Smels, and Lives,
> In them Affected is to whom he gives:
> In them ten thousand Ways,
> He all his Works again enjoys,
> All things from Him to Him proceed
> By them; Are His in them: As if indeed
> His Godhead did it self exceed.
> (ll. 71–78)

God's self exceeds itself because it is the Other. Traherne has here charted the inverse reflection of his earlier insistence that man is divine, made *in the image* of God. Extending the specular dialectic now to divinity itself, Traherne applies the principle of circulation announced in the third stanza of "The Circulation." From the perspective of this poem, that stanza offers an incarnational theory which posits God's very existence on the "Matter" of man: God, in short, is made the specular image of man, even to himself.

"The Demonstration" thus opens a view of God-as-Other grounded in lack, need, and desire. If God is "Affected" by the Other that is man, sees and lives only in him, then God must lack the capacity to know himself by himself. Like man, God's consciousness of self is dependent upon His structural relation to an Other. "The Anticipation" tries to develop the consequences of this thought. It begins by focusing on ends and means. God, of course, is "the End / To whom all Creatures tend," but He is also the end to which He himself tends. Thus, while "His Essence Perfect was in all its Features" "From all Eternitie," all ends *want* means. If "God is Himself the Means, / Wherby he doth exist," that want can only chart the bipartition of the divine Being. Traherne focuses on this lack:

Wants are the Fountains of Felicitie
No Joy could ever be
Were there no Want. No Bliss
No Sweetness Perfect were it not for this.
Want is the Greatest Pleasure
Becaus it makes all Treasure.
O what a Wonderfull Profound Abyss
Is God!
(ll. 64–71)

The means of God's perfection, which is his end, is his "Endless Wants," his "Eternal Wants":

He infinitly wanteth all his Joys;
(No Want the Soul ore cloys.)
And all those Wanted Pleasures
He infinitly Hath.

. . . .

Whose very Wants are Endles Pleasures.
His Life in Wants and Joys is infinit.
(ll. 73–76, 79–80)

Means and ends, needs and perfection, lack and completion: such structures identify an Other who, like man, is merely a locus of dialectical relations. The split between them is the irreducible ground even of God's existence. Possession and want, like self and Other, like creator and creature,

Both always are together:
No force can either from the other Sever.
Yet theres a Space between
Thats Endless. Both are seen
Distinctly still, and both are seen for ever.
(ll. 84–88)

Out of or within that "Endless" space or gap in Being Traherne inscribes the structural circulation or reflexivity of communication and defines its relation to desire:

His Essence is all Act: He did, that He
All Act might always be.

His Nature burns like fire;
His Goodness infinitly doth desire,
To be by all possest;
His Love makes others Blest.
It is the Glory of his High Estate,
And that which I for ever more Admire,
He is an Act that doth Communicate.
(ll. 91–99)

Communication is the systematic discourse within which all Being, all relations of being, are articulated: the infinite desire to cross the gap which fractures Being at its irreducible core or center. The reflexivities that discourse speaks bind man and God, self and Other, in terms of continual exchange, without which no comprehension of either self or Other is possible.

The opening stanzas of "The Recovery" push such exchange to its very limit:

To see us but receiv, is such a Sight
As makes his Treasures infinit!
Becaus His Goodness doth possess
In us, His own, and our own Blessedness.
Yea more, His Love doth take Delight
To make our Glory Infinite
Our Blessedness to see
Is even to the Deitie
A Beatifick Vision! He attains
His Ends while we enjoy. In us He reigns.

For God enjoyd is all his End.
Himself he then doth Comprehend.
When He is Blessed, Magnified,
Extold, Exalted, Praisd and Glorified
Honord, Esteemd, Belovd, Enjoyd,
Admired, Sanctified, Obeyd,
That is receivd. For He
Doth place his Whole Felicitie
In that, who is despised and defied
Undeified almost if once denied.
(ll. 1–20)

Although the last line hedges the final consequence, it is faithful to the dialectic Traherne has been exploiting in recognizing that God's divinity is absolutely dependent upon man, just as man's humanity is absolutely dependent upon God. Unless each can be the lost object, lack, of the Other's desire, neither can comprehend the self. Each "reigns," exists, in the Other as object of the Other's gaze, reflected in the gaze of the self. Giving that object and receiving it is the communicative exchange that structures all desire and all Being.

It is, I think, only when Traherne comprehends his own reality as the absent object of God's desire that he can begin to chart the progress out of the specular and imaginary confusions of the child's *stade du miroir* and into the adult field of the symbolic.[88] The "return" he stresses in the penultimate stanza as that which God most desires is not the involuntary love of the mirror phase, but "One Voluntary Act of Love" that "repays" the Other what both would otherwise lack. "Another" clarifies this "recovery" of an adult perspective by setting God's "Infinit Desires" against man's potential to be "Indifferent." Indifference, Traherne argues, is death, for unless the self is "Set forth . . . unto {its} whole Extent," neither self nor its object can exist. Man must be to God what God has been to man or neither can be what he is:

> Let that same Goodness, which is infinit,
> Esteems thy Lov with Infinit Delight,
> Tho less then His, Tho Nothing, always be
> An Object Infinit to Thee.
> (ll. 37–40)

To be an adequate object of the Other's desire, recognizing the dialectical structures upon which such desire arises and progresses, is, perhaps, to become resubjectified in full functional relation. Subjected to the Other, as well as to the self, the I can finally come to understand its function as a signifier. That consciousness, I think, is what Traherne tries to express in the final poem of this section of the narrative, "Love."

In some ways, "Love" is the most perplexing poem of the sequence, not only because its catalogue of metaphors is at extreme odds with Traherne's earlier deprecation of such figures, but also because its extravagant jubilation seems almost absurd in light of the careful thinking that has preceded it. My own sense of the poem, however, is that Traherne reverts to the figurative relations between self and God in order to attempt a revision of the dialectics he has been exploring. The last stanza can serve as an illustration:

> His Ganimede! His Life! His Joy!
> Or he comes down to me, or takes me up
> That I might be his Boy,
> And fill, and taste, and give, and Drink the Cup.
> But these (tho great) are all
> Too short and small,
> Too Weak and feeble Pictures to Express
> The true Mysterious Depths of Blessedness.
> I am his Image, and his Friend.
> His Son, Bride, Glory, Temple, End.
> (ll. 31–40)

Submerged in the middle of this stanza is an allusion to the Eucharist. I take this allusion as a crucial turning point, for it recognizes now that Other that holds both man and God in true functional and symbolic relation. As the God-man, God's Word become man's work, His essence become all act, Christ, not God, is the functional locus of communicative and circulating existence. As the discourse of the Other, Christ provides the self with the language by means of which its desire and the Other's desire can be both acknowledged and expressed. Freed from the imaginary identifications that have structured the confusions of the mirror phase and that have led the self to desire to *be* the Other, the subject can see in Christ the signifying site of communal relations that Lacan calls the Name-of-the-Father and the law. The concluding stage of the Dobell narrative, focusing on language as the discourse of this site, reimagines the self in its relation to that law—the law now of word made work, word working to draw self, God, and all men into a fully symbolic register or *epos*.[89] And it is precisely in terms of such a symbolic narrative, I think, that the blatant metaphors of "Love" must be interpreted. Each bespeaks one dimension of the functional and signifying relations between self and Other; together they insist that the self *is* nothing other than the systematic discourse of all of those signifiers.

One of the measures by which Traherne's transformed conception of the self can be seen is the depreciated status now accorded the Eye. In "Thoughts I," the opening poem of the concluding section, "The Ey's confind" and thoughts "taste" sweets "No Ey can see." Thoughts still offer mirror images, but here such images are not mirages. Instead, they are recognized for what they are: signifiers and "Representatives." Indeed, the functions of re-presenting and representing structure the entire poem. Thoughts are "machines," "Engines of Felicitie," functional mechanisms by which the self recovers its own lost past and the lost objects of its desire:

> Old Objects I
> Far distant do even now descrie
> Which by your help are present here.
> . . . .
> The Offsprings and Effects of Bliss
> By whose Return my Glory is
> Renewd, and represented to my View.
> (ll. 16–18, 21–23)

We have seen such returns before, but not the consciousness of re-presencing and re-presenting which structures them. That apprehension is totally new and it inscribes this entire stage of the narrative, as well as the *thoughts* upon which it is focused, in the field of Lacanian language. What Traherne is attempting to work out is how his own entry into that field reveals his condition as a signifier, a function, within a larger discursive system.

Presencing the absent, representing the object-Other, representing the lost: these functions of thought lead Traherne to reimage all of his earlier concerns:

> What were the Skie,
> What were the Sun, or Stars, did [thoughts] not lie
> In me! and represent them there
> Where els they never could appear!
> (ll. 43–46)

Earlier in the sequence we recall these same objects could appear only in the glass of the Other's gaze, but here the Other is "*in* me," an acknowledgment of the structural function of Otherness itself and a revisioning of the scopic stage in signifying (i.e., representational) terms.

> O ye *Conceptions* of Delight!
> Ye that *inform* my Soul with Life and Sight!
> Ye Representatives, and Springs
> Of inward Pleasure!
> Ye Joys! Ye Ends of Outward Treasure!
> (ll. 49–53)

Thoughts, in short, *communicate*; they mediate the abyss separating self and object, internal pleasure and external treasure.

Thoughts are also "free": they "Rove ore the World with Libertie: / Can Enter Ages, Present be / In any Kingdom, into Bosoms see" (ll. 66–68). Hence they are unbounded and timeless, "Immortal in their place" (l. 82). We can hear in these lines echoes of the child's first imaginary perceptions, but now such perceptions have been grounded in structural mediation not specular transfer. The desire that sets the thoughts in circulating motion is, of course, no different from that which incites the imaginary identification; but now there is no wish to supplant the Other, to *become* God, for the necessary dialectical structuring of desire is recognized and acknowledged.

Thus "Thoughts II"[90] extends the circulation of the thought-word to the Other: that is, it extends the function of thoughts in "Thoughts I" to return and re-present past time and lost objects to the more important function of reoffering the self to the Other in communication, discourse and its necessary reply. Like several of the poems in the preceding section, the present value of thought-as-reply is grounded upon the real acknowledgment that man is, in both Heideggerian and Lacanian terms, a being-toward-Death. To be "Indifferent," as Traherne said in "Another," "Tis Death"; here, indifference would be a refusal to ex-press thought. The word enclosed or bound within, not extended to the Other, "withers strait, and fades away" (l. 11.). "Every word contains its own reply," Lacan frequently reminds us. Failure to see in the word, therefore, this systematic function of exchange would be to deny the word its very nature and to bar any symbolic relation between the self and the Other. Such potential loss once again structures concurrent desire.

God's desire is to "Enflame / The Soul with Love to him" (ll. 35–36) who first spoke the word and whose desire must therefore be for its return. Man's desire is for God's desire, which grants to the thought "Which we conceive, / Bring forth, and Give" to Him such "Greater Value" that it can represent "*our* Paradice" (ll. 4–5, 6, 9). Man and God, then, both recover each other and maintain their eternal self-presence in the Other through the "Representation" discourse allows. Although Traherne does not yet mention him by name, Christ-as-Word mediating this man-God relation is already figuratively present, converting man's consciousness of self from an I-Eye to the tongue-ear of conversation.

In "Ye hidden Nectars," thoughts again prove the relations that structure the self. When they appear, "Even Heavn it self, and God, and all . . . / Come down on Earth, and pleas my Blessed View" (ll. 19–20). That blessed view, however, is of a blessed self, and thoughts thus answer to the desires the self's consciousness of its own lacks occasions:

> I never Glorious Great and Rich am found,
> Am never ravished with Joy,
>   Till ye my Soul Surround,
>   Till ye my Blessedness display.
> No Soul but Stone, No Man but Clay am I.
> (ll. 21–25)

Thoughts speak, that is, man's very being, inscribe and define him within the discursive functions of language itself, display and reveal the thing he is. Like Heidegger and Lacan, Traherne would seem to accept the fact that man is the creation of the Word, not the creator of the word.

"Thoughts III" is the most interesting poem of this section, a series of epigrams by which Traherne tries to express the functional structures of language itself. Two aspects of Traherne's meditation require special attention. The first is the sign-system, which links thought to what we have come to call Saussurian linguistics:

> The Matter of all Pleasure, Virtue, Worth,
> Grief, Anger, Hate, Revenge, which Words set forth,

Are Thoughts alone.
(ll. 25–27)

If the matter is thought (signified) and the word its image (signifier), then the relationship between thought and word replicates that between self and Other. It can do so, however, only so long as neither thought nor self is accorded any special privilege, for both of these are simultaneously—that is, dialectically and systematically—functions of another level: thoughts as signifiers of things; self as signifier of other men. The explicit connection between thought and language thus keeps open the essential question of the status of the signifier within a broader system. It is precisely this question that eventually offers to Traherne full entry into the discursive law by Christ-the-Logos in the Name-of-the-Father.

The second important consequence of Traherne's thinking about thoughts here is an understanding of the structural necessity of difference: thoughts are the "Best or Worst of Things," "all Misery or Bliss," "The Hony and the Stings," "all or Nothing" (ll. 59, 60, 22, 45). Bound to such dialectical possibilities, thoughts escape all attempts to define or contain them. In short, thoughts become purely *functional*: "rightly used" they can make a creature a king; wrongly used, they can turn a glorious sun to darkness. To me, this is a critical recognition on Traherne's part, for it means that the creature of thought, the creation and subsequent user of thought, must likewise be a function, a signifier that is used. As thought gives being, it must also structure the functions within which being speaks and works. And it is precisely this understanding that leads Traherne, in the next poem, to full acknowledgment of himself as a function of signifying desire.

If, in Lacan's terms, the end of the psychoanalytic process is to bring the subject to the point of being able to recognize and express his own desire, Traherne's poem "Desire" functions as an analogous end of the Dobell sequence. Here, for the first time in that sequence, desire is not only directly named and accepted as the very ground of the self's existence ("All" is "founded in Desire"), but also acknowledged as an insatiable demand born of the self's "deep profound Abyss." Desire, Traherne confesses, did

> ever ever me Enflame,
> With restlesse longing Heavenly Avarice,
> That never could be satisfied,
> That did incessantly a Paradice
> Unknown suggest, and som thing undescried
> Discern, and bear me to it; be
> Thy Name for ever praisd by me.
> (ll. 7–13)

Ever desiring, never fulfilled; ever wanting, never satisfied. Caught within these structures, the self lives and moves and finds its real being. To accept and to praise that desire is finally to recognize the signifying functions of its very Name and the law that name articulates. Thus freed from such imaginary captures as require the continual denial, sublimation, or transference of desire, the self can enter fully into the symbolic register of desire as such.[91]

"Thoughts IV," meditating on the blessings God has given man and the capacity of thoughts to bring the soul into presence with both those blessings and God himself, envisions a yet higher registration of desire: the desire for an Other who will see and accept us for what we are, even for the very worst that we can be. Thus the name of Jesus enters the sequence for the first and only time as the signifier of the Other whose "Blood refines [our] Soul from Sin," whose function in relation to us as this Other loves not in spite of but *because* of the lack that structures our being, and whose "Blood hath brought us [ever] new Desires." Subjected to the "constant Mirror" of this Love, this enactment of the law which makes possible all our "Conversation," the self openly perceives itself in radically symbolic terms and can turn, again for the first time in the sequence, to its own mediatory function of expressing God to other men and other men to God. Here, in the poem Traherne entitled "Goodnesse," the gaze that reflects upon the self from others serves not merely to exalt the self, but to incite the self to return that gaze *for* the others. The earlier "Ends" (*in* me) here extend and multiply as the suddenly eucharistic imagery of the final two stanzas remaps the self in the full symbolic community of creatures (again the plural is crucial) and creator feeding and drinking the signifying cup of prepared communion.[92] It is the only moment of the entire sequence in which the I that has been so conspicuous from its beginning is read in terms of its structural relations to "them" rather than to *moi*; it is the only instance, in short, in which the self the sequence has tried to fashion reaches a condition which we are able to recognize as fully Christian. That condition is made possible only by the sudden and late intrusion of the Name-of-Christ as the Father of such communion. I repeat the concluding stanzas in full because they are dramatically unique: the self is firmly grounded upon earth, firmly bound to other men, and, like them, functioning solely as a signifier of the God-Other whom it both desires and is:

> The Soft and Swelling Grapes that on [other men's] Vines
> Receiv the Lively Warmth that Shines
> Upon them, ripen there for me:
> Or Drink they be
> Or Meat. The Stars salute my pleased Sence
> With a Derivd and borrowed Influence
> But better Vines do Grow
> Far Better Wines do flow
> Above, and while
> The Sun doth Smile
> Upon the Lillies there, and all things warme
> Their pleasant Odors do my Spirit charm.
> (ll. 49–60)

I take the final lines here to be Traherne's imagined scene of all men returning to Christ the drink and meat He has been to them: "My beloved is mine and I am his: he delights in the lilies"; "My beloved has gone down to his garden, to the beds where balsam grows, to delight in the garden and to pick the lilies. I am my beloved's and my beloved is mine, he who delights in the lilies"; "Let us get up early to the vineyards; let us see if the vine flourish, whether the tender grape appear, and . . . there will I give thee my loves"; "I am come into my garden, my sister, my spouse: . . . I have eaten my honeycomb with my honey; I have drunk my wine with my milk: eat, O friends; drink, yea, drink abundantly" ("The Song of Songs"). In the echoes of the symbolic wedding between the soul and Christ and between Christ and the whole community of saints which is the Church, the self identifies both its place and its function.[93]

Their rich Affections do like precious Seas
Of Nectar and Ambrosia pleas.
Their Eys are Stars, or more Divine:
And Brighter Shine
Their Lips are soft and Swelling Grapes, their Tongues
A Quire of Blessed and Harmonious Songs.
Their Bosoms fraught with Love
Are Heavens all Heavens above
And being Images of GOD, they are
The Highest Joys his Goodness did prepare.
(ll. 61–70)

Human existence is here rewritten in pointedly sacramental terms, all beings feeding upon, being fed by, and being food for all other living beings, mortal and divine. It is as complete an enactment of the fullness of man and God in their mutual relatedness as anything Traherne ever wrote. And it is the only moment of the entire Dobell sequence in which other men become both the source and the object of the self's own joys rather than origins of its errors and sins. I think it remarkable how infrequently criticism has noted how absolutely unique this scene is within the manuscript. My own sense is that it arises directly out of, and thus is fully dependent upon, something like a Lacanian narrative of the structural relations between the self and an Other, the desire such relations inevitably generate, and the psychic progress through the various imaginary captures of the mirror stage and into the symbolic register of real humanity.

CHAPTER FOUR

Traherne and Derrida

The Economy of the Supplement

I must content myself for the moment with underscoring the supplementary aspect of this structure.

In certain respects, the theme of supplementarity is certainly no more than one theme among others. It is in a chain, carried by it. *But it happens that this theme describes the chain itself, the being-chain of a textual chain, the structure of substitution, the articulation of desire and of language. . . . It tells us in a text what a text is.*

While pretending to turn around and look backward . . . one is also in fact starting over again, adding an extra text, complicating the scene, opening up within the labyrinth a supplementary digression. —JACQUES DERRIDA

I SUPPLEMENTARITY AS ECONOMY

Supplement: "something added, especially to make up for a lack or deficiency."[1] For Heidegger and Lacan, as we have seen, lack is primarily a *manque d'être*, and the desire of being or the self to fill this void at and of its "center" structures all subsequent activity. Although neither thinker makes extensive use of the term, it is clear that the general notion of supplementation describes the dialectical relations (between, for example, Being and being, presence and absence, self and Other, want and desire) both attempt to chart. Indeed, it could be argued that without some such notion neither author could have challenged the conventional and hence comfortable binary oppositions of Western thought. That they did so, and in the process reopened the entire history of dialectics, has been made explicit by their one follower who has been most concerned with the supplement—Jacques Derrida.

According to Derrida, supplementarity is the operative mechanism or law of *différance*, the irreducible interplay of differing and deferring within which all thought—all conceptualizing, verbalizing, representing, or signifying—is "always already" captivated.[2] *Différance*, of course, is the concept most widely recognized as Derrida's contribution to modern thought, but for my purposes it is neither as central nor as useful critically as the supplement precisely because it does not require the sense of something added, of an excess which is simultaneously necessary and superfluous, of an insatiable demand or desire for more. Supplementarity, as the perceptual-conceptual operation that holds this excess constantly in view, is more directly relevant to what I see as the central characteristic of Traherne's imagination.

This is not to say that we can avoid the idea of *différance*, for part of my intention in this chapter is to explore in some detail the principal binary sets which structure Traherne's thinking. Many of these have already appeared in the preceding chapters: presence/absence, all/nothing, empty/full, center/sphere, mirror/image, part/whole, essence/act, origin/end, fact/value. But it is not, finally, the simple (or even complex) opposition of such terms that is of issue here; rather, the issue is the supplementary economy, the exchange value, of differences within Traherne's discourse. Let me offer a brief illustration. The first *Century of Meditations* opens as follows: "An Empty Book is like an Infants Soul, in which any Thing may be Written. It is Capable of all Things, but containeth Nothing. I hav a Mind to fill this with Profitable Wonders. And since Love made you put it into my Hands I will fill it with those Truths you Love, without Knowing them: and with those Things which, if it be Possible, shall shew my Lov; To you, in Communicating most *Enriching Truths*; to Truth, in Exalting Her Beauties in such a Soul."[3]

In this brief passage, one difference (empty/full) gives rise to another (nothing/all), which generates a third (unknown/known), promises a fourth (truth/profit), and predicts a fifth (the progress from the silent *tabula rasa* of the infant's soul to the "communicating" soul of the adult properly enriched and exalted). One of our tasks here will be to disclose both the logic and the consistency of these multiplying differences, and for that purpose Derrida's notion of *différance* will prove extremely helpful. But Traherne's passage does more than simply multiply differences; it accumulates differences in such a way as to stage them as a production of *value*. In fact, the paragraph progresses by a kind of doubled staging: the first syntactic unit (and by that I do not mean "sentence") ends in the production of "*Profitable* Wonders"; the second produces "*Enriching* Truths" and "*Exalting*" beauties. How Traherne's manipulation of the binary sets creates this increase and appropriation of values is what I take to be an economic question. Charting that economy will be the central task of this chapter.

Under the differences announced in the first meditation is a complex analogy between the souls of both author and reader and the book they are about to share.[4] The dedication of the volume, which immediately precedes the first meditation, states:

> This book unto the friend of my best friend
> As of the Wisest Love a Mark I send
> That she may write my Makers prais therin
> And make her self therby a Cherubin.

Here the literal and literally blank pages initially given Traherne by, presumably, Susanna Hopton, are returned fully inscribed. Hopton, reading what Traherne has now supplied, "writes" herself within the already filled pages and thereby adds to that fullness her own cherubic innocence. We can see here two distinct versions or dimensions of supplementarity. Remembering the opening of the first meditation, emptiness is equivalent to value-less-ness; fullness, here symbolized by writing itself, is worthiness. And yet the apparent plenitude of the fully inscribed pages is immediately undercut by the necessity of a "second" writing, a supplement of the supplement that, in fact, has obviously not "filled" the formerly blank pages. Emptiness and blankness remain no matter how many words attempt to complete the text: the field, as Derrida will say, is never saturated and it is precisely in the face of that void that the economic desires arise. The second level of supplementarity concerns again a sequence of exchanges whereby Traherne transforms a literal gift into a symbolic economy: through the series of analogous differences—book and soul, self and other, reading and writing, showing and making—he announces and offers another process of accumulative enrichment. How complex we conceive this latter economy will depend upon how we interpret Hopton's promised innocence. Is it, for example, a return to the soul's original "purity" and thus like the originally "blank" book (before it was stained with the inky marks of "exteriority"); or is it a progress to final purity and thus like the fully inscribed book?

The second and third meditations of the First Century supply additional differences: invisible/visible, absence/presence, expectation/desire, "Things Strange, yet Common; Incredible, yet Known; Most High, yet Plain; infinitly Profitable, but not Esteemed." Each of these oppositions will be expanded and extended throughout the remainder of the five *Centuries*, but all will find their functional value, their narrative or discursive *profit*, within an economy of supplementation that seeks constantly to enrich, promote, advance, magnify, enlarge, replenish, augment, exceed, improve, exalt; and that seeks to do so not only for the self, but for a self that can, like the book, be exchanged so as to supplement an Other, be that other God, or Susanna Hopton, or a supposed reader of the circulating volume. "Through this sequence of supplements," we can force Derrida to conclude, "a necessity is announced: that of an infinite chain, ineluctably multiplying the supplementary mediations that produce," within their structures of irrepressible substitution, "the articulation of desire"[5] and the appropriation of value.

Two distinct but related senses of economy must therefore be kept in mind throughout this chapter. The first is the system or organization of supplementarity and how that will account for the orderly arrangement and management of parts within the Trahernean text. In general terms, I have subdivided this organization into three levels of management. The first may be called the supplement of the predicate, which seeks to describe the differential logic of Traherne's various binary sets by means of the grammatical relations between nouns and verbs. The second is the supplement of the adjective, which tries to define the operation of appropriating or annexing terms of quality and value to ones of ostensibly neutral description. And the third is the imagination as supplement, which focuses more specifically on the paradoxical logics of excess and desire. The second sense of economy will emphasize that behind and motivating this system of supplementation is a carefully developed strategy for producing and distributing wealth of various kinds. Supplementarity generates, as it were, discursive capital, and that capital is then put to work within Traherne's text as an exchangeable commodity. The issue, therefore, is not so much how binary terms are arranged (Derrida's *différance*), but how their capacities for substitution and exchange affect all narrative expressions of worth and value—how that value is generated, how it is appropriated or expropriated, how it is either spent or invested.

I shall begin with a general sketch of the field called above the economic organization of supplementarity. The supplement of the predicate is the logic that structures each of Traherne's binary sets or differences. At its core, Traherne's text is continually exploring the structural relations between origin and end, cause and effect, essence and act. These relations are almost always explicated as a form of the necessary grammar whereby one of these terms functions as the predicate of the other. Interestingly, Traherne's own version of such supplementarity corroborates Derrida's broader project —which, as the latter frequently reminds us, is not a simple inversion of the usual hierarchies or privileges structuring Western metaphysical categories (speech/writing, soul/body, presence/absence, signified/signifier, self/other), but rather a reinstalling of all such oppositions within the "always already" interplay of *différance* as such.[6]

In Traherne, the supplement of the predicate may ultimately depend upon the elementary grammatical relations between noun and verb. God, for example, is Love. Love, as a noun, signifies essence; but as the syntax expresses, love-as-essence is already supplementary *différance*: God is Love; Love is God.[7] When Traherne subsequently argues that love can be only insofar as it loves, acts by loving or by willing to love, the predicate operates as a necessary and secondary supplement, a "superadded" substitution. The verb, in other words, supplements a difference already present within the noun. The economy of the supplement allows, however, that initial difference to be both displaced and deferred, submerged, in fact, under the value the verb appropriates as an essence put to worthwhile work. When Traherne comes to understand that economy and the profit of the supplemental exchange, he describes it as "communication," an *articulation* of supplementarity whereby all difference is deferred within the grammatical interval (time and space) of predication.[8]

"Originary différance is supplementarity as structure."[9] For Derrida, of course, that structure is always the irreducible complexity of the interplays of presence and absence, the re-presentations of a presence that never was and can never be, the attempt to fill or defer the ultimate absence (death) that will always be. The supplement, Derrida thus writes, the multiplication of supplements, "produce the sense of the very thing they defer: the mirage of the thing itself, of immediate presence, of originary perception."[10] To this extent, the supplement is always *différance* and, like *différance*, "the indefinite process of supplementarity has always already infiltrated presence, always already inscribed there the space of repetition and the splitting of the self."[11] Why, then, if the supplement is but "another name for différance,"[12] do we choose here to call it the more useful critical term? Part of the answer lies in what Derrida calls the "law of geometric regression," the process by which the supplement supplies an excessive or superfluous substitute for the thing itself, whether that thing be the self, another, presence, origin, or a signified. The supplement, as excess, as exorbitant surplus, must itself generate supplementary supplements: the supplement is always already the supplement of a supplement and the (lost or lacking) object of desire is deferred/differed by yet another level of representational registration.[13] Thus, where *différance* would reveal the binary structures of what might be called the syntactic level of the text, supplementarity discloses the semantic level on which those items are accorded or accrue both meaning and significance. Although it may be misleading in the long run, it is helpful initially to conceive the Derridean *différance* as systematically analogous to Lacan's imaginary; supplementarity is then analogous to the symbolic and therefore points more directly to an economy of substitution and exchange.

To return, then, to the notion of predication, the subject is replicated in the predicate; but the very fact of the predicate merely confirms the originary split always already fracturing that subject. After our discussions of Heidegger and Lacan, this fracture comes as no surprise. What may be surprising, however, is that discourse makes capital of the split: rather than announcing *différance*, the predicate supplements the subject in such a way as to substitute a registration of value for a definition of essence. God is Love. Love articulates God as a worth, as an entity that is valuable and exchangeable. Or, perhaps more dramatically, God is not anything of value until the predicate articulates it.

Obviously verbs can be transformed into nouns as easily as nouns can be transformed into verbs. In fact, it is precisely the reversibility of the grammatical positions that allows us to reconceive all structural differences as modeled upon the syntactic pattern. Origin *is* end and essence *is* act in the same supplementary fashion as noun *is* verb or God *is* loving. Again, however, it is the value that accrues to such exchanges, rather than their mere presence, that points to the economy I wish to describe.

Derrida's sense of the supplement as filling a void or lack with a surplus that can only refer and defer to additional representational substitutes is also helpful in revealing what I have called the supplement of the adjective. Adjectives (the term derives from *adjicere*, "to add to"), of course, are doubly supplementary: they supply an entity or object with an otherwise lacking quality, and they are themselves governed by a system of absent (that is, unspoken) comparison (a *good* thing, for example, in relation to a *better* or a *best* thing).[14] In effect, then, the supplement of the adjective offers an operative intersection or interweaving of what Saussure calls the syntagmatic and paradigmatic textures of signification. In each instance, adjectives supplement/substitute a value for a presence, a quality for a substance. And like all supplements, adjectival addition knows no bounds or limits; it continually expands according to what Derrida will call the law of supplementary acceleration.[15]

There are, then, two aspects of adjectival supplementarity that will concern us, but both are related to or structured by the economy of exchange. Nothing in Traherne's text can be said to have value in or of itself: value, like meaning or signification, is always an added surplus.[16] To prize a thing, therefore, requires more than merely seeing or noting it. The thing must be enjoyed, treasured, given thanks for by adding to it a serviceability, a usefulness. Usefulness, in fact, is the Trahernean value *par excellence*, for a thing that is useful is a thing that can supplement and be exchanged in order to supplement. Or, in slightly different terms, only a substance supplemented by quality or value can be received or given as a supplement desired in answer to either a need or a demand. This, as I will try to show, is the supplementary economy of what I have elsewhere cited as circulation.[17]

Circulation, as an economy of supplementary exchange, also suggests a different register of the supplement of the adjective. Derrida refers frequently to the notion of a chain or series: "all the possibilities of the supplementary series . . . have the relationship of metonymic substitutions among themselves."[18] If it can be shown that the split or lacking self we have already characterized in Traherne's text necessarily supplements itself with a definable series of differing and deferring substitutes, then we might also be able to demonstrate how those substitutions are metonymically associated. To do so, I think, would open to us a broader structural principle of Traherne's thought, namely the relation of part to whole that would make metonymy possible. It is, of course, an unforgivable cliché to argue that a whole is greater than the accumulation of its parts or that parts have value or meaning only in relation to a whole. But in the case of a Christian poet who, as we have seen, inscribes both God and man within irreducible structures of lack or want—that is to say, of non-wholeness—the part/whole relations must become problematical.[19] Traherne seems to have no difficulty in identifying parts, but what or where is the whole? The question can be put more dramatically by asking how relatedness can be established at all if the whole is precisely that which is inconceivable and unimaginable? In some sense, to ask the question this way is to invert Derrida's focus: it is not now the lost origin that requires or necessitates the supplement, but the desired end.

A part, of course, is not, strictly speaking, an adjective even though the word can assume this grammatical form. By subsuming part/whole relations under the general field of the supplement of the adjective, I mean to suggest that the part always functions in a way that is structurally analogous to the adjective: it appropriates value both for itself and for the whole to which it is subjected. Once again, however, it is the reversibility of these structural relations that best exposes the manner by which the text produces and consumes its expressions of value. If accumulated parts enrich by supplementing wholes, wholes themselves are always enriched by supplementary reinscription as simply other parts of yet richer wholes, and so on indefinitely. In the absence of any totality, all parts and all wholes serve only as items of economic discursive exchange.

A secondary consequence of Derrida's assertion about metonymic substitutions concerns the status of figure within the Trahernean text. As is well known, Traherne frequently disavows and discredits metaphor. Usually critics have taken such statements as either naive or disingenuous self-contradictions, but might there be more at stake? The critical issue may not be a Traherne who cannot see his own metaphors, but a reader who does not recognize metonymies or the associative relations that bind them to a supplementary series with its own internal logic or necessity. We can clarify the issue by recalling one of Saussure's more notorious assertions: in language, in the *system* of language, there are only differences.[20] If this is so, then one might argue that all signs function as a consequence of and in relation to an internal systematic contiguity. For Derrida, such a consequence can license the declaration that any signifier merely replaces, supplements, another signifier.[21] Extension of this principle would seem to strike a blow at the very notion of metaphor—if by that figure we mean the substitution of a similar sign for a known thing. That may not, of course, be an acceptable definition, but it does seem possible to argue that metaphor must assume the fixed identity, the presence and the essence, of one of its terms. Where all terms are only a systematic difference from all other terms, identity recedes in an infinite regression of speculation and supplementation. Under these epistemological conditions the privileging of metonymy over metaphor becomes not only predictable but necessary.[22] Applied to Traherne, such an argument seriously challenges those readings that see in his text only the calm assurance of a pietistic mystic. I do not mean to plunge Traherne into the despair of existential doubt or conscious skepticism. I want only to ask that we reconsider the broader implications of his stance against metaphor and that we make some attempt seriously to account for it. The resulting portrait of Traherne will not, I think, be as confident as we have been led to believe. At the very least, it will reveal a poet whose principal concern is not to announce matters of worth or value, however metaphorically stated, but in fact to produce such matters by manipulation of metonymic exchanges. That production will follow the strange logic that Derrida has defined as the structural principle of supplementarity.

In his extended meditation on the works of Rousseau, Derrida associates the process of supplementarity with the human imagination itself. "Imagination," he writes, "is the power that allows life to affect itself with its own re-presentation."[23] Representation, reflection, or speculation, as we have seen, always splits and doubles what is represented or reflected. And it does so by adding to, by supplementing; thus Derrida can write, "imagination . . . is . . . supplementary."[24] More important, however, than this doubling function is the relationship Derrida, following Rousseau, draws between imagination and desire. Rousseau's text is this meditation:

> To begin with, [Nature] gives [man] only such desires as are necessary for self-preservation and such powers as are sufficient

> for their satisfaction. All the rest she has stored in his mind as a sort of reserve, to be drawn upon at need. It is only in this primitive condition that we find the equilibrium between desire and power, and then alone man is not unhappy. As soon as his potential powers of mind begin to function, imagination, more powerful than all the rest . . . enlarges the bounds of possibility for us, whether for good or ill, and therefore stimulates and feeds desires by the hope of satisfying them. But the object which seemed within our grasp flies quicker than we can follow.[25]

Derrida comments: "If we desire beyond our power of satisfaction, the origin of that surplus and of that difference is named imagination"; "imagination, origin of the difference between powers and desire, is determined as difference"; and *différance*, we recall, is but another name for supplementarity.[26] Such, then, Derrida continues, is the supplementary "paradox of the imagination: it alone arouses or irritates desire but also it alone, and for the same reason, in the same movement, extends beyond" or exceeds desire.[27]

We can orient these thoughts to Traherne by following the brief exchange of a familiar opposition. With the kind of remarkable understatement with which he sometimes surprises us,[28] Traherne writes in *Christian Ethicks* that "if all the expansions of Time and Eternity should be void, and all the extents and out-goings of Infinity empty . . . [the soul] would hugely be displeased" (*CE*, 229). Two pages earlier, he explains why: "Omnipresence and Eternity fill the Soul, and make it able to contain all Heights and Depths, and Lengths and Breadths whatsoever. And it is the desire of the Soul *to be filled with all the fulness of GOD*" (*CE*, 227). Space and time in these two passages are the concurrent axes of both imagination and desire, and both are measured or charted by a supposed movement between a feared emptiness and an anticipated fullness. "Whatevers empty is accurst," Traherne says in "Circulation," and he thereby assigns to imagination the task of filling all the otherwise empty spaces and times. But imagined fullness, insofar as it is already itself a supplement (here heard in the simple repetition of "filled with fullness"), can only incite the desire for more. *More*, of course, is itself already a supplement and always therefore an object of further supplementation, and so on *ad infinitum*. Empty-full-fulfillment-more: such, schematically, is the generative organization of Traherne's supplementing imagination, an insatiable desire for more captivated and stretched out along the spatial/temporal poles of a premised nothing (absence) and a promised all (presence).

Ad infinitum indeed![29] We must attend to the structural necessities of the supplementarity of the imagination and desire. The *more* which must continually be both imagined and desired continually defers the *most* within whose horizon it must be thought. That most, I think, is how we must interpret the various and numerous expressions of "infinite" or "infinity" in Traherne's text. The infinite is precisely that supplement that forever escapes thought or conception: it is irreducible to expression even as Traherne tries to say it and it is transcendent to all imagination and desire even as they are in the process of supplementarily producing it. The infinite is, in effect, the determined failure of imagination, the mark that inscribes the regressive limits of desire.[30] But by the same logic, it is the final proof of the essential grounding of imagination in desire and of both in the indeterminate *ad infinitum* of the chain of supplementarity.

As with the supplement of the predicate and that of the adjective, the task of the imaginative supplement is to generate and appropriate worth and wealth. Whether that wealth is appropriated for the self or extended to another, it never reaches a point of fulfillment. It can, however, serve as the economic means to further imaginative investment or production. By charting the supplementarity of the imagination within Traherne's text we should arrive finally at an appropriate place to stop—not, it must be said, at the center of that imagination, but at the margins which define and mark at least its limits.[31]

II SCENES OF THE SUPPLEMENT

It may be helpful to survey a few of Traherne's central scenes of supplementarity before attending further to the particular economies that organize them. We can begin with the Fall, for here loss, want, and lack are originally bound to the fundamental structure of supplementary exchange. In *Christian Ethicks* Traherne describes virtue as "an *Aequivocal* offspring of the Fall": equivocal, of course, for "while there was no sin, there was no need"; virtues supplement sinful wants even as they mark man's sinning nature. Traherne thus calls virtues "Additions that are made upon the Fall of Man" (*CE*, 34). An addition is now a gain, a plus exchanged for a minus, a positive good for a negative evil. Traherne's thinking about this exchange inevitably invokes the supplementary pattern. "The Sinners Restauration makes it as *Natural* [here meaning also 'as necessary'] to grieve for his *Fault* as to rejoyce in his *Felicity*" (*CE*, 134). And that equivocation is possible because "what he hath lost in himself is regained in the perfection and Goodness of his Object" (*CE*, 134), the object of his desire that is God. God, in short, comes to replace and supplant originary Edenic felicity with a blessedness that is infinitely, supplementarily, *more*. The economy of that exchange is a frequent emphasis of Traherne's meditation: "But when *Adam* fell, and brought more Hazzards and Difficulties on himself GOD might justly leave him to them, for his *greater* Trial and *more perfect* Glory. Now we are *more* blind and Weak by Nature, yet *infinitely Beloved and more Precious*: For the *price* of the Blood of the Eternal Son of GOD *is laid upon* the Soul *as an Addition* to its *interior Value*" (*CE*, 168; my italics).

As Derrida suggests, the supplement is always an exterior added to an interior,[32] but its economic or exchange value is appropriated and registered within. The passage is a convenient illustration of the mechanics of that registration as the initial, negative "more" is, through repetition, not only reversed to a positive signification, but also rewritten in specifically economic terms: precious, price, and value. We might note in particular that it is not Christ's blood that supplements, "as an Addition," the soul's interior value, but "the price" of that blood. Redemption is here an economic investment. Throughout the *Centuries* Traherne continues to chart this added value: "Since therefor by the Second Adam, we are restored to that we lost in the first: unless we valu that we lost in the first, we cannot truly rejoyce in the second. But when we do, then all things receiv an infinit Esteem, and an Augmentation infinitly infinit, that follows after" (*CM*, II.5). We who were, through the Fall, originally empty have now become full, infinitely augmented by the value which Christ-as-supplement places upon us.[33] That God chose to exchange the Son for us, to offer the Son to supply the necessities his own internal Justice demanded, can only increase *our* value. It is important to note Traherne's qualification here. Although man's "interior Value" is augmented by the exterior supplement, his appropriation of that value is itself a secondary registration of supplementarity. Unless he values the "Addition," it would not effect the economic and specular exchange: man would remain a lost, first Adam rather than a restored second Adam.

"All our Disadvantages contracted by the fall are made up and recompensed by the Lov of God" (*CM*, IV.36). The *différance* of this supplementarity is the object of Traherne's thoughtful wonder:

> He [that is, I, your friend] thought that men were *more* to be Beloved now then before. And which is a strange Paradox, the Worse they are the *more* they were to be beloved. The Worse they are the *more* they were to be Pittied and Tendered and Desired, becaus they had *more* need, and were *more* Miserable. But his Meaning in that saying was this, Comparing them with what they were before they were faln, they are *more* to be Beloved. They are now Worse yet *more* to be Beloved. For Jesus Christ hath been Crucified for them. God loved them *more*, and he gave his Son to die for them, and for me also, which are Strong Obligations, leading us to greater Charity. So that Mens unworthiness and our vertu are alike increased. (*CM*, IV.26; my italics)

The supplementary *more*, the addition that occasions each of the better/worse differences, is simultaneously that which both lowers and heightens man's "inherent" value. It becomes, in effect, the supplementary coin whose circulation throughout Traherne's narrative continually produces images and tokens of capital. Invariably it leads Traherne to specific economic appropriations: "If you ask, what is becom of us since the Fall? . . . Truly Now we hav superadded Treasures: Jesus Christ" (*CM*, IV.53) In each of the passages examined thus far, the Son of God serves as a supplement "superadded" to the son-of-man, the addition clearly announced in its supplementary difference/sameness as First and Second Adam. What is most suggestive, however, in all the passages is that every account of that supplement is registered as an economic increase, as the production of value as such. The "price" of Christ's blood supplements the soul's interior value by marking it as valuable, by making it an object of another's desire, and therefore an object capable and worthy of exchange. As the supplement converts worse to better, less to more, unworthiness to beloved, it functions throughout the text as a structural economy regulating and organizing the production and consumption of "superadded Treasures."[34]

Supplementary economy, then, is always grounded upon an act of exchange in which a lack in one entity is supplied by another. Much of Traherne's thought is directed toward exploring the infinite variety of and desire for such exchanges. A particularly interesting example occurs in the Second Century, where Traherne tries to explain how "Objectiv Treasures" are always a product of two contrary desires. One is the avaricious "Lov of Propriety": the "desire to hav all alone in our Private Possession, and to be the alone and single End of all Things." The other is the equally insatiable need to share, to spread our delights abroad to others, to make our pleasures their treasures. True value resides in the interchange of these two desires, "Perfectiv to each other" (*CM*, II.79). Either humor, either desire, by and in itself, is defective, wanting; only in supplementary relation with the other can either be satisfied. In this instance, supplementarity serves as the structural law of an economy that must possess, dispossess, and repossess in continual and circulating fashion. By giving and receiving "private possessions," the subject appropriates to them the value of "Objectiv Treasures." We might see beneath this example one aspect of Traherne's broad structural patterning of parts and wholes. Anything to which something else or other can be added must, of necessity, be subject to supplementary relations and thus to the paradoxical and synecdochal logic of supplementarity itself.

The entire volume of *Christian Ethicks* is an elaboration of this principle. All virtues supplement the loss/lack incurred by the Fall. Each virtue, then, is not only itself a supplement, but the mark of an announced defect requiring further supplementation. The principle can be glossed by Derrida's notion of geometrical regression: supplement of a supplement, part of another part, addition of the superfluous but necessary surplus, each supplementary stage takes us further from the imaginary fullness we are presumed, originally, to have lost.[35] Without further supplementation, no virtue could be the supplement that it is; without being supplemented, in fact, any virtue becomes a vice. The "strange logic" of this supplementarity structures all of Traherne's discourse on Christian ethics. Traherne announces the theme early in the work by citing Saint Paul: "adde to your Faith vertue: and to vertue, knowledge; and to knowledge, temperance; and to temperance, patience; and to patience, godliness; and to godliness, brotherly kindness; and to brotherly kindness, Charity" (*CE*, 22). "To be filled with all the Fulness of GOD," to acquire that "perfect Soul . . . whereunto nothing can be added to please our Desire," is to achieve a final dispensation from all supplements by becoming full of all supplements. Short of that impossible and imaginary goal, supplementation, "adding to," is the structure of all experience.[36]

Virtue itself, Traherne argues, must be distinguished from the powers of the soul. "THE Powers of the Soul"

> are not vertues themselves, but when they are clothed with vertuous Operations, they are transformed into Vertues. For Powers are in the Soul, just as Limbs and Members in the Body, which may indifferently be applied to Vertues and Vices . . .
>
> AS the Members are capable of Various Motions, either Comely or Deformed, and are one thing when they are naked, another when attired, and capable of being modified with several Habits: so are the Powers and Faculties of the Soul. As they are in the Nature of Man without Exercise, they are void and Naked: But by many acts of Vice or Vertue, they put on a Habit. . . .
>
> *Vertue is a right and well ordered Habit.* A Habit is something added to that which wears it, and every Power of the Soul is naked, without the Quality wherewith long Custom cloaths it. (*CE*, 26)

It should be observed that no conception of the Fall is needed here to ground the human soul in originary lack. The naked[37] and void faculties must act in order to be; those acts, whether virtuous or vicious, supplement the void by clothing it in a habit. And the appropriated habit offers a significant supplementary exchange: for the transformation of essence to act is also the addition of quality to faculty. The exchange, in short, "adds" custom to nature, value to fact, and *différance* to indifference. Without such supplements, the soul "might be a piece of Dirt surrounded with Gold; but no imputed or annexed value could make it a Jewel" (*CE*, 31).

The necessity that defines virtue in general as a supplementary value added to a wanting soul also governs the internal relations of each particular virtue. We can see this most clearly in Traherne's chapter on Prudence, which begins as follows:

> CHARITY is that which entereth into every Vertue, as a main Ingredient of its Nature and Perfection. Love is the fountain and the End of all, without which there can be no Beauty nor Goodness in any of the Vertues. Love to one self, Love to GOD, Love to Man, Love to Felicity, a clear and intelligent Love is the Life and Soul of every Vertue, without which Humility is but Baseness, Fortitude but Fierceness, Patience but Stupidity, Hope but Presumption, Modesty but Simpering, Devotion but Hypocrisy, Liberality is Profuseness, Knowledge vanity, Meekness but a sheepish Tameness, and Prudence it self but fraud and Cunning. (*CE*, 152)

Like the naked powers of the soul, individual virtues must themselves be "modified" by another "right and well ordered Habit," here named charity. Added from the outside but appropriated within each virtue as its "main Ingredient," the supplement restages the originary *différance* that installs every virtue in binary opposition to its corresponding vice. But if all virtues need to be supplemented by charity, charity, as a virtue itself, requires the supplement of prudence in order to acquire or be expressed as value: "Its Office is to consult, and contrive . . . and so to mingle all Vertues in the Execution of our Duties, that they may relieve, and aid, and perfect each other, in such a manner as at once to be pleasing to GOD, profitable to his Creatures, and to our selves" (*CE*, 153). "So here," Traherne concludes in what can only be called at least a third stage of supplementary registration, "one Vertue supplies the Defects of another . . . WHILE all the Vertues conspire to supply what is wanting in each other" (*CE*, 153).

Traherne continues to explore the consequences of such supplementarity: "the Truth is, no Vertue is of any Value as cut off from the rest. We may as well expect all Beauty in a Nose divided from a Face, or an eye pluckt out of the head, all Perfection in an Ear, or a tongue cut off, all serviceableness in a Hand, or Foot dismembred from the Body; as a full and perfect Security from any one Vertue whatsoever. If one were sufficient, the rest would be Superfluous" (*CE*, 154). But, of course, "the rest," like the one, *are* superfluous at the same time all are necessary: "Supplies to make up the Defect of every single Sence" (*CE*, 155). The supplementarity that defines their function thus grounds the virtues in nothing less than the irreducible interplay of differences, the systematic law of *différance* itself: "There is an infinite Excellency in every Vertue, but it is to be sought in its Relation to all the Rest. It is Good for nothing in its Place but for that Particular End to which it is assigned, in attaining that end it is subservient to all other Vertues; and while it serves all, is aided by all" (*CE*, 155).

Supplement of a supplement, supplemented by all supplements, virtue becomes a true Derridean *pharmacon*: the mark of the dangerous excess which measures either beneficial value or contaminating loss:[38]

> All kind of Vertues must concur to Compleat [man's] Perfection. The Want of any one Denominates a Vice, and makes him Vicious. Nay the Want of any one destroys the form and Essence of the rest. Vertue is not Vertue but in order to felicity [now *another* supplement to supply the want of all supplements]. If it hath lost its force, it hath lost its Nature. As a little Poyson turnes the best Meat from Nourishment into Poyson so doth one Vice cherished and allowed corrupt and viciate all the Vertues. (*CE*, 156)

The chain of supplementarity here opens the abyss that threatens it from within, the indifference to supplementary relatedness which is death to think and the cessation of life altogether. We have not gotten far enough in Traherne's own thinking to see clearly what this negative void might be, but we might take a clue from the notion of "concurring." Whatever is isolated, privileged and held for itself, severs all relations to all else. Movement ceases: the movement that charts the differing/deferring of *différance*, the supplement of the supplement, and is the only guarantee of life itself.

It is exactly this idea of motion that leads Traherne away from expected conclusions about God. For Derrida, God is the name of In-difference itself, the one being who can dispense with the supplement.[39] Traherne initially seems to agree: God is "Him . . . To whom Nothing can be Added" (*CM*, III.65). And yet, as we have already seen, the fact that God dispenses supplements—"the Charity of Men ought to supply the [fallen] Earth's Sterility . . . But since this also faileth . . . What is wanting . . . God will supply" (*CM*, IV.23)—does not mean that He escapes supplementation. Holiness, for example, is "The infinite Excess of his Eternal Goodness" (*CE*, 87); in giving all to man and receiving all from man, "His Godhead did it self exceed" ("Demonstration," l. 77). The structures of supplementary desire thus bind God as well as man and Traherne's assertion that "we desire to live that we may do something else" applies equally to divine as to earthly existence. Being is doing, and doing, acting, is the supplement added to essence in order to let it be, the movement always outside and beyond itself.

That movement, moreover, is invariably expressed within Traherne's text as an economy, as a differential exchange in which being produces, takes on, or appropriates supplementary worth or value. Whether Traherne's focus be the conversion of naked powers into virtuous actions, deformed and severed members into a comely and coherent body, deforming vices into exalting virtues, or merely sensual pleasures into enriching treasures, the economic exchange structures all forms of human relatedness. To the extent that exchange always moves outside and beyond the self, therefore, the supplement always already instigates the difference of the Other. Other men are defined as "supernumerary persons" who are "enrichers of" man's "inheritance"; elsewhere they are "Superadded Treasures" of both God and man (*CM*, I.35). God too becomes a valuable addition: knowing God, man loses himself in wonder and admiration, "But it is an Happy Loss to lose one self . . . and to find GOD in exchange for oneself" (*CM*, I.18).

In the *Centuries* this supplementary exchange is described in terms that are again appropriate for both God and man, terms which can return us to the central images of the circulation of entity and image, mirror and its reflection or representation. In love, "The same Thing is Multiplied by being Enjoyed. And He that is Greatest is most my Treasure. This is the Effect of Making Images. And by all [man's] Lov is evry Image infinitly Exalted" (*CM*, I.74). Or again, in the Second Century: "Lest therfore the other Depths and Faculties of our Souls, should be Desolat and Idle, [other men] also are Created to entertain us. And as in many Mirrors we are so many other selvs, so are we Spiritualy Multiplied when we meet our selvs more Sweetly, and liv again in other Persons" (*CM*, II.70). Creatures are multiplied that the treasures of one may be multiplied, just as the self seeks constantly to replicate itself in order to meet itself "more Sweetly." The geometric acceleration of supplementarity affects, then, not only the exchange of God for man or man for God, but also relations between man and other men, as well as those between man and that Other that is himself. Within the complex economy of all these multiplying additions, all value is produced, appropriated, and distributed.

Nothing in Traherne's text, as I have said, is inherently valuable. A corollary to this assertion is that anything can become a value. But value as such is a purely structural signification: it is the product of an economy whose essential capital is *différance* (and especially the constant reversibility of the primary binary sets) and whose systematic registration is always by means of the supplement (that is, value is always *added on* as surplus or excess). "Misapprehension" is perhaps Traherne's clearest statement of the economic ground of his thought:

> Men are not wise in their Tru Interest,
> Nor in the Worth of what they long possest:
> They know no more what is their Own
> Than they the Valu of't have known.
> They pine in Misery,
> Complain of Poverty,
> Reap not where they hav sown,
> Griev for Felicity,
> Blaspheme the Deity;
> And all becaus they are not blest
> With Eys to see the Worth of Things:
> For did they know their Reall Interest,

No doubt they'd all be Kings.
(ll. 1–13)

As a supplementary excess produced by and accruing to what men own, sow, or see, "Tru Interest" is unknown even as it is covetted and desired (l. 14). To take possession of such interest, to make it "Reall," man must reconstruct the economy which produces it. The sequence of key terms in the stanza—worth, possess, own, value, poverty, reap, sown—sketches the rudimentary mechanics of the system within which this "Interest" is both produced and consumed as "Reall" profit. In the three sections to follow I will try to flesh out that system by illustrating the economic structures that are most prevalent in Traherne's narrative.

III SUPPLEMENT OF THE COPULA

Toward the end of the Fourth Century, Traherne engages in an extended dialogue with Pico della Mirandola's *Oration on the Dignity of Man*. Discussing the creation Traherne invokes a familiar Renaissance principle to argue that "All Things were already full" and to reiterate that God is "he to whom nothing proper to himself could be added" (*CM*, IV.75). If we recall Derrida's notion that the supplement is always added to a plenitude,[40] we will not be surprised by Traherne's next thought. Although God is already full, the particular supplement now added is man himself, last created even as he is always already inscribed within the creative act. Man is, Traherne cites, the "*Creaturarum Internuncius . . . Naturae Interpres. Stabilis Aevi et fluxi Temporis Interstitium, et . . . Mundi Copula*" (*CM*, IV.74). Supplement of the copula, to adopt a Derridean phrase, man is messenger, interval, interpreter; the added link which binds each to each and each to all; he who brings the spatial and temporal coordinates of meaning and worth to ford the abyss of nonmeaning and infinite, eternal emptiness. Man, in short, is the supplement, the "necessary surplus," as Derrida phrases it, that God and nature need in order to confirm existence by assigning it a value. In this economy, it is man, not God, who pronounces all things good. And he can do so, Pico argues, because God has placed him "in the Middle," paradoxically outside and unbounded by the "certain Laws" that constrain all other things, including his Creator. As that being added to Being as a "last Production," man can thus behold every thing "more commodiously"—that is, more profitably, as if everything were, in fact, a commodity. The copula, therefore, connects and joins, announces and pronounces: it lets all things *be* and it assigns the meaning and the worth of that being by registering it as capital.[41]

Almost exactly a full Century earlier Traherne had cited Gregory Nazianzus also speculating on the creation: "*Becaus it was by no means sufficient for GOODNESS to move only in the Contemplation of it self: but it became what was GOOD to be Diffused and Propagated, that more might be affected with the Benefit (for this was the part of the Highest Goodness:) first He thought upon Angelical and Celestial Vertues, and that Thought was the Work, which he wrought by the WORD, and fulfilled by the Spirit*" (*CM*, III.65). By diffusion and dissemination, creation is here presented as a verbal narrative added to God's interior thought, a supplement roughly equivalent, by the way, to Saussure's distinction between sound-image and concept.[42] For Derrida, this particular supplement would immediately predict at least three crucial consequences: (1) that what is added is always already registered as *différance* (external/internal, created/creator, word/thought, communication/contemplation); (2) that differences are joined by a copula that forces them constantly to double back upon themselves so as to effect a hierarchic registration of value (in the series just noted, each of the second terms would assume priority over its paired term); and (3) that existence is experienced and structured like a language, that Being is always articulated (that is, arranged *and* expressed) according to conventional grammatical and syntactic categories. For Traherne, I would suggest, there are two additional implications. The first is a reasonably direct analogy between the principal parts of speech—noun and pronoun, verb and adverb, article and adjective—and the structural categories of existence. The second is that the accumulation or production of what is here called "Benefit" is an economy whose laws are primarily a syntactic management of those grammatical parts.

What I am calling the supplement of the predicate, therefore, encompasses two distinct kinds of management. The first is the essential narrative condition that requires a second term to affirm or declare an initial one—as "grass" predicates "greeness" or as "the wind" needs the predicate "blows" in order to complete a meaningful statement. To give two common Traherne examples, "origin" will have meaning, signification, or value within Traherne's text only so long as it predicates or is predicated on "end"; similarly, "Idea" or "essense" is virtually inconceivable and never expressible without a predicated "act." To this extent, predication, as I am using it, describes the supplementary operation of textual *différance*. And precisely for that reason the predicated relations are never reducible to a subject and its complement, for the logic of supplementarity insists that the added term generates an excess, turns the ostensibly complementary operation into an incessant exchange, and that it is only in relation to such an exchange that value comes to announce itself. As origins become ends, as ends become further origins, and so on *ad infinitum*, the value-adding economy of supplementation begins to assert itself and to inflict further necessities upon relations that might have appeared complementary. Such exchanges I have elsewhere called the principle of circulation, although here I want to focus on the special verbal nature of that transference by subsuming circulation under the more restricted Trahernean notion of communication.[43]

Communication or articulation—or, more generally still, expressibility—suggests a second kind of supplementary management. Traherne's discourse proceeds largely by articulating the syntactic consequences of predication: those narrative "modifications" by which a virtual state, usually expressed by a noun, of necessity predicates an actual deed, expressed by the verb. Nouns and verbs, of course, exchange or reverse positions as insistently as origins and ends. Obviously, this cannot be posited for nouns and verbs in general, but it is certainly valid for those constantly privileged within Traherne's text (e.g., seeing, being, loving, etc.). Indeed, it is precisely because his key words are capable of serving in multiple syntactic positions that Traherne can manipulate them within a supplementary economy. "Love loves" would be the simplest illustration, the supplement of the verb clearly appropriating a value in excess of that expressed in the noun it doubles.[44]

The supplement of predication, in its broadest sense, is the narrative chain that links all verbal exchanges within Traherne's text into a complex economic system. The system is one of *différance*, to be sure, but more fundamentally it is a structural manipulation of differences in order to produce or generate ever more value and worth. Like Derrida's "writing," this system is not capable of totalization: the very principle of supplementarity precludes all closure and promises only the infinite replication and interplay of its differing/deferring terms.

One place to observe this interplay is in Traherne's continual meditation on end or ends, on the end in its differing relations to origin, effect, means, and goal or purpose. *Christian Ethicks* opens several of these equivocal relations:

> IT is the Prerogative of Humane Nature to understand it self, and guide its Operations to a Known End: which he doth wholly forfeit, that lives at random, without considering what is worthy of his Endeavors, or fit for his Desires.
>
> THE End is that which crowns the Work; that which inspires the Soul with Desire, and Desire with a quick and vigorous Industry. It is last attained, but first intended in every Operation. All means which can be used in the Acquisition of it, derive their value from its Excellency and we are encouraged to use them only on the Account of that End which is attained by them. (*CE*, 13)

The limits that close human existence within an imputed origin and a known termination describe a temporal interval whose duration is the relation between desire and purpose, intention and attainment. End is both first and last, cause and effect. These equivocations are not random: every act or operation is structured by the value ends add to the desire its origin creates.

> SINCE the Consideration of the End is that alone, which does animate a Man, to the use of the Means, they that treat of Virtue do worthily propose the End in the beginning . . . For it is a vain thing to discover the Means, unless the End be desired by those to whom the Nature and use of them, in their tendency to that End, is taught and commended; for if the End be despised, all endeavors are but fruitless . . .
>
> THAT Reason, whereby Man is able to Contemplate his

> End, is a singular Advantage, wherein he priviledged above a Beast. (*CE*, 13)

Man's origin, as man, lies in his contemplation of his end, and the means by which he achieves that end are the ends that he desires. The "account" of his end is an economy that crowns man's endeavors with worth, his knowledge with advantage, his desire with legitimacy, and his means with excellence. The supplementary economy here is roughly analogous to Lacan's *Fort! Da!* If throwing the reel over the bed predicates pulling it up, and pulling it up predicates throwing it off, it is only as a secondary registration that either act (or term) assumes value or incites desire. Value, in short, like desire, is always a systematic consequence, never an independent or isolated origin. So the end of any single deed accumulates or appropriates added value only as it repeats the infinitely repeatable succession of origins and ends, ends and means.

What is repeatable here is also, of course, reversible: Da/Fort, means/ends. Reversibility, in fact, is precisely the ground upon which all economic exchange operates, for the substitution and the supplementation it makes possible is the only guarantee that the system itself would not shut down, that the value-producing supply will always be full. Traherne must therefore keep all his ends open. God, for example, as the assumed origin of all things is also the acknowledged end of all things. But, Traherne argues in meditation 15 of the First Century, God-as-end is revealed only in His endlessness, in, in fact, His infinite desire to make "evry [other] one the End" (*CM*, I.15). Dutifully appropriating the worthiness God apparently desires, Traherne announces, "So that I alone am the End" (*CM*, I.15). As the end that I am is the means by which God fulfills His own end, so "the Soul that Enjoys [Him is] . . . the End of His Desire in Creating it" (*CM*, I.10). By meditation 69 Traherne is exalting in the fact that God "hast made me the End of all Things, and all the End of me. I in all, and all in Me" (*CM*, I.69). By this point in the *Centuries*, God, man, and all things are simultaneously means, ends, and origins.

It could be argued, of course, that Traherne is merely exploiting that kind of "equivocal predication" Heather Asals finds so pervasive in Herbert,[45] but such an argument would distort his purpose. The multiplication of "ends" is not equivocation as much as supplementation, a constant accumulation or replication that seeks to generate heightened senses of worth. As origins become ends and ends become means each exchange carries with it a prior investment, a previous registration. Each exchange either appropriates or announces an imported value. And only insofar as ends are stamped with value are they worthy of being exchanged. What begins, therefore, as a kind of doubled interplay of *différance*—origin/end, ends/means—is soon mapped within Traherne's text as a complex systematic economy.

That the economy is complex is not merely a factor of Derridean *différance*, but that the individual differences by which value is produced or announced soon begin to appropriate additional "coins" within the systematic exchange. "The Anticipation" offers a convenient illustration: although the poem begins by again contemplating an equivocal "end," by its conclusion Traherne has superimposed upon that original term of difference several other sets, each of which adds a clearly marked sense of supplementary value. The poem illustrates, therefore, how such value accumulates.

> My Contemplation Dazles in the End
> Of all I comprehend.
> And soars abov all Heights,
> Diving into the Depths of all Delights.
> Can He becom the End
> To whom all Creatures tend?
> Who is the Father of all Infinites!
> Then may He Benefit receiv from Things,
> And be *not Parent only* of all Springs.
> (ll. 1–9)

That God is both origin and end is hardly a radical thought. If God's own end is to "becom the End" of His creatures, then the creatures must become the means by which He achieves that end. And insofar as He becomes *their* end, the supplement accumulates the now doubled end as "Benefit receiv[ed]."

In the second stanza, Traherne slightly shifts the terms:

> The End doth Want the Means, and is the Cause,
> Whose Sake, by Natures Laws,

Is that for which they are.
Such Sands, such Dangerous Rocks we must beware
From all Eternitie
A Perfect Deitie
Most Great and Blessed he doth still appear.
His Essence Perfect was in all its Features
He ever Blessed in his Joys and Creatures.
(ll. 10–18)

The lack of means is the cause of ends. Traherne immediately conceives a danger in imputing a lack or want to God, but he also understands that without that lack no supplement would be necessary and thus no value possible. God's want, then, must itself be registered within the supplement of predication—the differing/deferring interval which both separates and yet draws into relation source and destination, cause and effect. In the gap of that interval, need is announced:

From Everlasting he these Joys did Need,
And all these Joys proceed
From Him Eternaly.
From Everlasting His felicitie
Compleat and Perfect was:
Whose Bosom is the Glass,
Wherin we all Things Everlasting See.
His Name is NOW, his Nature is forever.
None Can his Creatures from their Maker Sever.

The End in Him from Everlasting is
The Fountain of all Bliss.
From Everlasting it
Efficient was, and Influence did Emit,
That caused all. Before
The World, we do Adore
This Glorious End. Becaus all Benefit
From it proceeds. Both are the very same.
The End and Fountain differ but in name.
(ll. 19–36)

The end is the beginning, the final end is the efficient cause, the present now is the preceding was, and that which is perfect is that which must move outside of itself, emitting influence, adding to and receiving thereby the supplementary "Benefit." Difference is but the name of the same, the structural exchange by which value supplements existence as desire supplements need.

In the following stanzas the value that accrues to both ends and means is recirculated again as a supplementary exchange in order to heighten the worth of each:

> That so the End should be the very Spring,
> Of evry Glorious Thing;
> And that which seemeth Last,
> The Fountain and the Caus; attained so fast,
> That it was first, and movd
> The Efficient, who so lovd
> All Worlds and made them for the sake of this
> It shews the End Compleat before, and is
> A Perfect Token of his Perfect Bliss.
>
> The End Compleat, the Means must needs be so.
> By which we plainly Know,
> From all Eternitie,
> The Means whereby God is, must perfect be.
> God is Himself the Means,
> Whereby he doth exist:
> And as the Sun by Shining's clothd with Beams,
> So from Himself to All His Glory Streams,
> Who is a Sun, yet what Himself doth list.
> (ll. 37–54)

The "Glass" of stanza 3 here becomes the Sun clothed in its own beams, the split in God himself between origin and end, cause and effect, ends and means, creator and creature. God, in short, *is* and that copula situates Him in the irreducible register of predicated supplementarity. The copula keeps repeating itself, each repetition turning God back upon Himself and in the process adding "necessary surplus" to the already supposed plenitude:

> His Endless Wants and His Enjoyments be
> From all Eternitie;
> Immutable in Him:

They are His Joys before the Cherubim.
His Wants appreciat all,
And being infinit,
Permit no Being to be Mean or Small
That He enjoys, or is before his Sight.
His Satisfactions do His Wants Delight.
(ll. 55–63)

"Appreciate" is the key supplementary term here: the relations between desire and satisfaction, wants and enjoyments, Being and beings, sight and delight all advance the value of the exchange. No being can *be* without also being subject to and of a predicate economy. Being *is* as Being *adds* its own appreciating interest/investment. That notion leads Traherne again to the fundamental question of want:

Wants are the Fountains of Felicitie
No Joy could ever be
Were there no Want. No Bliss
No Sweetness Perfect were it not for this.
Want is the Greatest Pleasure
Because it makes all Treasure.
O what a Wonderfull Profound Abyss
Is God! In whom Eternal Wants and Treasures
Are more Delightfull caus they both are Pleasures.
(ll. 64–72)

In this stanza the earlier equivocations provide the structural categories for a new registration: "want" here becomes both origin and end, means and end. Supplementing and substituting for the prior difference, want now announces further values—pleasure become treasure, joy become bliss. We might also note the logic by which want deploys a syntactic cluster of negatives (no joy, no want, no bliss, no sweetness, were it not) in order to make the appropriation of value "more Delightfull." In this light we might recall Derrida's gloss on a different "Profound Abyss": "An entire theory of the structural necessity of the abyss will be gradually constituted in our reading; the indefinite process of supplementarity has always already *infiltrated* presence, always already inscribed there the space of repetition and the splitting of the self. Representation *in the abyss* . . . is not an accident of presence."[46] Not an accident, perhaps, but certainly grammatically accidental, for the supplement generates the entire series of differential "accompaniments"[47]: comparisons of degree (height and depth), of tense (now and ever), of person (creator and creature, him and me), of mood (joy and bliss). "The structural necessity of the abyss," then, is the law of supplementary predication that inscribes each lexical item in differential relation to either its opposite or its consequent and that accumulates the added terms as appropriated value.

If *want* now names that supplement, Traherne continues to expose its economy:

> He infinitly wanteth all his Joys;
> (No Want the Soul ore cloys.)
> And all those Wanted Pleasures
> He infinitly Hath. What Endless Measures,
> What Heights and Depths may we
> In his Felicitie
> Conceiv! Whose very Wants are Endless Pleasures.
> His Life in Wants and Joys is infinit.
> And both are felt as His Supreme Delight.
>
> He's not like us; Possession doth not Cloy,
> Nor Sence of Want Destroy.
> Both always are together:
> No force can either from the other Sever.
> Yet theres a Space between
> Thats Endless. Both are seen
> Distinctly still, and both are seen for ever.
> As soon as ere he wanteth all his Bliss,
> His Bliss, tho Everlasting, in Him is.
> (ll. 73–90)

The copula that identifies the same simultaneously preserves the interval of *différance*, the "space between" origin and end, cause and effect, that is itself an "Endless Abyss." *Différance*, in short, preserves distinction only in order to appropriate identification. The copula that articulates existence upon the economy of wants inexorably predicates possession: *is* becomes *has*, both always together in the inseparable exchange of value or worth. The supplementarity that structures that exchange is most evident in the final two lines, where want produces the need for bliss and bliss, thus needed, affirms the worth of what is. What is, moreover, is what is *in*, what is reappropriated as what one has.

That act of appropriation is the subject of the following stanza, which now supplements both the initial origin/end, ends/means and their substitutes wants/possessions with yet another supplementary registration:

> His Essence is all Act: He did, that He
> All Act might always be.
> His Nature burns like fire;
> His Goodness infinitly doth desire,
> To be by all possest;
> His Love makes others Blest.
> It is the Glory of his High Estate,
> And that which I for ever more Admire,
> He is an Act that doth Communicate.
> (ll. 91–99)

Origin to end, desire to possession, being to doing, essence to act: the economy of such exchanges reveals its structural core as the predicated relation between self and Other, "I" and "He" in communication. Both always together: no force can either from the Other sever, and "to be" has now become "to communicate," to invest that Other with the value of a supplementary predicate.

In the final three stanzas Traherne returns to the initial register of the poem's expression of *différance* in order to demonstrate how man must replicate the divine economy of origins and ends/ends and means in order to appropriate for himself the values that economy promises and produces:

> From all to all Eternity He is
> That Act: An Act of Bliss:
> Wherein all Bliss to all,
> That will receiv the same, or on him call,
> Is freely given: from Whence

Tis Easy even to Sence,
To apprehend That all Receivers are
In Him, all Gifts, all Joys, all Eys, even all
At once, that ever will, or shall appear.

He is the Means of them, they not of Him.
The Holy Cherubim
Souls Angels from him came
Who is a Glorious Bright and Living Flame,
That on all things doth shine,
And makes their Face Divine.
And Holy, Holy, Holy, is his Name.
He is the Means both of Himself and all,
Whom we the Fountain Means and End do call.

In whom as in the Fountain all things are,
In whom all things appear
As in the Means, and End
From whom they all proceed, to whom they tend.
By whom they are made ours
Whose Souls are Spacious Bowers
Of all like His. Who ought to have a Sence
Of all our Wants, of all His Excellence,
That while we all, we Him might comprehend.
(ll. 100–126)

The logic of the supplement, the installing of supplementarity within the economic exchange of *differance*, predicates the act whereby "all" are means and ends, givers and receivers, seers and objects, pleasures and treasures, wants and satisfactions. The chain that links each installment of this economy is generated by the internal necessities of the *differance* initially opened by the "Profound Abyss" that is the God Traherne attempts to define, the want that structures his acts, the need that articulates his Being, and the communication that must fracture that Being in its grammatical origins. To be is to differ and to defer; but within the modifications of that predicate an economy appears which masks those losses and converts all lacks. To "have a Sence" of want is to incite an economy of desire, and within the logic of that economy the creature who owes all gradually and subtly appropriates "all." It is therefore striking that of the eighteen times "all" is repeated in these last few lines, only the first two can unequivocally refer to God; from that point on, the being that was nothing, wanting all, in fact assumes all. Although the lines seem to return to the poem's opening—that is, to the meditation on means and ends—that return is at best a deflection; the real drama lies in the "all" that has supplemented the initial difference and that now registers the value that has been produced.

We can perhaps gain a firmer sense of this supplementarity and the economy it generates or predicates by glancing at a few other passages in which Traherne explicates one of the differences at the center of "The Anticipation"—that between idea, or essence, and act. As before, we can begin with *Christian Ethicks*. In the preface, "To the Reader," Traherne argues that "The things we treat of are great and mighty; they touch the Essence of every Soul, and are of infinite *Concernment*, because the Felicity is eternal that is acquired by them. I do not mean *Immortal* only but *worthy* to be *Eternal*" (*CE*, 4). Essence become act is an acquisition of value, the supplement that *has* adds to *is*. "Concernment" describes an operation of supplementary interest, an appropriation of value by a process of replication or duplication: "actions of Men," therefore, "must *concur* aright with [those] of GOD." God's essence "becomes" (in both senses) our actions; our actions articulate and thus become God's essence (*CE*, 6). Insofar as these relations are structured by the narrative logic of communication, they inevitably announce yet another supplementary value. In *Christian Ethicks* that value is most often expressed as the economy of predicated glory or righteousness, but the precise term used to name the supplement is not here the issue. Instead, the point I wish to insist upon is that value is always the product of supplementarity as such. A few passages will illustrate.

The essence of the soul, Traherne argues shortly after the opening of the volume, is the powers it contains. Immediately, however, essential powers predicate necessary acts, as seen in this passage we have already had occasion to cite:

> The Powers of the Soul, are not Vertues themselves, but when they are clothed with vertuous Operations, they are transformed into Vertues. . . . As the Members [of the body] are

> capable of Various Motions, either comely, or Deformed, and are one thing when they are naked, another when attired, and capable of being modified with several Habits: so are the Powers and Faculties of the Soul. As they are in the Nature of Man without Exercise, they are Void and Naked: But by many Acts of Vice or Vertue, they put on a Habit. . . . A *Habit* is something added to that which wears it, and every Power of the Soul is naked, without the Quality wherewith long Custom cloaths it. (*CE*, 26)

The metaphor of clothing[48] here orders the supplementary operation whereby essence is and must be act and whereby the exchange of essence and act effects value as such. Quality is thus an economic addition, a supplement that is acquired only through the necessary logic of *différance*. Without the irreducible *différance* that requires such supplementation—act to essence—"no Treasure can be . . . of any value" and no "intrinsick Goodness and Glory of the Soul" can shine with "imputed or annexed value" (*CE*, 30–31).

The mechanics by which this supplementarity operates can also be seen in chapter 5, "Of the Necessity, Excellency, and Use of Knowledge":

> THE understanding Power, which is seated in the Soul, is the Matter of that Act wherein the Essence of Knowledge consisteth: Its form is the Act itself, whereby that Power of knowing apprehendeth its Object.
>
> ITS nature is invisible, like that of all other Spirits, so simple and uncompounded, that its form and matter are the same. For all Powers, when transformed into Act, are Acts themselves. And the faculty of understanding, in a Compleat and Perfect Act of Knowledge attains its Perfection; and is Power exerted, or an Act in its Exercise. For every Act is Power exerted. (*CE*, 36)

The same cannot be thought without the irreducible differences of *différance*, and what is purportedly "intrinsick" is in fact a supplementary relation of ex-ergon: the *exergue* of Derridean economy which both marks and announces all forms of ex-ecution, ex-pulsion, ex-ertion, and ex-ercize. Only in throwing itself outside of itself does ex-istence appropriate value, make itself, in Traherne's terms, "more useful and Excellent," or "impute to itself" the clothing of worthiness. Thus knowledge-as-power requires the supplement of understanding-as-activity in order to "*reflect* a Lustre, and *add* a value" (*CE*, 38; my italics). Here "perfection" names the supplementary predicate, as "quality" did in the preceding passage. In the following one, "righteousness" and "glory," themselves supplementary additions to the differential relation of essence and act, are supplemented in turn by "perfection" once again: "His Essence is an infinite and Eternal Act of Righteousness and Wisdome, which filleth his Kingdom with the Majesty of its Glory, and by coming into Being in a voluntary Manner giveth to all Things their Essence, and Perfection" (*CE*, 76). The economy of essence/act supplementarity clearly defines God as well as man: "In God, to *Act* and to *Be*, are the same thing. Upon the suspension of his act, his Essence would be gone. . . . And if his Act existeth, by Acting, his Righteousness is, and existeth of it self, and by it self compleateth its Essence forever" (*CE*, 76). Essence *is* Act, but the supplementary predication supplies an addition, a surplus, without which the same could not exist at all. Here "righteousness" names the first registration of the supplement, the value imputed or annexed to the exchange by which essence becomes act or act fulfills essence. That supplement is immediately supplemented in turn by "compleateth" and "forever," and here two further observations might be drawn. First, no grammatical form is outside or unusable within the supplementary system; and second, every grammatical "place" the mere fact of predication requires or makes possible is therefore an opportunity of economic production.

I have said above that this economy affects God no less than man, but it would be more accurate to say that it would not affect man at all if it did not always already define God and would not affect God at all if it did not always already define man. For God and man, as we have seen in the chapters on Heidegger and Lacan, are already in supplementary relation and the only value either can appropriate comes directly from that predicated relation. Being is being as the self is the Other.

Appropriation of value, then, is the fundamental principle behind Traherne's communication, and communication, in turn, is the supplementary exchange of and with the Other. Whether that exchange is discursively staged as the *différance* of person (I and he, I and me, mine and his), or of thing (essence or act, origin or end, ends and means), communication always has the production of value, not the transfer of knowledge, as its aim. The fact that I have classified this narrative operation as one form of the supplement of predication means only that every term in Traherne's economy is subject to and subjectified by a predicate object. The "and," for example, which links many of these differences is never to be interpreted as a simple conjunction: rather it marks an addition, an excess that accumulates as clearly as 2 *and* 2 *makes* 4. Essence and act, means and ends produce added value. In subsequent sections of this chapter we will see other binary sets Traherne subjects to this economy, but at the moment let us turn to the second form of predication, the grammatical laws linking nouns to verbs, verbs to subsequent adverbs, and nouns to consequent adjectives. Again the supplementarity is inherently verbal and again its driving or motivating force is economic.

"All is Love variously modified," Traherne announces in *Christian Ethicks* (p. 44). Although "love" is certainly not the only privileged term in Traherne's vocabulary, it is arguably the one he subjects most consistently to grammatical modification. As essence or origin, love functions as a noun; as end and action, it functions as a verb. It can serve as well as an adjective of quality and as a predicate object and objective (as in the statement "God is Love"). We might, then, follow some of these modifications in order better to see how Traherne manipulates love's grammar and how that manipulation is directed by a supplementary economy. Here again are three passages from *Christian Ethicks*:

> The Life of GOD is *Love*; nay the Apostle saith, GOD is *Love*: By *Loving* he begot his *Love*. And if his *Love* be his Godhead, his Essence is an infinite and Eternal Act of *Love*, by extending which through all infinity, and by *Loving* Eternally, he begot his infinite and Eternal Essence: which is the *Love* that filleth all Worlds with Beauty and Glory. When you consider it well, An Act of *Love* is begotten by *Loving*: And if his Wisdome, and Goodness, and Blessedness, and Glory be seated in *Love*, his *Love* is his Wisdome which is the Son of GOD, and his Good-

> ness, and his Glory, and his Blessedness. For all these, tho we conceive them diversly, are the same Thing. (*CE*, 50; my italics)

> For he *Loves*, that he may *Love*, and begets that *Love* which is his Essence. . . . FOR the better understanding of this *Love*, we will consider it in the power of *Loving*, in the inclination *to Love*, in its act and Perfection. (*CE*, 47; my italics)

> THE Capacity of Love being so exceeding vast, multiplies and heightens in the Soul of man, that is apt to overflow of its own Accord. For nothing is so prone to communicate it self as that Active Principle of Love. (*CE*, 48)

Let us note first that the necessary supplement of the predicate, the grammatical law by which love generates loving, is the same supplement that derives act from essence or end from origin. If Traherne calls that generative operation "communication," it is because he recognizes in the structural mechanisms of language—and particularly those of a grammar becoming a meaningful semantics—an analogue to the economy of supplementarity as such. Syntax, in other words, is a system of arranging or organizing discrete grammatical elements; semantics is the system within which meanings are assigned or accorded those elements. "Tho we conceive them diversly," the two systems "are the same thing"; only insofar as syntax is reprocessed or received as semantics, however, can "meaning" as such be exchanged in a communicative act. To that extent, semantics serves as the supplement of syntax and "meaning" is the surplus it generates. In Traherne's economy, meaning and semantics are equatable with, "the same thing" as, value as such.

In the present passages, then, it is precisely the capacity of "love" to serve in various syntactic modifications that announces, or rather produces, both its semantic and its economic value. As love replicates and reproduces itself throughout the passages, the very repetition of the same is saved from tautology only because it is experienced as a supplement in something like the Derridean sense.[49] Each repetition marks an additional accumulation of value and each is intended not, as we might initially conceive, to prove that love is all-inclusive, but exactly to create that sense of value.

In the immediately following passage, Traherne subjects the term to a slightly different kind of supplementary economy:

> All his Laws are the Laws of Love, all his Attributes and Counsels are Love, in several formes, acting upon several occasions. When his Love communicates it self in Joys to innocent Creatures, it is *Goodness*; when it attains the most perfect End by the most perfect means, it is *Wisdome*; when it rescues guilty Creatures from Hell, it is *Mercy*; when it punishes the Rebellious it is *Justice*; when it inspires Obedience into any obstinate Person, it is *Grace*; when it delights in the Beauty of all its Works, it is *Blessedness*; when it appears in the perfection of its works, it is glory. (*CE*, 51)

Here love is, by turns, both essence and act, and the "law" that regulates its exchange from one grammatical position to the other is a complex supplementarity characterized by a sequence of excesses appropriated and communicated as values. Obviously, love becomes "variously modified" by the virtues with which Traherne aligns it and which "name" the value its modifications produce. But the reverse is also true, for were love removed from the virtues named, they would point only to "meer Privation and Vacuity." Love and the virtues, then, supplement one another in order that either can appear as valuable. We might also see here a convenient illustration of why Derrida calls the supplement the operation of *différance*, for it is only insofar as love differs from and defers itself from each individual virtue that it can conserve itself as the supplementary excess added to and thus producing worthiness for all.

We have already seen that Traherne conceives of virtues as supplementary actions clothing the naked powers of the soul. Grammatically, however, this axiological position of the virtues is inverted, for by themselves virtues are empty abstractions (nouns) unless and until they are supplemented and "filled" by particular loving actions (verbs). Traherne calls this new supplementary relation "the Application of *Actives* to *Passives*," "a mystery in Nature of very great and General Importance" (*CE*, 72). Supplement of a supplement, the predicate now fosters a further production of economic exchange:

> He [God] was infinit LOV, and being Lovly in being so, Would prepare for Himself a Most Lovly Object. having Studied from all Eternity, He saw, none more Lovly then the Image of His Lov, His own Similitude. O Dignity Unmeasurable! O Exaltation Passing Knowledge! O Joy Unspeakable! Triumph O my Soul and Rejoyce for ever! I see that I am infinitly Beloved. For *infinit Lov hath exprest and pleased it self in Creating an Infinit Object*. GOD is LOV, and my Soul is Lovely. God is Loving and His Image Amiable. (*CM*, I.67)

Structured as the paragraph is upon the specular *différance* confusing subject and object, seer and seen, image and similitude, it is not surprising to find its new supplement—the adjective "lovly"—floating equally between love, lover, and beloved. Just as God replicates himself and thereby appropriates the value the adjective adds, so man, assuming God's image, assumes as well the supplement which imputes value to that image. What is particularly interesting, however, is Traherne's surprising decision to suppress the expected repetition in the final, climactic word of the passage. But while "amiable" marks an anomaly in the grammar, it clearly participates in the general supplementarity which motivates the argument. And to that extent, the reader is directed away from its more obvious meanings to its etymology, from Latin *amabilis* (worthy of love) and *amare* (to love). Even when Traherne's repetitive syntax seems to violate its own characteristics, it is still subject to the logic of supplementary economy, the constant production of ever more worth or value.

Although this passage seems not to acknowledge it, Traherne is, of course, fully aware that earthly love differs from heavenly love, but once again difference itself occasions an economy of the supplement: "in a lower Acceptation Humane Love differs from Divine; it being founded upon Temporal Causes, Vivacity, Wit, Learning, Beauty, Behaviour, Moral Honesty, Fidelity . . . and the like. But all these may be exalted . . . and made Divine by the superadded concurrence of Coelestial Causes. For when a Man loves another, because he is made in the Image of God, and by the Beauty of his Soul is something more than Humane, this Love is made Sacred" (*CE*, 46). Supplements abound here, and all are grounded upon a logic of *différance* which argues that the "same" always involves an appropriated "concurrence" on the basis of something "superadded." And the addition, as we have come to expect, is always registered as an increase in worth—a "something more than." When that principle is itself brought to bear upon both the specular relation and the necessary "Application of *Actives* to *Passives*," we get a passage like this: "By Loving all Things as GOD Loveth them, we transform our Wills into an Act of Love, which is most Sweet and Blessed. We enrich and Beautify our selves with the Image of his Goodness, while we communicate our Souls (in our Powers) to all Objects" (*CE*, 70). Here Traherne returns to the elaboration of the idea of communication—an inclination become an act, a potential become a power, a word become a reality. At whatever level we interpret that supplementarity, its function is solely to "enrich" the self by means of an investment in the exchange.

In the middle of the Second Century, Traherne engages in his most sustained exploration of the supplement of love. Through ten meditations Traherne interweaves most of the terms we have been tracing in this section and discloses the economy by which love predicates a communication of exchanged value. He begins, in meditation 39, with Love's originary act: "*GOD by Loving Begot his Son*. For GOD is Lov. And by loving He begot His Lov. He is of Him self, and by Loving He is what he is *Infinit Lov*. GOD is not a Mixt and Compounded Being, so that His Lov is one thing and Himself another: but the most Pure and Simple of all Beings, All Act, and Pure Lov in the Abstract. Being Lov therfore it self, by Loving He begot Lov. Had He not loved He had not been what He now is, the GOD of Lov" (*CM*, II.39). Although it seems ludicrous to speak of God as a split or fractured being, that in fact is what Traherne here describes. In Derrida's terms, the supplement of love loving takes the form of the *différance* of the same.

In the next meditation Traherne opens this same to the particular differences of its mode and manners of production:

> In all Lov there is a Lov begetting, a Lov begotten, and a Lov Proceeding. Which tho they are one in Essence, subsist Nevertheless in Three Several Maners. . . . The Lov from which it floweth, is the Foundation of Love. the Lov which streameth

> from it is the communication of Lov, or Lov communicated. and the Lov which resteth in the Object is the Lov which streameth to it. So that in all Lov the Trinity is clear. . . . The Lov that lieth in the Bosom of the Lover, being the Lov that is perceived in the Spirit of the Beloved: that is, the same in Substance, tho in the Maner of Substance, or Subsistence, different. Lov in the Bosom is the Parent of Lov, Lov in the Stream is the Effect of Lov, Love seen, or Dwelling in the Object proceedeth from both. Yet are all three one and the self same Love: tho three loves. (*CM*, II.40)

Production here is re-production, the generation, in effect, of grammatical categories. Love loves a lover who loves love in return. Traherne's familiar specular scene lies behind such expression and we should recall that, as Derrida tersely phrases it, whatever can see itself is three.[50] Within the mirage of reproduction and representation, the same differs from and defers itself: essence becomes act, substance becomes subsistence, self becomes a relation to an object-Other. The sentence, even the *sententiae*, thus generated by the supplementary predicate maintains the difference of the same by assigning grammatical and syntactic sites to the same's replication of itself: love loves loving. If these grammatical categories are reassigned as origin, means, and end, then we have the syntactic structure of communication itself.

Traherne continues to unfold that structure: "Lov in the Fountain, and Lov in the stream are both the same. And therefore are they both Equal in Time and Glory. For Lov communicateth it self: And therfore Lov in the Fountain is the very Lov communicated to its Object. Lov in the fountain is Lov in the stream, and Lov in the stream is Equaly Glorious with Lov in the Fountain. Tho it Streameth to its Object it Abideth in the Lover, and is the Lov of the Lover" (*CM*, II.41). Communication now supplies its own additional surplus, here named "Glorious." The economy of exchange produces a value that supplements both substance and subsistence. In the next three meditations (*CM*, II.42–44) Traherne focuses on the initial lover love produces—the Son who becomes the very symbol of all economic exchange, "willing to redeem us by His own Blood" and therefore the "Means of all our Glory." Glory remains the name of the supplementary value, but its object varies according to the predicates originary love-as-essence produces along the grammatical/ syntactical chain. In meditation 45, Traherne pauses to respond to the benefit, the glory, that man achieves in this exchange:

> How Wonderfull it is, that GOD by being Lov should prepare a Redeemer to die for us? But how much more Wonderfull, that by this means Himself should be: and be GOD by being Lov! By this means also He refineth our Nature, and enable us to Purge out the Poyson and the filthy Plague of Sin. for Lov is so Amiable and Desirable to the Soul that it cannot be resisted. Lov is the Spirit of GOD. In Himself it is the Father, or els the Son, For the Father is in the Son, and the Son is in the Father: In us it is the Holy Ghost. The Lov of GOD being seen, being GOD in us. Purifying, Illuminating, Strengthening and Comforting the Soul of the seer. (*CM*, II.45)

Purifying, illuminating, strengthening: here love is not only redemptive but reformative, clothing its object in the refashioning glance of its own gaze, reproducing that object as the "lovely" and hence worthy Other of itself. In the next three meditations Traherne extends these thoughts to explicate the full potential of love's supplementary exchange: "In all Lov there is some Producer, som Means, and som End: all these being Internal in the Thing it self. Lov Loving is the Producer . . . Lov produced is the Means . . . The End of these Means is Love. . . . What can be more Desirable then the most Delightful Operation. . . . There being in it the Perpetual Joy of Giving and Receiving infinit Treasures" (*CM*, II.46). As earlier, the production of supplementary exchange effects a surplus, an excess; it converts pleasures to treasures within the communicative circulation of giving and receiving. The generation of something *more* desirable produces the "*most Delightful*," "*most Glorious*" being. And thus, in meditation 48, Traherne can focus on the process of reproduction itself and the economic surplus that process effects: "By Loving a Soul does Propagat and beget it self. By Loving it does Dilate and Magnify it self. By Loving it does Enlarge and Delight it self. By Loving also it Delighteth others, as by Loving it doth Honor and Enrich it self. But abov all by Loving it does attain it self. Love also being the End of Souls, which are never Perfect, till they are in Act, what they are in Power" (*CM*, II.48).

Loving, therefore, becomes the supplementary predicate without which the Soul-that-is-Love would be vain, comfortless, idle, "Narrow and Little and Dishonorable." Re-placing itself, substituting for itself, the soul in loving supplements the want or lack of and at its own center. Communicating itself outside of itself, it thereby regains and attains itself, honors and enriches itself in its own supplementary replication.

Traherne's extended analysis of love suggests that he conceives of human existence—indeed any existence—as necessarily structured as a language. The linguistic preconditions for meaning require that any noun be replicated in an equivalent grammatical verb as well as in a predicated object. Meaning as such, however, is a consequence of syntactic structuring, of the exchangeability or economy of supplementary displacement. That is to say that Traherne's view of syntactic structure—$S + V + O$, for example—must of necessity include of possibility of grammatical inversion. Love's object, the beloved, must simultaneously serve as supplemental subject (be-love) to Love-as-object. Indeed, it is precisely this reversibility of love's grammar that guarantees its economy. Meaning and value arise only in a certain doubling back, a predicated supplement folding back upon itself and recomposing itself in relation to an originary/secondary predicate. Love, like language, like means and ends, like all existence in Traherne's text, locates its value, its enrichments and enlargements, in this exchange. The economy of the structure is a linguistic version of the Möbius strip: each twist of the strip, each exchange of obverse to inverse, adds a surplus—the supplement of the supplement, there registered and appropriated as value.[51]

Grammar, then, as noted earlier, reveals a signifying semantic. It defines the irreducible structuring of supplementary differences—origin and end, ends and means, essence and act, noun and verb, subject and object—that make communication an economic operation and a systematic chain of unlimited exchanges. My own sense is that for Traherne the grammatical relations between noun and verb provide the mechanism for the entire system and that, as a consequence, the logic of predication best discloses the process and the operations of supplementarity.

This, perhaps, could explain the broader significance of Pico to Traherne's thinking. We have already had occasion to cite Pico's assertion that man himself is the copula. That assertion finds its context in Pico's larger point that man is dis-placed: God tells him that he has created him in no special place, that he has the power to place himself where he will, and that his worth or value will accrue from such placements as he chooses. In Traherne's view, these "places" are grammatical. Man can be subject (origin, essence), verb (means, act), or object (end, effect). Each grammatical place imputes or annexes a supplementary value; man's capacity to exchange one place for another, or to serve in multiple places simultaneously, imputes *more*. The economy of predication is precisely the operation of shifting grammatical function so as to assure maximum worth and value. To conceive human existence as "structured like a language" is thus to conceive supplementary predication as the continual re-placement of man in meaningful relation to all principal grammatical categories.

IV SUPPLEMENT OF THE ADJECTIVE

Supplementarity itself, however, structures other economic exchanges—one of which I earlier called the supplement of the adjective, the operation by which a particular subject or object annexes to itself a surplus registered as worth or value. I have named such supplements adjectival because they too are "structured like a language," but the general field of supplementarity I wish to address by that name is not limited to adjectives. For example, continuing our focus on the verb "to love," we might observe a different kind of supplementary accretion in the following two passages. The first is from the Dobell poem, "Innocence," in which Traherne tries to define the relations between the child's wondering Eye and the objects of its gaze: "While it those very Objects did / Admire, and prize, and prais, and love" (ll. 17–18). The second occurs a few poems later, in "Silence": "See, Prize, Give Thanks within, and Love / Which is the High and only Work" (ll. 25–26).

In these two passages love, as both principle and activity, is an imagined whole of which seeing, admiring, prizing, praising, and giving thanks are all synecdochic parts. The *value* of love, however, is not to be measured by its wholeness as by its accretive syntactic position: it is the surplus, the excess, the supplementary addition that cumulates and accumulates interest and profit.[52] The relation between parts and wholes, the interrelatedness of parts and wholes, is also a supplementary structure of exchange. Ultimately, Traherne will name this particular economy "circulation" and in its various operations it is perhaps the most consistent supplementarity within his entire text. I have grouped it under the general category of adjectival supplementation primarily because both "part" and "whole" tend to function as qualifiers within that text. Moreover, nothing in the text is called either part or whole without invoking as well a clear assumption of value.

We might also observe the other significant repetition in these two passages, the verb "to prize." Traherne's preference for and almost obsessive use of this verb has been noted, but we need to bring its etymological resources more openly into discussion. Both prize and praise derive from Old French *preisier* (to price, value, prize), subsequently leveled to Middle English and French *prisier*. In modern English "prize" appropriates the meanings of to value, to estimate, or esteem the value of, to appraise or fix the price of; "praise" retains the more tropical sense of the Latin *laudare*, to honor or extol or commend. This etymological exchange announces a fundamental economy within the Trahernean text. The gifts that man receives from God must be prized as valuable before the giver can be praised as glorious. The praise man accords God is subsequently received and prized by Him, who then praises man in turn. Prize to praise become prize(d) and praise(d) in turn: each verbal act "imputes or annexes" added or supplementary value. Or, more exactly, the verbal exchange itself appropriates the surplus an economy requires. It is perhaps not too much of an overstatement to say that the entire Trahernean text is an attempt to initiate this exchange: to incite proper appraisal (prizing) of gifts so that man will afford God appropriate praise and thereby re-present himself as a supplementary prize. In the final section of this chapter we will examine more closely the mechanics of prizing as appropriation, but that operation is equally important to the economic system at issue here. And to this extent, we can see that prize and praise operate within the same circulating structure as parts and wholes; indeed, insofar as both are parts of the other, they contribute to Traherne's overall part/whole economy.

By describing one field of Traherne's supplementarity as adjectival, then, I want to direct attention to two different but associated mechanisms. The first involves the rather uncomplicated assignment of qualification. All things are, in themselves, neutral. They acquire value only when an additional term (fair, beautiful, good, wise, etc.) is annexed to them. But they also accrue added value by the manner in which they are used or the context in which they are experienced: "A farthing is *good* and pleaseth a Beggar in time of distress; but a piece of Gold is *Better*. An Estate of a thousand pounds a year is better than a Piece of Gold; but our Ambition carries us to" what is Best. Thus, where "Good, Better, and Best, are subservient to each other . . . the Good are bad in comparison of the Better, and the Better worse than the Best of all" (*CE*, 15). Qualification, therefore, produces value in a double motion: as quality supplementing the thing as such, and as itself qualified in comparison to potential supplementary addition. The second mechanism, supplement of a supplement, derives from the first, and all such systematic accumulation is governed by the law of relation, particularly between items conceived as partial and others conceived as wholes. To prize a thing is one registration; to understand its value or usefulness in relation to another thing is a second; to value it in relation to all things is a third. The economy that refuses to grant either permanent place or fixed value to any single thing is thus an incremental process of continual exchange. It is of some significance, therefore, that the passage we have just cited to illustrate adjectival qualification and systematic comparison grounds itself in the imagery of coinage.

Much of Traherne's imagery, in fact, is drawn from this economic system. The world is always full of riches, riches that achieve supplementary value by being either received or given (prized) as treasures. Worth, in such a worldview, is always relative or systematic and the imaginative urgency is to conceive a value outside—that is, over and above—the *différance* that originally captivates worth. As with other aspects of Trahernean supplementarity, the desire is for transcendence. That desire, however, is not here the issue, for I conceive transcendence itself as the third field of the supplement and would defer its analysis for a few moments. Here we can focus on the relatedness of part to whole and the economy of exchange that relation fosters.

We can close in on the subject with a series of passages from across the Trahernean text:

> The Noble Inclination wherby Man thirsteth after Riches and Dominion, is his Highest Virtu, when rightly Guided: and Carries him as in a Triumphant Chariot, to his Soveraign Happiness . . . all Satisfactions are near at hand . . . They are immediately near to the very Gates of our Sences. . . . The Way to Possess them is to Esteem them. And the true Way of Reigning over them, is to break the WORLD all into Parts, to examine them asunder. And if we find them so Excellent that Better could not Possibly be made, and so made that they could not be more ours, [we are] to rejoyce in all with Pleasure answerable to the Merit of their Goodness. We being then Kings over the Whole World, when we restore the Pieces to their Proper Places, being Perfectly Pleased with the whole Composure. (*CM*, I.23)

> That any thing may be found to be an infinit Treasure, its Place must be found in Eternity, and in God's Esteem. For as there is a Time, so there is a Place for all Things. Every Thing in its Place is Admirable Deep and Glorious; out of its Place like a Wandering Bird, is Desolat and Good for Nothing. How therfore it relateth to God and all Creatures must be seen before it can be Enjoyed. . . . Did it not relate to others it would not be Good. Divest it of these Operations, and Divide it from these Objects it is Useless and Good for Nothing. And therfore Worthless, because Worthles and Useless go together. A Piece of Gold cannot be Valued, unless we Know how it relates to Clothes, to Wine, to Victuals, to the Esteem of Men, and to the Owner. . . . It enjoys its valu in its Place, by the Ornament it gives to, and receives from all the Parts. (*CM*, III.55)

> Reason is a transcendent faculty, which extendeth to all Objects, and penetrates into all misteries, so far as to enquire . . . what

Agreement or repugnance there is in the Nature of the Things revealed; what Harmony of Contradiction there is in the Things themselves, what Correspondence in all the Circumstances, what consistence between those Things which we certainly *Know*, and those which we are perswaded to *believe*, what Authority the Relation is of, what is the Design and integrity of the Relators, what is the Use and End of the things (*CE*, 109)

When first Eternity Stoopd down to Nought,
  And in the Earth its Likeness sought,
When first it out of Nothing framd the Skies,
  And formd to Moon and Sun
That we might see what it had don,
  It was so Wise
  That it did prize
Things truly Greatest Brightest fairest, Best.

. . . .

By Merit and Desire it doth allure:
  For Truth is so Divine and Pure,
So Rich and Acceptable, being seen,
  (Not parted, but in Whole)
That it doth Draw and force the Soul.
("The Designe," ll. 1–9; 28–32)

It is never easy to disentangle the strands that weave passages into an identifiable Trahernean texture, but here we seem to have three primary ones: the question of what esteem is proper, the complex relations between parts and wholes, and the economy that derives from those relations. On an initial level of registration, esteem may be said to be proper when it is appropriate or answerable to the merit of the thing prized.[53] The merit of the thing, however, is dependent upon whether it is conceived as a part or a whole. Since all things are always both part and whole, merit can only be a product of comparative relation, a supplementary factor of relatedness itself. A thing may *be*, but only a thing that *relates* has any value. To this extent, then, the initial question of the propriety of esteem becomes an issue of the ownership or property of the thing: appropriateness becomes appropriation. Esteem motivates, "draw[s] and force[s]" the exchange that defines both value and possession.

Appropriate esteem is esteem that appropriates: what I value I own; I own whatever I value.

Value is a function of systematic relatedness. Were a thing void of relations, it would necessarily be void of value. Relatedness, then, is the operation of drawing and re-drawing part/whole relations in order to appropriate added value. Every thing, as a thing, must be a whole that "receives" harmony, ornament, beauty from the coherence of its parts. And every thing, God has told us, is good. "Goodness," however, is at best an equivocal value, for any good whole that is not also a useful part of some better whole, is "Good for Nothing." Only by relating a thing to other things can merit be generated. What is received must be given, what given received again. In that exchange, that economy or "operation" of part/whole relatedness, the supplement keeps supplementing itself, announcing itself as "Truth" only when *good* has been converted to "Great*est* Bright*est* fair*est*, B*est*."[54]

Somewhat surprisingly, though, adjectival superlatives do not appear in Traherne's text as often or as centrally as might be expected. The comparative forms—greater, brighter, higher, fairer, better—are far more common.[55] This fact is all the more curious in light of the Traherne criticism has drawn for us—the ever-expanding voice, the aggressive ambition, the imaginative presumption. What the supplement of the adjective reveals, however, is the systematic necessity of remaining at the comparative level. That is, as either the registration of value or the motivation of desire, the qualitative supplement must anticipate and defer its potential fulfillment. The same principle governs the economy of parts/wholes: it is precisely the absence of any verifiable "whole" that propels the entire supplementary system. The narrative, like the imagination or desire, can be committed only to generating ever more parts. Any whole temporarily conceived as such—as highest or brightest or best—would escape the systematic generation of value if it were not immediately re-presented as a part.

A convenient illustration of this deferring mechanism occurs in the opening meditations of the First Century. Attempting to incite his reader's ambition and desire, Traherne, from the second to the seventeenth meditation, keeps pointing toward that highest and brightest end, the world: "the Whole World" (*CM*, I.6); "the End of the World" (*CM*, I.15); "all the World" (*CM*, I.16), and the "Whole WORLD," which is not a thing as much as "the most Beautiful Idea in all Worlds" (*CM*, I.17). Then, in meditation 18, the perspective alters: the world we have been following, the heavens that bound it, even the "Heavens of Heavens" are only "Parts of the World"; and "WORLD," as a whole, is suddenly "unknown." All we can see or consider are "the Beauty and the serviceableness of its Parts." Almost paradoxically, once the world has been imagined as "an illimited field" of constituent parts, its wholeness collapses altogether: "Alas the WORLD is but a little Centre in Comparison of you" (*CM*, I.19). We can readily predict, of course, that the newly installed whole—here the individual reader's soul—will undergo the same expansion and contraction. It too must ultimately become only another part of yet another differing and deferred whole.

The systematic registration of parts and wholes—and this means the systematic exchange that must rewrite any whole into a subsequent part in order to imagine a new whole—is in Traherne's text a supplementary economy. Only the relation between part and whole makes serviceability and usefulness available or accessible as economic values. And we must never forget that value is the desired end: in the "vulgar Exchequer" of the human imagination, supplementary accumulation of wealth and profit, a kind of supplemental interest, is the economic means to that end. Usefulness is one of the markers of this exchange; in fact, as I have already argued, it is the primary coin of the supplement of the adjective.

Traherne's discussion of the value of knowledge will show some of the mechanics of the economy of usefulness. Knowledge, of course, is both a power and an act. The initial registration of the supplement occurs when the power to know becomes exerted as the act of knowing. But the act of knowing requires an object: extending its power to act upon an object, knowledge appropriates a reflected lustre from the object of its comprehension and thereby "add[s] a value" to itself. Even before the particular worth of the object itself can be imagined or imputed, we are already engaged in the supplement of a supplement. Usefulness now heightens the registration one more degree: "AS for the *Use* of Knowledge, it is apparent enough. For the Relation between the Use and Excellency of things is so near and intimate, that as nothing Useless can be at all excellent, so is every Excellence in every Being founded in its usefulness. The use of Souls is as great as their Excellency: The use of Knowledge as endless in Variety, as in Extent, and Value" (*CE*, 38–39). Use and value are here obverse and inverse of the same economic coin. It hardly matters whether Traherne is discussing an object in the world or a faculty perceiving the world, value accrues always in relation to imputed usefulness.

The *Centuries* is perhaps more insistent on this point than any other Traherne work. At the opening of the First Century, Traherne promises his reader all manner of incredible and wondrous things, infinitely profitable. As he begins to explain what these "Great Things" are, he pauses to address the relation between their innate value and their added usefulness: "True Lov, as it intendeth the Greatest Gifts, intendeth also the Greatest Benefits. It contenteth not it self in Shewing Great Things unless it can make them Greatly Usefull. For Lov greatly Delighteth in seeing its Object continualy seated in the Highest Happiness. Unless therfore I could advance you Higher by the uses of what I give, my Love could not be satisfied, in Giving you the Whole World" (*CM*, I.6). To be "Sensible of . . . Use and Value" (*CM*, I.9) is here a double register: in order to make my gifts valuable to you, I have also to make them useful to you; if I do make them useful to you, then they are valuable to me. Usefulness, as the coin of adjectival exchange here, is at the same time and for that reason the production of supplemental value: the process by which "Great Things" can become "the Greatest Gifts," or a "Higher" seat can be advanced to the "Highest Happiness." Use and value, therefore, are not simply two terms arbitrarily yoked together: the "and" that conjoins articulates the very structure of supplementary *différance*.[56]

In the Fourth Century, Traherne's "and" inscribes a different term of value, but the supplementary economy of usefulness remains the same: "For can the World be Glorious unless it be Usefull? And to what Use could the World serv Him, if it served not those, that in this were supremely Glorious, that they could Obey and Admire and Lov and Prais, and Imitat their Creator? Would it not be wholy useless without such Creatures?" (*CM*, IV.46). The economy of this passage is almost identical to the one we have just cited. Although it is here God rather than man who gives the great gift, all value—of the gift itself, the giver, and the recipient—depends upon the supplemental structure of usefulness. Useless and useful are thus registers of meaningless and meaningful, value-less and value-full. Use, as economic coin of exchange, is therefore another way for Traherne to map his fundamental difference of empty and full. Useful is full of value; useless is empty and void of value. So it does not matter here that "glorious" has replaced the term "value" from the earlier passage, for glorious is merely another name for the supplemental value use generates. The next meditation thus repeats: "things when they are usefull are most Glorious, and it is impossible for you or me to be usefull, but as we are Delightfull to GOD." To "be useles, as it is improportioned to the Glory of the Means . . . is . . . the utter undoing of all his Glory" (*CM*, I.47). "Use-full": the surplus announced in the very term is the economy of the exchange it offers and the reason why Traherne is so insistent in employing it. Once a thing can be imagined as useful it can be imagined and imaged as full of value, meaning, love, and glory. That such fullness is charted only in relation to the mechanism of exchange is another sign of the operation of circulation upon which the supplement of the adjective is based.

We have already discussed circulation from a number of different perspectives, but here the issue is the economy of the supplement. That circulation is a supplementary process should, by now, be obvious enough. That it is also an economic one should be equally easy to demonstrate.

> All Things to Circulations owe
> Themselvs; by which alone
> They do exist: They cannot shew
> A Sigh, a Word, a Groan,
> A Colour, or a Glimpse of Light
> . . . .
> But they anothers Livery must Wear.
> ("Circulation," ll. 29–37)

Circulation, in this stanza from the poem of that title, is merely an existential necessity: to be at all a thing must be subject to the irreducible law of exchange itself, receiving and giving. In stanza 4, that exchange is described in revealing terms:

A Spunge drinks in that Water, which
Is afterwards *exprest.*
A Liberal hand must first be rich:
Who blesseth must be Blest.
The Thirsty Earth drinks in the Rain,
The Trees suck Moysture at their Roots,
Before the one can Lavish Herbs again,
Before the other can afford us Fruits.
No Tenant can rais Corn, or pay his Rent,
Nor can even hav a Lord,
That has no Land. No Spring can vent,
No vessel any Wine afford
Wherin no Liquor's put. No Empty Purs,
Can Pounds or Talents of it self disburs.
(ll. 43–56)

Purse and disburse, rich and lavishing, blessed and expressed, rent and vent: circulation is always already a re-circulation and always an accumulation of value by giving value away. Traherne tries over and again to articulate this paradoxical economy: "Lov knows not how to be Timerous, becaus it receives what it gives away. And is unavoidably the End of its own Afflications and anothers Happiness. Let him that pleases Keep his mony. I am more rich in this Noble Charity to all the World" (*CM*, IV.58). The supplement that receives by giving is conventionally expressed as charity, but what is important to note, both here and in the preceding passage, is the almost inevitable recourse to monetary terms: accumulating money, growing rich, "refilling" an already full purse. What Traherne calls, two meditations further, the exertion of supply, is nothing less than the production and accumulation of supplementary capital. And what is particularly revealing about this economy is that it is always already the supplement of a supplement, a surplus added or appropriated to value already annexed by the law of supplementary addition. It is perhaps for this reason that Derrida prefers to emphasize supplementary cumulation rather than accumulation: the distinction is one of degree, but it focuses attention on the mass of wealth that is constantly being generated.

In the Second Century, Traherne again points to the economic register of circulation: "The World within you is an offering returned. Which is infinitly more Acceptable to GOD Almighty, since it came from him, that it might return unto Him. Wherin the Mysterie is Great. For GOD hath made you able to Creat Worlds in your own mind, which are more Precious unto Him then those which He Created: And to Give and offer up the World unto Him, which is very Delightfull in flowing from Him, but much more in Returning to Him" (*CM*, II.90). Here the particular terms are not as pointedly monetary as those in the preceding passage, but the economy by which each stage of the exchange takes on or adds to itself a supplemental excess is clearly the production and consumption of wealth and therefore "more Precious." In addition, we can see here that circulation, like the part/whole relations examined earlier, is subject to the logic of *différance*: receiving and giving inevitably invoke one another as necessarily as the *Fort* invokes the *Da* in a cycle of continuous reregistration that knows no termination and whose sole function is to reproduce its own supplementary value. "More Precious," therefore, already a doubled supplement, comes to add itself to a self already supplemented. At each level, the economy seeks only to generate and appropriate "much more."

Regardless of his particular subject, Traherne's sense of circulation is always grounded in such an economy:

> The Heavens and the Earth and all the Creatures are Gifts and Tokens of his Love, Men and Angels are a Present of his Love, which he hath infinitely adorned, and made endlessly serviceable to every Soul that is Beloved. All these his Love would have us to receive with a due Esteem . . . and Love them as much as their Goodness deserveth. When we see and understand their Excellence, and Esteem them according to the transcendent value that appeareth in them, we adorn our selves with their fair Ideas, we enlarge and beautifie our Souls with Bright and Clear Apprehensions, and which is much more, with regular and well ordered Affections, we enrich our selves, and increase our Greatness . . . we are lively, and pleasant, and vigorous Creatures, full of knowledge, and Wisdome, and Goodness, and fit to offer up all these things unto him *again*, while

> we empty them as Helps and Advantages in that Service which we pay unto him. (*CE*, 57)

The registration of supplements here is especially evident and carefully orchestrated. The gifts God offers are themselves good, but insofar as they are prized (both appropriated and esteemed) they accrue a "transcendent value." In turn, that value serves to supplement—to enlarge, beautify, enrich, and increase—the worth of the soul that receives them. That worth is now appropriated by means of the adjectival supplements qualifying the soul: pleasant, lively, bright, clear, well ordered, vigorous, and, most important, full. Finally, as man offers "unto him again" both the original gifts and his own revalued self, in effect disbursing and emptying himself, he paradoxically "increase[s]" the value of both gifts and self. This accumulation of supplementary and circulating exchange Traherne names "service" or "serviceable[ness]": a production and consumption both generating and generated by an economy in which God and man together "pay" and thereby "enrich" themselves."

Even when, on occasion, Traherne uses the correlative notion of communication, the economy of circulating exchange still structures the exposition and determines the course of the imagery he fastens on. As examples, we might look at two passages from the end of *Christian Ethicks*. In the first, Traherne imagines God speaking to man:

> You give trifles, and give them but to one, I give Worlds and give them to every one. You divide and disperse your Gifts, and lessen by dispersing them, I communicate and unite my Gifts, and augment by giving them . . . You think your interest is abated, and your fruition endangered by the communication of your Treasures to many, I know they are increased and multiplied by the number of the Enjoyers. (*CE*, 249)

At issue here is what might be called the decorum of exchange: the difference between an economy that wastes its investment by conceiving all expense as probable loss and an economy that augments and increases its investment by regarding expense as self-expansion. In this context, communication and circulation are merely different terms for the same economic thing. The self projects itself outside of itself in order to appropriate to itself the pleasure of a value disbursed to and desired by a prizing/praising Other. Without that extension and the *différance* by which it is structured, no value accumulates and the economy itself is abated or dispersed. With it, the economy is driven by its operative functions of augmentation and multiplication.

Value, as this passage implies, is always the economic object of desire.[57] The relation between supplementary circulation, desire, and that supplement I have called the imagination can be seen in the second passage from *Christian Ethicks*:

> To receive all is sweet, but to communicate all (adorned thus within the sphere of our own lives) is infinitely beyond all that can be sweet in the reception, both for our glory and satisfaction. There is ever upon us some pressing want in this World, and will be till we are infinitely satisfied with varieties and degrees of Glory. Of that which we feel at present we are sensible: when that want is satisfied and removed, another appeareth, of which before we were not aware. Til we are satisfied we are so clamorous and greedy, as if there were no pleasure but in receiving all: When we have it we are so full, that we know not what to do with it, we are in danger of bursting, till we can communicate all to some fit and amiable Recipient, and more delight in the Communication than we did in the Reception. This . . . is a Principle so strong, that Fire does not burn with more certain violence, than Nature study to use all, when it hath gotten it, and to improve its *Treasures* to the acquisition of its *Glory*. (*CE*, 258–59)

Giving and receiving is the accumulation of value, not, we must emphasize, because man thereby acquires more, but because this exchange offers an imaginative context within which desire can generate infinite "varieties and degrees" of self-promotion and production. "To talk of overflowing," as Traherne does here and further on in the same chapter, is to attempt to imagine a self that is so full of itself that it is "in danger of bursting," as outrageous a desire as Traherne ever manages. Outrageous or not, however, that desire is structured by the same economy of the supplement that adds quality to essence and act to power. Once that supplementary operation is set in place it can find no logical or necessary end. Bursting, overflowing, is merely a "certain violence" employed to "improve" treasure and "acquire" self-glory. Even violence is here subjected to the orderly exchange of a fundamental economy in which production and consumption are the principal tasks and the only objectives.

V IMAGINATION AND DESIRE

What I have called the third primary field of Traherne's supplementarity concerns relations between the imagination and desire. For Traherne, no less than for Derrida, the imagination is the supplementary faculty and its function is solely the production of desire. This means, first of all, that we must carefully distinguish in Traherne the sensory and the rational faculties from the imaginative faculty: the former work actively on and are consequently bound to the objects they perceive. Imagination, however, knows no such bounds. More often than not, imagination works only with the specular representations of "thoughts," an extremely equivocal category in Traherne's mental scheme. However the status of the imagination is derived, the fundamental point is that it is itself already a surplus in the faculty hierarchy, not quite essential to the minimum requirements of perception and understanding, but paradoxically necessary to the economy of psychic desire. Given this status, whatever is produced by the imagination must also be a surplus or excess, supplement of a supplement, as Derrida phrases it.

We can clarify the nature of the imagination in Traherne by recalling the five "Thoughts" poems at the conclusion of the Dobell folio. Two themes run throughout these poems: first, that thoughts are purely re-presentational, the "only mirror" wherein any thing appears to "the Glass of Imagination" (*CM*, III.10); and second, that because of this specular registration, thoughts are always free and unconfined. In one sense, both themes emphasize the same distinction between knowledge and sight, which are limited to the objects presented to them, and thought, which is always "transcendent" to any object. Thoughts are the productions of an imagination driven by desire, and while they may be "free" of objective reality, they are clearly subject to a systematic logic and represent desire raising itself to a second power. And this, perhaps, is why it is possible to argue that for Traherne the imagination, like desire, works only upon itself, upon the methods, manners, and objects of its own production or re-production.

It is not, therefore, coincidental that Traherne places the poem called "Desire" in the middle of the "Thoughts" sequence.[58] As both product and producer of desire, imagination is already inscribed within the doubled folds of a supplementarity generating itself out of its own excesses. If "thought" is here interpreted as the site of this staged or represented desire, then two of the themes I have been urging in this study—that Traherne is a serious thinker and that he is fundamentally a poet of desire—converge in an unexpected way. What should be of particular interest at the moment is that that convergence again signals an economy: desire is registered upon and within thought as value and thought is produced and consumed by an imagination bent upon increasing and reconfirming its own worth.

I have just said that the imagination in Traherne's text continuously "stages" itself, re-presents itself to itself along an axis of narrative supplementation (what Lacan calls *epos*). That axis may be said to originate in a conceived want or lack (emptiness), to progress through various registrations of the desire for more and for fulfillment, and to culminate in deferral to an unimaginable condition of infinity. To conceive Traherne's narrative in this way ought to reveal the chain of supplements by which imagination and desire continually supply each other with the terms of indefinite difference and deferral, the irreducible exchange which makes the constant production of value not only possible, but necessary.

In the chapter "Of Hope" in *Christian Ethicks*, Traherne offers a dramatic illustration of the imagination at work:

> All the Honor, Advancement, Exaltation, Glory, Treasure, and Delight, that is conceivable in Time or Eternity, may be hoped for: all that the Length, and Breadth, and Depth, and Height, of the Love of GOD, which passeth knowledge, is able to perform; All that Ambition or Avarice can desire, all that Appetite and Self-Love can pursue, all that Fancy can imagine Possible and Delightful; Nay *more than we are able to ask or think*; we are able to desire, and aspire after. . . . And the more Sublime its [the imagination's] Objects are, the more Eagerly

> & violently does our Hope pursue them, because there is more Goodness in them to ravish our Desire. (*CE*, 121–22)

Though perhaps unconsciously, Traherne confesses here the very structure of supplementarity: we desire more than we are able to imagine; we imagine more than we are able to desire. But what exactly is the object sought by an imagination that cannot conceive it or a desire that cannot attain it? The italicized phrase suggests the object is the desiring imagination always already supplementing itself by generating *more*. As Traherne continues, the nature of this auto-object becomes clearer: "For it is the property of a true and lively Hope to Elevate the Soul, to the Height of its Object . . . the Soul extends itself with a kind of Pleasure in its Wishes and in touching the Possibility of such Goodness, as it proposes to its self in its own Imagination" (*CE*, 122). The objects of imagination "do really surpass all Imagination" even as, paradoxically, they *are* the imagination. Desire here is the pleasure imagination proposes for and appropriates to itself in reproducing itself as the "possible" object of its own imaginings—which is to say that the imagination proposes itself to itself as that which is "purely Superadded, and increasing the same" (*CE*, 123). Supplement of a supplement, the imagination is desire captivated by its own specular image, by the spectacular sublime imagery of the self exceeding itself.

The *Centuries* define the imagination in similar terms. What begins as a reasonably orthodox conception of the freedom of the imagination[59] becomes ultimately the supplementary return of a self trying to gaze at itself as a surplus generated by and out of itself:

> Creatures that are able to dart their Thoughts into all Spaces, can brook no Limit or Restraint, they are infinitly endebted to this illimited Extent, becaus were there no such Infinitie, there would be no Room for their Imaginations; their Desires and Affections would be cooped up, and their Souls imprisoned. . . . the Everlasting Expansion of what we feel and behold within us. . . . is an Object infinitly Great and Ravishing. . . . all Glorious within, as infinit in Light and Beauty, as Extent and Treasure. . . . Evry Man alone the Centre and Circumference. . . . A Cabinet of infinit Value. (*CM*, V.3)

If "The Glass of Imagination [is] the only Mirror, wherin any thing [is] represented" (*CM*, III.10), then this must also be true of imagination itself. And yet imagination is precisely that one object that is "transcendent to all Imagination." This is so, of course, because of the fundamental logic of supplementary *différance*: imagination re-presents itself to itself only in the production of desire—desire, ultimately, for its own self-presence. As its own surplus, however, imagination can never seize its own specular image. The same logic governs the desire that drives the imagination: desire reproduces itself upon its own inability to satisfy itself, deferring satisfaction in order to generate an imaginative surplus. In both cases, the desired or imagined surplus itself becomes the only adequate object of production, supplanting and supplementing both desire and imagination. That surplus, as I have already suggested, bears the structural significations within the Trahernean text of "more," "full," and "infinite."

On the last page of the Fifth Century, immediately following meditation 10, Traherne wrote the number 11 and left the rest of the volume blank. This gesture has frequently been read as an intentional incentive—either literally in regard to Susannah Hopton or figuratively in terms of a general audience—to the reader to take up the task of writing the praise of God or thanksgivings to God. Numerologically, however, the gesture is more interesting. Ten is the number of unity and perfection; eleven is a transgression, a striving beyond completion, an insatiable demand or desire for more. Paradoxically, eleven has also been seen as symbol of infinity and thus it is appropriate that this otherwise silent meditation voices simultaneously Traherne's imaginative desire for more and his registration of that desire under the inexpressible (that is, nonverbal) sign of the infinite.[60]

The desire for more is, as we have already said, grounded upon lack or want. "A perfect Soul," Traherne argues in *Christian Ethicks*, "is that whereunto nothing can be added to please our Desire" (p. 20). But since desire is precisely that which can never be satisfied, the soul is always perceived as imperfection being supplemented: "Unless all [objects and creatures] be perfect in their Nature, Variety, Number, Extent, Relation, Use and Value, our fruition cannot be simply perfect, because a Greater and more perfect fruition might, upon the production of better Objects, be contrived [e.g., presented in the imagination]. . . . The more Beautiful the Object is, the more pleasant is the enjoyment. But where Delight may be increased, the Fruition is imperfect" (*CE*, 20). The want or lack of perfection ensures the generation of the supplement: either the *more* valuable object proposed by the imagination or the *more* enjoyable one demanded by desire. The quest for these mores is insistent across Traherne's text, and its economy is exactly stated as "the production of better Objects."

In two passages we have already cited in a different context the Trahernean more is clearly generated out of a lack. Both occur in the Fourth Century:

> He [the author-friend] thought that men were more to be Beloved now then before. And which is a strange Paradox, the Worse they are the more they were to be beloved. The Worse they are the more they were to be Pittied and Tendered and Desired, becaus they had more need, and were more Miserable. tho the Better they are, they are more to be Delighted in. . . . They are now Worse yet more to be Beloved. (*CM*, IV.26)

> If you ask, what is becom of us since the Fall? becaus all these things now lately named seem to pertain to the Estate of Innocency; Truly Now we have superadded Treasures: Jesus Christ. And are restored to the Exercise of the same Principles, upon higher Obligations: I will not say with More Advantage. Tho perhaps Obligations them selvs are to us Advantage. . . . For GOD is more Delightfull then He was in Eden. Then he was as Delightfull as was possible but he had not that occasion, as by Sin was offered, to superad many more Delights then before. Being more Delightfull and more Amiable, He is more Desirable, and may now be more Easily yea Strongly Beloved. (*CM*, IV.53)

Each passage is structured largely by comparative accretion, the first in terms of the *différance* announced in worse/better, the second in terms of then/now. "More," in both cases, names the supplement that *différance* incites or produces. And in the second passage, we can also see how the reproduction of the accreted more also, of supplementary necessity, heightens or increases desire as well. Although other passages in Traherne do not always invoke the lack or want here ascribed to the Fall, they do progress from that silent point of supposed origin to the constant re-imagining of additional mores.

In the First Century, the production of more is suggestively related to the specular mode: "But had He Determined to Creat no more: there had been no Witnesses of thy Glory" (*CM*, I.68). Such specular registration reaches its narrative extension in the next century:

> How Happy we are that we may liv in all, as well as one; and how All sufficient Lov is, we may see by this: The more we liv in all the more we liv in one. for while He seeth us to live in all, we are a more Great and Glorious Object unto Him; the more we are Beloved of all, the more we are Admired by Him; The more we are the Joy of all, the more Blessed we are to Him. The more Blessed we are to Him the Greater is our Blessedness. We are all Naturaly Ambitious of being Magnified in others, and of seeming Great in others. Which Inclination was implanted in us that our Happiness might be Enlarged by the Multitud of Spectators. (*CM*, II.61)

The self here projects itself as an object of others' gazes, but the imagination must supplement that object with an entire chain of incremental mores in order to magnify its own value and to prove itself "All sufficient." Self-sufficiency, of course, is an imaginative illusion, for the whole supplementary process is grounded in the structural *différance* of self and Other. As we saw in the preceding chapter, desire is the desire of the Other, now conceived as value.

Magnification, with its residual implications of specular staging, incites many of Traherne's chains of the supplementary more. In the Fourth Century, we find this excessive, almost obsessive, passage, which, although it seems to describe God rather than man, issues a dramatic exhortation to invert that perspective in the final line:

> He magnifieth Himself in Magnifying them [his Creatures]. . . . The more he loveth them the Greater he is and the more Glorious. The more he loveth them the more precious and Dear they are to Him. The more he loveth them the more Joys and Treasures He possesseth. The more He loveth them the

> more he Delighteth in their Felicity. The more he loveth them, the more he delighteth in himself for being their felicity. The more he loveth them, the more he rejoyceth in all his Works for serving them: and in all his Kingdom of Delighting them. And being Lov to them the more he loveth Himself and the more jealous he is least himself should be Displeased, the more he loveth them and tendereth them and secureth their Welfare. And the more he desires his own Glory the more Good he doth for them, in the more Divine and genuine maner. You must lov after his similitude. (*CM*, IV.65)

The most obvious feature of such a passage, of course, is its repetitiveness, and, like much else in Traherne, we can regret the repetition or simply dismiss the passage as ludicrous because of it.[61] In fact, the repetition is crucial to Traherne's argument: it is only by means of the incremental exchanges of the supplementary more that the economy can produce and reproduce either worth or value. More incites more! The exchange that takes place under that production increases the value of both parties: the more God adds to man, the more he appears to Himself; the more man imagines God adds to him, the more he appropriates to his own conception of himself. Both man and God add the supplementary more to the Other in order to stage themselves as more to themselves.

It is precisely this economy binding self and Other to a repetition of supplementary exchange that Traherne's extended references to more announce. Here, for example, is a passage from *Christian Ethicks*:

> The more Great, the more High, the more Excellent [God] is; the more blessed is [the Soul] it self, the more joyful, and the more contented. . . . All overtures of Pleasure, Beauty, Glory, Power, Exaltation and Honor it would have added to its happiness. The more Great, the more Good, the Wiser GOD is, the greater is its Happiness. The more he is admired and praised, the greater is its Happiness. The more he is magnified and pleased, the greater is its Happiness. . . . For the very true reason why it enjoyes *it self*, and all its *own* Treasures, is because it loves *it self*: And the more it loves *him*, the more it will be delighted with *his* fruitions. It is more concerned, it feels

> more, it sees more, it tastes more, it possesses more, it rejoyces more in its Object than it self. The imagination and fancy that is in Love frames all the thoughts of its Beloved, in it self . . . Loving GOD more than it self, it is more happy in GOD, than if it were a GOD. Could his Deity be taken away, and seated in it self, the Soul of a Grateful Creature would be grieved at the exchange. (*CE*, 274–75)

And yet, of course, this is the fiction the self proposes to itself, for that exchange is precisely its desire. What is here announced as possible grief is merely the irreducible law of *différance* upon which the economy of more and its exchange is grounded. The Other and the self must be kept apart so that each can add more to both. The imagination can "frame" its exchanges on no other terms, for desire "would have [All] added to it."

A few pages after this passage is another extended illustration of the incremental production of the supplementary more, this time identified as the "Hing" upon which "all a mans Interests turn." We should read "Interests" in two distinct senses: as both that which most concerns man as man, and as that which supplements his economic profit:

> As [man] hath more encouragements to believe in GOD, and to delight in him, so he hath more concerns to engage his fear, more allurements to provoke his desire, more incentives to enflame his love, and more obligations to compel his obedience: More arguments to strengthen his Hope, more materials to feed his Praises, more Causes to make him Humble, more fuel for Charity to others, more grounds of Contentment in himself, more helps to inspire him with Fortitude, more rewards to quicken his Industry, more engagements to Circumspection and Prudence, more ballast to make him Stable, more lights to assist his Knowledge, more sails to forward his Motion, more employments in which to spend his Time, more attractives to Meditation, and more entertainments to enrich his Solitude. (*CE*, 277)

Nor is this all. The imagination and desire continue to grind out more supplements—more aids, more avocations, more wings, more gates, more withholders, more aggravations, more waters, more motives, more consolations, more hopes, more bounds, more comforts, more Hallelujahs, more delights, more arts, more feasts, etc., etc.—until finally concluding that, "From this Spring of *Universal Fruition* all the streams of Living Waters flow that refresh the Soul. Upon this Hing all a mans Interests turn, and in this Centre all his Spiritual Occasions meet" (*CE*, 277). "Universal Fruition" is the continuous production and consumption of more. Hinge or center, spring or ocean, all "interest" accumulates around and through this term. Nothing, in fact, can bring that production to any necessary or logical conclusion, for desire and imagination can always seek more.[62]

And yet Traherne does manage to contrive a *sort* of culmination to this urgent supplementation by adding another surplus: "We shall lov Him *infinitly more* then our selvs, and therefore liv *infinitly more* in Him . . . and be *infinitly more* Delighted" (*CM*, II.52; my italics). Even more, that is, can be supplemented, perhaps itself generates another level of supplementation. Supplement of the supplement, the infinite, infinitely, or infinity comes to supplant more as the registration of *most* value. And here, of course, we can see the fuller implications of Derrida's logic of supplementary *différance*, for although "more" accumulates value as a "necessary surplus," it also defers value to a secondary or maybe tertiary register. The same principle, as we will see, governs "infinite" as well: supplement of a supplement, it must necessarily produce further supplementation.

Imagination, even more than reason, "never rests, but in the production of a Glorious Act, that is infinite in Perfection" (*CE*, 15)—which is to say, it can never rest but in the production of infinity itself. The Traherne text is, at its core, the insistent attempt to imagine that complete fulfillment of all desire and the equally consistent frustration at its inability to do so.[63] A few brief passages will disclose this structure and we can begin by again situating the (un)imaginable infinity within the field of desire: "[God] is enjoyed only when his essence and his Works satisfie the Desires of perfect reason, and exceed all Wishes in filling and delighting the soul: That having filled the soul with infinite Wisdome, he has laid infinite Obligations upon us, and set infinite Rewards before us, made Laws infinitely amiable, and given us Duties infinitely Desirable" (*CE*, 43). The economy of this passage begins by announcing its own supplementarity: "exceed[ing] all Wishes," the imagination fastens upon a term of value which it then obsessively affixes to everything it can conceive. What "satisfies" our infinite desires is the excess that imagines things infinitely desirable, or, in a kind of Lacanian register, desire infinitely desires infinite desire.

Traherne makes this point over and over: "FOR infinite Goodness must needs desire with an infinite violence, that all Goodness should be compleat and Perfect: and that Desire . . . must infinitely avoid every slur and Miscarriage . . . and infinitely aim at every Grace and Beauty, that tends to make the Object [self *or* Other] infinitely perfect, which it would enjoy. It cannot desire less than infinite Perfection, nor less then hate all Imperfection, in an infinite Manner" (*CE*, 88). If infinite desire must desire infinitely, then "upon the least subtraction, that which is infinite is made finite, and the Loss is infinite" (*CE*, p. 89). Beneath the wit of this assertion again lies the Derridean law, for desire cannot escape, even in its imagined failure, its own infinity.

It is perhaps Traherne's recognition of this supplementary captivity that leads him to attempt to imagine the surplus or excess of infinity itself. The question is initially posed in terms of a divine supplementarity: "His Love being Infinite and Eternal, in sacrificing it self in all its Works for its Objects welfare, became an infinite and eternal Act; which was not contented, unless in all its Works, it added [Act] unto Power, and exerted its Wisdom in all its Productions" (*CE*, 179).[64] It should be noted, albeit in passing, that God's desire is immediately conceived in relation to structures of the supplement, to the manner by which divinity adds to and exceeds itself.

The meditation continues: "Had it made one Infinite, some are of Opinion, it had exceeded it self; at least done all that was possible, both for it self, and for its Object, and that one Infinite, being so Created, must be its only Object. *For more than Infinite what can be?* We are apt to think that nothing can be beside. But to show that GOD is infinitely more"—again we must interrupt Traherne's argument to observe how the two terms ("infinite" and "more") we have identified as supplementary stagings here function to intensify one another[65]—"than what we conceive, while we think him infinite;

and that we infinitely wrong him, while we limit his Essence to one single Infinity; Who is every way Infinite, in Himself, in all his Works, in all his Waies. . . . He hath made every thing either Infinite, or better than so" (*CE*, 179).

What more than infinite can be? Traherne does not, cannot, answer his own question, but he has already announced that the imagination must propose something better. The supplement of the infinite, in these final five words, has already been displaced and deferred: "whereever GOD is, he is able to Act; and his Omnipresence is infinite Wisdom and Power; which filling Infinity is able to exert it self beyond the bounds of Space in an infinite Manner all at once. If it so do, it cannot rest in a less Attainment, than one that answers the measure of its Operation: if it did, that Attainment would be infinitely defective: For infinite Wisdom could certainly conceive one infinitely Better" (*CE*, 180). If "attainment" here means achievement or success in reaching, it is clear that Traherne's logic is only partially correct: *any* attainment would be defective and thus infinity functions as a supplement only so long as its own achievement is deferred. Traherne can therefore conclude: "But this I will aver, that GOD hath wrought abundantly more, than if he had made any one single Effect of his Power infinite" (*CE*, 180). Once again the "more" that "infinite" previously replaced now comes to replace it in turn. Supplement of a supplement, each becomes the object of the other's surplus or lack. Within the economy of that exchange, *différance* reiterates itself as the logic of supplementarity.

How, then, can Traherne escape his own question: what more than infinite? One way is to allow the infinite to defer its other by supplementing itself. The infinite must become infinite in supplementary tautology, Traherne's version of Derrida's "necessary surplus." Two passages from the Second Century can suggest the strategy of this attempt: "unless we value that we lost in the first [Adam], we cannot truly rejoyce in the second. But when we do, then all things receiv an infinite Esteem, and an Augmentation infinitly infinit, that follows after" (*CM*, II.5); "The Exceeding Glory of [man's] Primitiv Estate being so Great, that it made His Sin infinitly infinit" (*CM*, II.35). In effect, man is that creature suspended between two supplementary possibilities: an augmentation that ever heightens or increases his value as his valuing, or a lack that ever deepens and hollows out his emptiness and his want. But the real question here is what we read in the apparent absurdity of this language. My sense is that Traherne recognizes several consequences of his own thinking here. First, the phrase "infinitly infinit" concedes that the supplementary logic has nowhere to go except to multiply and replicate itself. Once Traherne has questioned the totality of infinity, subjected it to the difference of more, then the only end imaginable is one that is, paradoxically, "end-less." This also means, I think, that Traherne recognizes that supplementary doubling is an inevitable deferral. The "infinitly infinit," that is, does not bring a desired infinity about, but defers it once again even as it attempts to call it forth. Thus the phrase concedes the necessary frustration of desire. "Infinitly infinit," therefore, marks the extreme limits in the Traherne text of both imagination and desire. It announces the inexpressible law of replication to which both are bound and it defines the supplementary sameness within which their difference is captivated. We can read in the phrase the "strange logic" of both a supplementary desire and supplementary imagination: that the precondition of an economic production is precisely the impossibility of full possession.

"Creatures that are able to dart their Thoughts into all Spaces," Traherne argues in the third meditation of the Fifth Century that we have already had occasion to cite, "can brook no Limit or Restraint, they are infinitly endebted to this illimited Extent, becaus were there no such Infinitie, there would be no Room for their Imaginations." Three meditations on, Traherne's imagination has already found infinity to be insufficient room and has already begun the supplementary process of "Everlasting Expansion" by again using one of the privileged adjectives of surplus to force the other back upon itself in double registration: "One would think that besides infinit Space there could be no more Room for any Treasure. yet to show that God is infinitly infinit, there is Infinit Room besides, and perhaps a more Wonderfull Region making this to be infinitly infinit" (*CM*, V.6).

If "more" is here the trigger of desire that requires the imagination to reformulate infinity in such a way as to raise its own infinite status, the hypothetical "perhaps" signals the imagination's completion of the task desire incites. Here, therefore, we can distinguish the two faculties more carefully than we have yet done by suggesting that desire is always structured in terms of more whereas imagination is concerned with infinity. Such an alignment, of course, returns to the point that desire and imagination function as supplementary and economic *différance*.

If God is "infinitly infinit" and the world is "infinitly infinit," obviously desire requires an imaginative expansion and "augmentation" of man himself: "That you are a Man should fill you with Joys, and make you to overflow with Praises. The Priviledge of your Nature being infinitly infinit" (*CM*, II.24). Behind this passage lie two interrelated supplementary operations: that by which an empty self re-presents itself as so increasingly, excessively full that it must overflow itself; and that by which a finite being re-presents itself as so excessively infinite that it can only be imagined as infinitely so. Fullness overflowing does not seem to bring us to the same level of the paradoxically unimaginable or inexpressible as infinite infinity, but it is clearly organized by the same supplementary mechanics.

Before turning to explore these mechanics of fullness more closely, let me add a further thought on the unimaginable. I have said that Traherne's "infinitly infinit" is the determined failure of imagination and the marked limit of desire. The whole attempt to say the thought or the desire this phrase signals is grounded on its own impossibility.[66] In a sense, we can hear in the phrase only the operation of supplementarity itself, and the "strange logic" to which that operation is irreducibly bound. Traherne frequently imagines this infinite infinity in terms of center and sphere imagery. The more appropriate image would be a vortex whose center is a vacuum too deep to be conceived and whose particles whirl too fast to be perceived. All that registers on either eye or mind is the motion itself, continuous, unstoppable, inexorable.

VI RESTRUCTURING DOBELL

We have already had several occasions to note the central position of the empty/full difference in Traherne's thought and narrative. To be filled with all the fullness of God, to be brought into the presence of a continuously overflowing fullness, these are the constant pleas of both *Christian Ethicks* and the *Centuries of Meditations*. It is easy enough to understand that structures of supplementarity underlie the opposition:

> Infinite Lov cannot be Expressed in finit Room: but must hav infinit Places wherin to utter and shew it self. It must therfore fill all Eternity and the Omnipresence of God with Joys and Treasures for my Fruition. (*CM*, II.80)

> Your Soul being naturaly very Dark, and Deformed and Empty when Extended through infinit but empty Space: the World servs you in Beautifying and filling it with Amiable Ideas. . . . And we are to Grow up into Him till we are filled with the Fulness of his GODhead. (*CM* II.84)

If it can be said that desire drives the first of these passages as imagination drives the second, the supplementary operation is much the same as those we have been charting. In the second passage, in fact, the supplementary fullness that is imagined and desired is produced by the very failure of a supplement already discussed: infinity, already a supplement, must itself be supplemented by emptiness/fullness in order to be registered as value. Here again, as in the first passage as well, we see the economy the supplement generates.

It would not be too difficult to show that "fill," "full," and "fulfillment" serve the same supplementary functions throughout Traherne's text as "more" and "infinite." However, it may be more revealing to examine a single work in terms of the structural coordination this particular supplement makes possible. I have again chosen the Dobell poems because here it seems to me the chain of supplements is most easily displayed, in part simply because this is the shortest work, in part because here the supplements are more narrowly controlled. I shall begin, then, with the following graphic outline of the sequence.

The exterior columns identify, by poem number and line reference, all occurrences of the overarching difference, empty/full; the interior columns suggest, again by poem reference, the range of supplementary differences that function as both products and producers of that central opposition.

EMPTY	Supplementary	Differences	FULL
	1 silent dust/ chaos	speaking brighter regions	
	2 concealed	revealed	(2:32) full of bliss (3:14) full of immortality (3:18) filled with joy
	4 outward	inward things	(4:8) full of light
(5:51) empty powers (5:64) empty intelligence	5 devoid/ unbodied	prepared	
	11 inner temple speaker dumb	outer noise world speaks	(11:40) full of deities (11:48) filled w/pleasure
(12:30) an empty voice	12 inward work men's words	outward work heaven's words	
			(15) "Fulnesse"
(16:77) empty spaces	16 custom	Nature	(16:75) filled with joy
	17 false	true	
	20 dressed metaphor ornament toys	naked true worth true value real joys	
(23:40) empty is accurst	23 from received	into returned	(23:8) the places full

(23:55) empty purse			
	25 from Him	to Him	
	26 needs/ wants	complete treasures	
(27:64) empty dross/loss	27 despised, defied, denied, undeified refuse Him	extold, exalted, glorified receive Him	(27:53) full esteem
	28 man gives Nothing	God gives All	
			(29:34) fill the Cup
	30 distant	present	(30:26) fill the soul
	32 fades away	displays	
	34 Nothing worst/misery	All best/bliss	(34:42) fill hemisphere
(35:33) empty things	34 material toys	heavenly joys	(35:14) full of groans (35:51) full proprietie (36:epig) (36:34) fills worlds (36:74) fills worlds (36:75) fills us (36:76) drink our fill (36:82) full of joy
	37 goodness given	blessedness received	

God fulfills himself by emptying Himself	Man empties himself in fulfilling himself

We have already seen, in the preceding chapter, that the Dobell sequence tries to reenact the development, the maturing process, of the Christian self from a point of imagined emptiness to one of anticipated fullness. What we did not show in the earlier treatment was the operation by which that fullness comes to serve as necessary but exorbitant supplement to the self Traherne represents. Here, then, two arguments can be made. The first is that the economic value of fullness depends not only upon its structural relation to a haunting and fearful emptiness, but more centrally upon the systematic exchange of secondary supplements. If we conceive the imagined "self" of the sequence as occupying the exact center of our graph, then we might say the appearance of that self occurs only by means of the structural differences that name it. Silent/speaking, outward/inward, toys/joys, absence/presence—these differences both situation and evaluate the self to whom they are applied. That we are dealing with a situational self, that is, with a self that is conceived and fashioned out of structural relations, can be seen in the fact that any of these differences might be reversed with no harm at all. Feared emptiness can be imagined as either external or internal, and the privilege accorded nakedness or ornamented depends solely upon the perspective. The sundry differences are merely additions the self accumulates and appropriates in order to present itself to itself. But—and this is the crucial point—the economic value of these supplements is registered in the surplus that fullness names. Fullness is precisely that imagined/desired excess which itself accrues and accumulates as surplus all other terms of supplementary value. The economy of this exchange is systematic and structural, as the remainder of this chapter will show.

The second argument will have to account for the more concentrated and dominant occurrences of fullness at the end of the sequence. I do not mean simply that the self grows progressively more "full" or that Traherne stages that "fulfillment" or maturation by increasingly emphasizing the central term. Whether that operation is at work in the last four poems or not, fullness has, by this point, deferred itself, transposed itself onto a different stage and into another register. This is to say that the supplement of the supplements that fullness is must now be subjected to further supplementation or cease to function as a coin of desired economic exchange. What we have at the end of the Dobell sequence, I believe, is a perfect illustration of Derrida's law of *différance*: fullness is of value because it enables the self to empty itself; emptying itself, the self makes fullness more desirable. Without the doubled direction of these exchanges, value as such could not accrue and the self would be emptied of all desire. But desire continually reproduces and reenacts itself exactly as the self does, and thus must continually hollow out its own center in order to set itself forth as the object of its own desire.

Having suggested what my graph implies, I would immediately add two caveats. The supplementary differences that I have identified here are certainly not the only ones present in the sequence, nor are they always as clearly charted within a given poem as they are on the graph. I have selected only those differences that seem to me to operate consistently across the whole of Traherne's work, but there is no economic totality or systematic plenitude here. Fullness, in fact, could not serve at all as the supplementary excess if we could exactly tell its component coins. In terms of an earlier argument, we could say that each and any difference is but a metonymic synecdoche of all differences and consequently of *différance* itself staged here as empty/full.[67] Of more concern at the present would be to understand that the graph can only suggest the economic operation; it cannot recapture or present it. The chain of supplementation is not a narrative progress that we can reproduce. That limitation aside, there is still no question that such a chain is operative here, and that it links difference to difference as supplement to supplement in economic production and exchange.

Both "The Salutation" and "Wonder" record the astonishment with which the child first experiences the sensible world, but already *différance* is announced and registered along a doubled chain. The past is represented variously as abyss, chaos, nothingness; the tongue is silent; limbs and bodily parts do not appear. Against that re-collected prospect, the present world is a "Glorious Store" and "Brighter Regions"; as this world speaks to the previously silent tongue ("And evry Thing that I did see / Did with me talk"), discrete organs begin to appear—lips, hands, eyes, ears. What "appears" as well is the difference of inner and outer, an interior world within and an exterior world without the imagined or reimagined self. And that difference is projected forward in time as re-collection grounds itself upon the necessary temporal stages that make it possible: future oppressions, tears, cries, envy, properties, and avarice are still "conceald"; presently past joys, beauty, welfare, and wonders are "reveald." Although the central term has not yet been announced, the child's entry into experience is already enacting itself upon an imagined emptiness which, by means of these secondary differences, now produces the first supplementary fullness: "The State of Innocence / And Bliss . . . / Did fill my Sence."

"Eden" and "Innocence" expand the initial differences in terms of a self divided against itself. That is, by imagining the self as "Divided" from the vanities, sloth, errors, and sins of other men, the child re-collects himself as "undivided"—full of immortality. Thus freed from, by having expelled and thrown outside the self, all consequences of sin, the imagination is also free to accumulate fullness:

> Joy, Pleasure, Beauty, Kindness, Glory, Lov,
> Sleep, Day, Life, Light,
> Peace, Melody, my Sight,
> My Ears and Heart did fill, and freely mov.
> (ll. 14–17)

In "Innocence" the child's soul is "full of Light," not because no darkness exists, but because darkness and its concomitants (stain, spot, shade, guilt, and night) have again been split off and cast outside. Inner and outer, along with presence and absence, come to supplement the earlier revealed/concealed within the field of imaginable fullness. In other words, the paradoxical law of divisionary *différance* generates a supplementary fullness over and above the fullness originally conceived. Each further and particularized difference is registered as a metonymic value produced and appropriated by fullness at a higher economic stage.

The differences and divisions within which the self has thus far imagined itself constitute a doubled problem.[68] On the one hand, the desired fullness must be conceived as distinct from an originary and feared emptiness. On the other hand, fullness itself is fractured, for sin and darkness and fraud also fill the soul. In order to imagine fullness as value, then, the self must cast outside of itself (into its past or future, for example) such fullness as would darken or taint desire. Fullest fullness—supplement of a supplement—is fullness divided, fullness registered as *différance*.

It is, perhaps, the sudden awareness of the *différance* that insinuates itself within fullness that forces Traherne, in "The Preparative," to return to a different conception of emptiness. The intention to "becom a Child again" at the conclusion of "Innocence" is obviously an attempt to empty the self of all negative fullness. What remains, then, is a fuller emptiness, emptiness now staged not as an object of fear or scorn but as an object of desire. "Pure Empty Powers . . . did nothing loath" and intelligence is "Empty and . . . Quick," disentangled, naked, unpossessed, disengaged. What is most interesting here is that emptiness as such is first recorded in the sequence not as the other of fullness but as the same. This means, I think, that the larger project by which empty and full are identified as poles of economic exchange is always already captivated by the urge to restage difference as a principle of geometric registration, a kind of interest that accrues within each term once divided in itself and between the terms as differing from each other. Differing and deferring, the supplement is already supplement of its own supplementarity, "appears," therefore, only as the desired object of its own "Endless Ey." And that Eye, the gaze by which and in which the Eye appears to itself as itself, is already an Eye differing from its gaze. It must thus "retire," defer itself within the difference of empty/full, in order to "admire" itself as "all."

In terms of the supplementary chain I am trying to follow here, the next several poems break into two groups. "The Instruction" and "The Vision" are generally oriented toward the opening of the sequence and their broad differences are primarily extensions of ones already announced. Thus the contingents and transients of "Instruction" and the woes of men in "Vision" are conceived in terms of a worldly order and beauty or a solipsistic bliss. In effect, these are much the same antinomies already seen in "Eden" and "Innocence": a pure self imagines itself as full by imagining all others as empty.

This, of course, is an impossible point of view to sustain, for others are also full—but full of opprobrium. Fullness as such, therefore, becomes a fragile, even dangerous, investment and must be reconstituted in its economy. "The Rapture" begins that task by altering the differential terms. Here it is not the relation between the self and other men, but between a "magnified" I and its creator—in short, between the self and the Other, not others. Deferring the negative fullness of others by differentiating it from the positive fullness of God, fullness-as-value can be reconstituted and reappropriated as an object of desire.

"The Improvment" structures its economy in terms already familiar to us: "Tis *more* to recollect, then make." "Recollect" is a word whose ambiguity must not be evaded by transcription, for it points not only to God's (or man's) uniting or conjoining all power, wisdom, and goodness in one observer, but also the ability of the self to "think" the beauty and the glory of the world by recalling its creator. The exchange the word incites, then, makes both producer and product "more *Great*" and "more *Divine*." By the end of the poem the trinity of divine powers has itself been supplemented by the excess recollection promises: in the phrase, "Power, Wisdom, Goodness and Felicity," felicity names the surplus of economic interest accrued and accumulated.

"The Approach" continues to stage the difference between the self and the Other, man and God, by questioning value itself as the necessary object of desire. God woos and sues, but man remains care-less because he has not yet imagined himself as an economic object. He thus slights both his lover and himself because he disregards the exchange for which the Other prepared him and in which the Other employs and needs him. Here, in effect, Traherne reconceives man's originary dumbness: born of nothing, as nothing, silent, disregarding, while all around him shines in its plenty and speaks in concernment and glory. "Dumnesse" makes such differences explicit and consequently sets the stage for the sequence's next enactment of fullness.

The registration of fullness in this poem is a complex interweaving of several of the metonymic differences already charted. The poem opens by distinguishing between "*Mortal Words*" and immortal thoughts, between, that is, those external objects which corrupt, deprave, and disturb man's "Speechless" meditation of "inward Things." To be "in himself profoundly Busied" is to be "Distinct and Separat from all Men" in order to be in and to enjoy all "the World my Self alone." The condition of the self is here the same curiously distanced one we have noted earlier: only by enacting itself within a scene of radical difference from other men can the self produce itself as valuable. And yet that "Business Serious" in which the ostensibly isolated self immediately engages is, of paradoxical necessity, "to see all Creatures full." The exchange that now occurs is charted by a sequence of verbs syntactically structured by synecdochic supplementarity: to see, to admire, to be pleased with, to enjoy, to feel, and to inherit, thus "to be fild" oneself, to fill the self, "with Everlasting Pleasure." Dumbness, in short, is a closed textualizing of the self or a staging of the self as a closed and hence protected field. Emptied of words, of mortality, full of itself and filling itself, this text is opened in the final thirty lines of the poem to betrayal from the outside, the external: by noise, by wounding words, by invisible but hurtful vanities.

"Silence," the following poem, represents the self as divided by the differences such "*Mortal Words*" convey. The initial registration of difference here is hierarchical: "The Inward Work is the Supreme," "the High and only Work." Again Traherne charts this work in synecdochic infinitives: to view, to admire, to rejoice, to sing, to see, to prize, to love. Opposed to such work are those "outward Busy Acts": building churches, administering justice, preaching peace, visiting the sick. Internal and external divide, in other words, even ostensibly virtuous actions. Only the work within is privileged, because only that is "better than an Empty Voice." The voice, words, language itself can always be supplemented, magnified and enriched by the self staging itself as interior. Whatever dreams such a self may encounter or experience in the external world, interiorly "it is far more." It is this conception, I think, that always lies behind Traherne's need to imagine the self as "an Endless Sphere / Like God himself." Although that "like" defers to an irreducible *différance*, the image of the sphere inscribes the Other within and in the simplicity of that inscription protects itself against the pollution that threatens from without. As Traherne says in "Eden," "Simplicitie / Was my Protection."

And yet, as we have come to expect, no protection is ever possible and all simplicities are betrayed by originary *différance*. Thus the "Naked Simple Life" that "My Spirit" proposes as ground or origin of the self cannot be thought or sensed outside of the play and exchange of *différance* as such. Or, in terms more suitable to the present discussion, the "Naked Simple" self cannot appropriate any desired value outside of the supplementary exchanges of various differences. "My Spirit," then, repeats all of the previous binary terms in order to re-present and re-presence them as supplemental freight, as interest by which value supplements itself. Essence/act, sense/substance, thing/thought, distance/presence, elsewhere/here, external/internal, nothing/all—whatever difference Traherne takes up is appropriated "by Dame Natures" supplementary "Law" as an infinite self "Dilat[ing] it self even in an Instant, and / [in] an Indivisible Centre." That that appropriation accumulates and is apprehended as value is obvious in the poem's final stanza, in which the self, now firmly returned to the present tense, reacts in admiring wonder at the "Wondrous Self" it has enacted before itself, jubilantly captivated by, as we have shown earlier, the gaze that exalts and "prizes" as it perceives.

As a consequence of that enactment, the poem entitled "Fullnesse" announces both the supplementary facts and the supplemented value of the self, but it also opens the necessity of further appropriation. As a supplement always already, fullness as such is only a condition or occasion for further desire: the soul is still "kept alive" by being "Thirsty"; perfect being is an "Act of Seeing" grounded upon a fearful failure of "Enjoying"; and the "Spark" that makes the soul an "Endless Benefit" must also "encourage" it to rise, dilate, extend and expand itself. Fullness, that is, articulates both promise and its inevitable frustration, satisfaction and its inevitable failure. It marks, therefore, not so much "The Centre and the Sphere / Of . . . Delights" as the locus of desire. "Nature," the succeeding poem, must now accede to that desire and try to reconstruct the supplementarity within which it is caught.

The essential theme of "Nature" is how the centered but dilating soul/imagination inhabits the world in which it finds itself; but because habitation is inextricably bound to desire, the functions of inhabiting quickly expand to issues of appropriation and possession.

What "more" could imagination "encompass, and possess" and how does it impute value to its objects so as to appropriate that value to itself once it acquires them? As Traherne re-stages this imaginative activity he engages in a bit of Bachelardian topography:

> The Spaces fild were like a Cabinet
> Of Joys before me most Distinctly set:
> The Empty, like to large and Vacant Room
> For Fancy to enlarg in, and presume
> A Space for more . . .
> (ll. 75–79)

As Bachelard reminds us, an empty cabinet is inconceivable; cabinets, like chests, drawers, and wardrobes, are always full.[69] And their fullness is precisely of the sort that promises a rich adornment. Thus Traherne focuses not on particular objects, but on the principle which makes anything "so rich tis Worthy," and on the mechanisms by which things "twere enrichd." Emptiness or vacancy becomes only an incentive to such enrichment, the space of supplementary exchange. Imagination expands in such empty spaces in order to convert them into rare cabinets filled with invaluable treasures.

Out of the difference between "Things fals," forced and elaborate and "Things pure and true" and obvious, "Ease" continues the process of generating and appropriating supplementary value. Whereas earlier in the sequence "all Men" had to be excluded from the self in order to protect the self from their empty but polluting voices, here men are reappropriated as "Living Treasures" by which the self adorns and enriches itself. The exchange thus initiated is twice repeated in the poem:

> That all we see is ours, and evry One
> Possessor of the Whole . . .
>
> . . . .
>
> That all may Happy be, Each one most Blest,
> Both in Himself and others; all most High,
> While all by each, and each by all possest,
> Are intermutual Joys . . .
> (ll. 17–28)

Joys possessed become supplementary treasures subject to continual exchange, and each exchange supplements in turn the value that accrues. "Intermutuality," here roughly analogous to what Traherne elsewhere calls conversation and circulation, is the law of *différance* operating as supplementarity. "Speed" extends that operation. "The Usefull and the Precious Things" are quickly and easily known, but knowing them is not, in itself, an appropriation of their worth. Value is again a function of possession:

> The Sacred Objects did appear
> Most Rich and Beautifull, as well as mine . . .
>
> . . . .
>
> New all and mine.
> (ll. 23–27)

For me, to me, in me—each syntactic staging of the elementary self/Other or self/object difference articulates the economy by which the worth of another is subjected to appropriation by the simple supplementation of "and mine," the pronominal possessive annexing to itself whatever value the self conceives/perceives outside itself. "The Designe" completes this mini-drama of appropriation by imputing the supplementary operation to God himself, and thus both vindicating and validating its own action. The economy of possession is here licensed by the fact that the law of created *différance* has always already "preposesse[d] our Soul, and proves / The Caus of what it all Ways moves." "Being all possest / Even in that Way [of prepossession] is the Best."

"The Person," "The Estate," and "The Enquirie," although not specifically announced in the precise terms of an empty/full exchange, do prepare the ground for the sequence's next enactment of that exchange by distinguishing first between those "fals Ornaments" with which the self may dress itself and the true "Ornaments of Joy" that *are* the self. That distinction, in turn, allows Traherne, in "Enquirie," to re-present the self not as a valuing subject but as valued and hence valuable object. Both stages are necessary preludes to the communicative economy of "The Circulation."

At the center of this poem, Traherne states with epigrammatic terseness "Whatever's empty is accurst." And yet the conviction of that assertion is challenged by the surrounding lines. The ideas and images of the poem's opening richly beautify the mind/soul that receives them and which they subsequently fill precisely because that soul is initially empty. Similarly, unless something or someone has made man's "Empty Purs" full, he cannot subsequently enrich himself by disbursing his own riches. Circulation, then, is the economy of the empty/full exchange, each state valued as the necessary precondition and inciting of the other. Neither, in these terms, is valuable in and of itself; only in supplementary relation to the other does either accumulate worth within an exchange of excess or surplus. Receiving and giving, emptying and filling—or better, receiving in order to give and emptying in order to fill; giving in order to receive and filling in order to overflow and empty—this is the mechanics of circulatory supplementarity.

"Amendment" further describes this economy. The things that are mine are, by the supplementary logic already exposed, rich and sweet. But insofar as I use them by returning them to God they become "more Rich": "they more delight" "And sweeter be." My use, my acceptance of them as coins of an economic exchange, as excess or surplus that I can re-disburse, doth "refine, Exalt, Improve" them. Amendment, then, is economic increase, the production and appropriation of surplus value by the work of a supplementarity that always "Exceed[s] the End" to which that "Work so Wonderfull[y] doth tend." "The Demonstration," like "The Anticipation," adds more differences to this exchange: springs and fountains, origins and ends, things and evaluations, needs and wants, his and ours, essence and act. All, as we have come to expect, "are the very same" and "differ but in Name." Difference, however, is the necessary structuring of exchange by which that same "more value get[s]." As we noted in the preceding chapter, the irreducible ground of that exchange is self and Other:

> there could be no Worth at all
> In any Thing Material Great or Small
> Were not som Creature more Alive,
> Whence it might Worth Derive.
> (ll. 55–58)

Emptying and filling themselves with things—with the objects of the other's filling or emptying—self and Other accrue and appropriate all and any value.

"The Recovery" applies the economy of preceding poems to God himself. "To see us but receiv" His treasures is, to God, a "Beatifick Vision," because He then knows that He too is enjoyed and prized (in both senses). The thematic crux of the poem is the voluntary nature of man's receipt of God. If His treasure and Himself are enjoyed with "A free, Profound, and full Esteem," God is "repaid" and his desire is made "More Precious."[70] If they are not received, "All Gold and Silver is but Empty Dross," "but Loss," and even God himself is "despised and defied / Undeified almost." If the empty/full scheme of "The Recovery" charts the imaginative exchange by which God receives more than He gave, the economy of "Another" must necessarily invert that pattern to show that man is subject to the same law:

> Thy Lov is Nothing [by] it self, and yet
> So infinit is his, that he doth set
> A value infinit upon it.
> (ll. 33–35)

"What's aught but as 'tis valued," Troilus asks in an earlier moment of dramatic economics.[71] Traherne, though not so naive as Shakespeare's besotted lover, is nonetheless very close to his sense of value as an external supplement. To value God, to give value to God, is to receive "value infinit" in return. Worth is always dependent if not upon the rate then certainly upon the fact of that "return." Within the economy of exchange, where self and Other are inscribed within the logic of *différance*, "Tis Death . . . to be Indifferent." Indifference, that is, empties both self and Other; differential exchange, however, makes both full by supplementing each with the valuation of the other.

"Love" offers the next occasion of the empty/full registration in Traherne's text, but here, somewhat surprisingly, the context does not initially seem to involve an economy. Traherne imagines himself God's Ganymede:

> Or he comes down to me, or takes me up
> That I might be his Boy,
> And fill, and taste, and give, and Drink the Cup.
> (ll. 31–33)

In a text with remarkably few allusions to classical mythology this particular reference is all the more notable. My own sense is that behind this cup lies the entire operation of emptying and filling in order to accrue supplemental value, and that the cup, therefore, offers the first hint in the sequence of the ultimate object of exchange between man and God. As the sequence now turns inward to meditate upon the capacity of imaginative thought itself, this cup and the economy it incites serve as the "Object Infinit" to be both conceived and received. Not until the penultimate poem will the imagination prove equal to that task.

In order to make thought capable of understanding the supplemental economy within which man and God are bound, Traherne reemploys all the particular differences that have structured the sequence to this point. In "Thoughts I" the dialectical focus is on objects past and objects present, on objects within and those without, on the Eye confined and the imagination free. At issue is the imagination's power to re-produce and re-present, "As in a Mirror Clear," "Yesterdays-yet-present Blessedness." Such reproduction supplements the soul:

> Ye Thoughts and Apprehensions are
> The Heavenly Streams which fill the Soul with rare
> Transcendent Perfect Pleasures.
> (ll. 25–27)

"Thoughts II" subjects the temporal powers of "Thoughts I" to economic exchange. If thought is the "Quintessence" of all God wrought, it is also that

> Which we conceive,
> Bring forth, and Give,
> Yea and in which the Greater Value lurks.
> (ll. 4–6)

Precious and fragile because so precious, thought is both production and reproduction, presentation and representation of value both given and received. It is precisely because thought is always caught in that supplementary *différance* that it can represent for Traherne the operation of economic accumulation.

In "Thoughts III" Traherne further explores the *différance* within which imagination is bound: object and image, nothing and all, confined and free, the best or the worst of things, origin and end, product and producer. What is most crucial, however, is that thought is inextricably bound to desire: "what it self doth pleas a Thought may be." As both origin and end of desire, thought "fils the Hemisphere" and clothes itself with all accumulated treasure. Thought, in short, is the operation by which imagination enriches itself.

With that observation, Traherne returns to the urgencies of desire, to a self that conceives itself as "full of Groans" and as the potentially indifferent observer of "all these . . . poor and Empty Things." Things that were treasures earlier in the sequence are now stripped of value so that thought may reappropriate them as values. The objects themselves will not satisfy desire; only the "sense" of those objects can "dispence" value by the accumulation of "full Proprietie" or possession. That is, thoughts make objects "mine" and hence of value, convert "Dead Material Toys" to "Heavenly Joys."

"Thoughts IV" begins Traherne's final stage of registration by citing, as epigraph, one of his favorite Biblical passages, Psalm 16:[72]

> In thy Presence there is fulness
> of Joy, and at thy right hand there
> are Pleasures for ever more.

Surrounding and filling, God's glory converts all to blessing. Traherne conceives that glory as a stream that replenishes, enriches, and fulfills, and he comes finally to locate its source:

> Men are like Cherubims on either hand,
> Whose flaming Love by his Divine Command,
> Is made a Sacrifice to ours; which Streams
> Throughout all Worlds, and fills them all with Beams.
> We drink our fill, and take their Beauty in,
> While Jesus Blood refines the Soul from sin.
> (ll. 71–76)

Feeding on sacred self-presence, drinking our fill from God's overflowing cup, filling our souls with Christ's refining blood, man is filled with all the fullness of God. That fullness is specifically a conversion and its effects in Traherne's text are immediate and dramatic. The image of Christ as the winepress or the bunch of grapes that fills itself by emptying itself "prepares" the soul for the sacramental exchange, the circulation and the conversation, that "Goodness" dramatizes. Here, for the first time in the sequence, value, as economic product, expands far beyond the simple and single difference of self and Other to include all in an operation of giving and receiving that "multiplies" the worth of all at once and infinitely. Although Traherne does not here use the term, his subject now transcends the dialectic of emptiness and fullness by inscribing both within the exchange that is fulfillment.

My own language here betrays, however, the supplementary logic, because transcendence is precisely what does not occur. Fulfillment is merely the final registration of the supplement of the supplement, supplementarity doubling back upon itself in order to produce its own excess as value. We should thus read all such moments as full-fill-ment, as verbal act in the process of appropriating adjectival value in the hope of producing a nominal essence or condition. Interestingly, Traherne's most consistent use of the redoubled term, and here we must go outside the Dobell sequence, is almost invariably in the context of the law. Filled with all the fullness of God, man can then be fulfilled under the system of judicial exchange which tries to effect, within the constraints of an ultimate and authoritative law, a fixed ground of value beyond which no economy can progress: "It becometh us to fulfill all Righteousness" (*CE*, 72); "He that loveth another hath fulfilled the Law" (*CE*, 95); "The veracity of God obliged him to fulfill the Denunciation of the Sentence" (*CE*, 101); "Love is the fulfilling of the Law" (*CE*, 136); "Felicity . . . is hid in the fulfilling of God's Laws" (*CE*, 146); "In the love of every one, the concurrence [is] fulfilling the Law" (*CE*, 146); "[Modesty] fulfills the Law" (*CE*, 237); "The Rule of Trial shall be the fulfilling of its Laws" (*CE*, 241). The law in these passages is the economy and the boundary of the supplement, the operation of *différance* that structures all human thought and human interaction. And the logic of that law requires that the supplement replicate and duplicate itself in order to present and to possess itself as either fact or value. As with the notion of an infinite infinity, imagination here reaches its furthest limits by redoubling back upon itself. Transcendence of these limits is impossible and inconceivable: it would be, quite simply, an untenable violation of the law of the supplement.

Afterword

From what has been said, and from a perusal of the poems, the reader will be able clearly to perceive the object which I had in view: he will determine how far it has been attained; and, what is a much more important question, whether it will be worth attaining: and upon the decision of these two questions will rest my claim to the approbation of the public. —WILLIAM WORDSWORTH

I began this study with some general observations on the current state of critical practice, on the theoretical problems raised and evaded by various forms of historicism, and on the position of my own work in relation to those critical modes. In the course of the study itself, these issues have necessarily been relegated to implicit rather than explicit status, but in the few remaining pages I want to return to them in order to draw three conclusions about the present and future course of Renaissance criticism.

Part of my concern here is to clarify the claims this study has made, but I would also like to address another issue, namely that political and historical themes have become so insistent in the current Renaissance discourse (indeed, in those of virtually all periods) as to encourage, even at times to coerce, a wholesale condemnation of alternative methods and issues as socially irresponsible, intellectually naive, and historically unsound. The certainty and the force of such judgments need to be challenged—not only because the judgments themselves are wrong, but also because the rhetoric with which they are promoted threatens to tyrannize and terrorize an entire generation of critics. "If you want your work to count," the modern critic is being told, "to be taken seriously, or to have any significant impact on the general direction of literary studies, then you must 'do' New Historicism." The conclusions I make here are intended to challenge such critical prescriptions.

My first conclusion involves the issue of canonicity. Insofar as we could agree that Heidegger, Lacan, and Derrida articulate some of the central themes of the present historical moment and thus condition not only the subjects we expect to find in a work of literature, but also the ways in which we analyze literary treatments of those subjects, their applicability to Thomas Traherne constitutes a renewed claim for Traherne's place in the seventeenth-century canon. By the same token, or at the same time, the demonstration that the three moderns can illuminate thematic urgencies as well as structural organizations of a classical Renaissance text constitutes a claim for their continued central position in the canon of contemporary critical models.

The second argument posits that the similarities between the discourses of Traherne and the three moderns raise important questions about the extent to which the twentieth-century critique of Western metaphysics and logocentricity has escaped its own entanglements with the past. At stake here is our sense of modernity itself and the ways in which the thoughts and themes of Heidegger, Lacan, and Derrida are inextricably bound to historical prefigurations that must be underemphasized in order to establish the perception of novelty out of which any definition of the present arises. A corollary to this problem is the historical status of Heidegger, Lacan, and Derrida themselves. The dialogue constructed here may well suggest that the historical moment in which these three spoke on behalf of an interventionist discourse capable of dissociating the present from the past has now come to a definitive end.

The final conclusion concerns the future course of Renaissance criticism. By deliberately eliding crucial questions of difference —especially of the relations between the historical/cultural conditions that compel Traherne's analyses of being, the self, and a supplementary economy and those that motivate or shape the modern investigations of the same issues—this study should serve to reopen the question of the conditions under which a clearer historical sense might begin to be constructed. What I mean here is that an understanding of historical difference can arise only out of a sharpened insight into historical continuity. But it is an open question whether any single critical approach is capable of working both sides of this historicist task. For that reason I would argue the necessity of a new critical pluralism as the most pragmatic way of identifying both our historical attachments to and our historical alienation from the Renaissance texts we treat.

Each of these points can only be sketched in these few pages, but together they raise important questions for Renaissance criticism in general. If I am correct in arguing that the current predominance of a so-called historicist agenda has actually dehistoricized Renaissance literature by rendering history itself as an unexamined and unproblematic concept, then it seems to me that the present need is to articulate the critical conditions that would encourage a reproblematizing of history as such or at least our self-assured sense of what an historical criticism really is. Here, I think, it is not so much a question of appropriating a particular modern critical theory to an analysis of prior texts as trying to establish a kind of historical triangulation between our own contemporary situation and the doubled attachments to which that situation commits us. That is, we must more carefully thematize and theorize the difficulties of keeping separate yet related two distinct pasts (here Traherne's and the three moderns'), of describing the affiliations each has with our historical present, and of recognizing the kinds of necessary blindness about our own historical alienation both of those tasks seem to require.

Let me return, then, to the question of canonicity. In an important sense, the canon is established on the basis of accessibility. Whether we are discussing a literary text or a theoretical position, our determination of what is historically "central" or "essential" is largely dependent upon whether it is accessible to present concerns and present modes of thinking. By showing that Traherne thinks consistently and seriously about problems of being, desire, and supplementarity, this study has made his writing not only accessible to a certain line of contemporary critical discourse, but essential to such historical generalizations as that criticism makes about the seventeenth century. In the same way, the fact that the application of Heidegger, Lacan, and Derrida to Traherne reveals important aspects of his thought and writings not seen before makes the three moderns also more accessible to current interpretive practice. Obviously I do not mean to assert a particular novelty to "deconstructing" a Renaissance text (and I do not think that is what I have done anyway), for criticism has been doing that for some time now. What I do mean is that the line of inquiry instigated by Heidegger, Lacan, and Derrida forces into the open the problematic historical relations between the Renaissance text and our capacities or urgencies to make that text accessible to a modern reader. And it does so without focusing on any particular historical or political themes, but simply by making certain canonical claims about past and present concerns.

Let me put this argument in more pointed terms. If the ideas and critical methods of someone like Michel Foucault make accessible and noteworthy the negotiations that certain female writers—Mary Sidney, for example—must conduct with the shapes and forms of Elizabethan patriarchy and thus reopen the question of their position within the sixteenth-century canon, that fact is no more nor less definitive of an historical recovery than Lacan's disclosure of Trahernean desire. And yet, for the New Historicist, Foucault is the *necessary* context within which canonical questions must be posed. I have implied throughout the present study that the line of Heidegger, Lacan, and Derrida is an equally necessary context. But the "necessity" of either case is an a priori assumption, not an argued certainty. It means only that we have made a choice of and a judgment about particular kinds of questions as relevant to present literary concerns. Such questions, we assume, provide entry into a given field of contemporary interest and thus marshal a certain persuasive force to our canonical claims. But they also exclude other kinds of questions, especially those that would contest or challenge our very notions of what in the Renaissance text is predominant, interesting, or worthy of contemporary attention. To this extent, it seems to me that any interpretive act must assume a level of transhistorical continuity at the same time that it elides issues of historical discontinuity. Whether that is a reasonable assessment or not, the more important question is the extent to which any single critical approach can address both past concerns and modern ones, both historical continuities and discontinuities at the same time and in the same frame of reference.

Canonicity, therefore, is one theoretical issue in which the convergence of past text and present interests allows the registration of historical sameness and difference to be observed. Yet the very moment in which a claim is made for inclusion or exclusion of a certain writer from the canon, historical certainty eludes us because that claim will have to assume an historical homogeneity. This is what I take the urgency to keep canon questions open to mean, for only by foregrounding the entire issue of literary or critical canonicity can we keep open the question of history as such. At a certain level, all criticism is overtly or covertly making canonical claims—either attempting to solidify a given writer's or text's status within the canon by redefining its affiliations with present concerns, or challenging that status by demonstrating the work is inaccessible to those concerns. In either case, and implicitly or explicitly, criticism is making assumptions about its own historical moment.

I have assumed throughout this study that particular themes of being, identity construction, desire, and supplementarity are indexes of the present historical and critical era. The New Historicist would insist that those indexes are themes of power, gender, and subjectification. Neither assumption, however, is self-evident, and both would have to be argued afresh if a compelling sense of history or historical situation is our aim. Without challenging the idea that that is, in fact, one of our central goals, I would nonetheless propose that accomplishing this goal can only be by means of discrete critical activities which, for want of better classifications, I would call the partial recovery of historical continuities, the partial discovery of historical discontinuities, and a theoretical investigation of what both may tell us about our own historical situation. What I have urged above as a critical pluralism is a pragmatic concession to the fact that no one approach to Renaissance literature can hope to accomplish all of these tasks and that if a clearer sense of historicity is our joint end, then we must be willing to accept the consequence that ours is a cooperative venture in which no one critical mode can have priority over any other or any greater claims to doing "historical" work.

This argument can be clarified, perhaps, by my second point. There can be no question any longer that a significant portion of our own historical sense has been shaped by what I earlier called the interventionist discourse of Heidegger, Lacan, and Derrida (as well, of course, as by that of a number of other theorists and philosophers). By so thoroughly and disconcertingly critiquing the normative tradition of Western metaphysics, that discourse has succeeded in articulating a difference between concerns and pressures of the present historical moment and those that preceded it. My own sense, however, is that this intervention has had its greatest impact on literary theory, and that as Heidegger, Lacan, and Derrida became normative agents of literary interpretation, then, by definition, they lost their interventionist capacity to keep historical questions at the forefront of our concerns. Over the last ten years, the philosophical issues these three have raised have become less urgent than the need to replicate with specific Renaissance texts the kinds of deconstructive analyses they conducted upon those of Aristotle, Plato, Rousseau, Hegel, and a few others. And though this activity has certainly proved the usefulness of Heideggerian, Lacanian, and Derridean terms in revealing hitherto unacknowledged and perhaps unreadable aspects of the Renaissance texts in question—and thereby answered those who only a few years ago could charge that modern theory has little to contribute to exegetical and critical *praxis*—it has also in tangible ways domesticated and reappropriated what had been disorienting in their thought. The resulting security—some would call it simply a loss of a sense of novelty—may have led, in part, to their apparent replacement by such figures as Foucault. But as Foucault too is now primarily an enabling agent of specific critical practice, his own capacities for intervention will also have to be reevaluated.

Obviously, new studies of Heidegger, Lacan, and Derrida are being published constantly, Lacan's work is still not totally available, and Derrida continues to write. And yet the signs seem very clear that their interventionist moment is over. My own appropriation of them is but one of those signs. Others that come to mind are such diverse present discourses as "Against Theory" polemics, the New Historicist obsession with "culture-specific practices," and even reader-response or speech-act criticisms. If I am correct in seeing behind these various activities a widespread disaffection with and resistance to theory and a concurrent demand for pragmatic historical specificity, then it seems to me that an altogether different kind of work will be required to retrieve any of the modern thinkers for interventionist service in a more self-critical historicism.

Indeed, I would like to think that one effect of the work I have done here is to reopen the necessity of bringing Heidegger, Lacan, and Derrida into a more active historicist dialogue with others of our contemporary begetters. One step in this direction would be to subject Traherne to a Foucauldian approach and to ask what more that approach will tell us about either his situation or ours that mine has not? Would that "more" be more "historical," and in what ways? My own suspicion is that a fuller sense of the historical could be obtained only by refocusing both inquiries upon a totally different level of analysis—say that in which the Heideggerian, Lacanian, Derridean, and Foucauldian readings are evaluated not by how effectively they seem to resolve historical questions (continuities *or* discontinuities), but rather by how effectively they raise and problematize such questions. At this level of investigation (and I mean nothing "hierarchical" by speaking here of a *level* of inquiry), it is hard to see how criticism could avoid a considerable reinvestment in and recommitment to theory of all kinds—critical, literary, philosophical, psychological, political, and historical. Questions of this nature simply cannot be settled on the grounds of historical specificity.

I have here broached my final point about the future of Renaissance criticism, but I want to put that argument once more in polemical terms. As I said in chapter one, the claims of both the old and the new historicisms to historical recovery are unsupportable. History is never recoverable in the sense that these methodologies seem to imply or assume, and thus there is no legitimate reason to privilege their strategies, figures, or propositions over any other critical approach—even if we accept some sense of history as our primary goal or interest. This is not to deny that both historicisms have made significant and even brilliant contributions to our general understanding of the conditions of literary production in the Renaissance and of discrete Renaissance texts. But it is to deny that only those methodologies that focus on blatantly historical themes are doing historicist work. "Always historicize," exhorts one of my most widely read and respected colleagues, and his injunction has been accepted wholeheartedly by most Renaissance critics writing today. But there are at least two questions that should be raised about this exhortation. How to historicize, and what tools, models, and methods are best adapted to doing so, is perhaps the easier of the two. Why historicize and what that compulsion means or tells us about our present pressures and needs is no less urgent and no more capable of hasty resolution. Only by holding both questions in full view and by developing a multiplicity of critical approaches by which to force them to interrogate each other will we be able to keep in play the entire issue of the historicity of any particular moment or text, ours or the Renaissance's.

I would conclude, therefore, by suggesting a specific theoretical agenda for future Renaissance criticism. Recognizing that individual approaches are suitable for differing kinds of literary questions, we need to develop a fuller conceptual model of exactly what each one might contribute to a more comprehensive historical understanding of Renaissance literature and of our historical relations to it. As an initial step, we need to subject all of our current approaches to more open theoretical inquiry. Neither old historicism nor new, neither old New Criticism nor new can be exempt from this return to theory itself or from the need to make explicit their particular theoretical assumptions. The pragmatic pluralism I have suggested above might represent a second essential step. By sketching the theoretical arguments for such a pluralism and by carefully distinguishing it from the critical pluralism promoted in certain utopian quarters in the 1950s and 1960s, we should be better equipped to understand the legitimacy of the claims any one approach is justified in making, the particular field of inquiry each is appropriate for treating, and the full scope of the historical project to which each is, in its own way, contributing. To the extent that these two steps would resituate current critical *praxis* within the broader concerns of literary, critical, and historical theory, they should promote a clearer sense of the complexities of the tasks we set for ourselves and of the historical challenges continually posed to us by the literature we have chosen to study. More importantly, perhaps, such a recommitment to theory will force us to keep ever before us the often unacknowledged assumptions that enable our more pragmatic acts of critical interpretation.

Not everyone, of course, will be eager to return Renaissance discourse to theorizing about its own agendas, or willing to participate in these kinds of arguments. My own sense, however, is that a continued resistance to such theorizing will preempt any rigorous interrogation of our historical assumptions and presuppositions, and thereby render suspect any conclusions we may draw about either the conditions of Renaissance literary texts or our texts of the Renaissance. Here I would certainly agree with the New Historicist demand that we engage more actively in questioning our own methodologies; I disagree only that a confession of self-consciousness about those methodologies is sufficient. If we are serious about critiquing our own assumptions and methods—and that is an injunction our present historical moment makes inescapable—we will have to bring each interpretive approach into conscious and critical dialogue with competing or alternative approaches, and thereby articulate more honestly the capacities and the limitations of all. Such a dialogue will inevitably be grounded in theory—not a theorizing that floats above questions of historicity, but one that is centered directly on those questions. Until that dialogue is established, our various notions of history itself, as well as those about which methodologies are historical, will be not only partial, but potentially self-deceiving.

NOTES

JOURNAL ABBREVIATIONS

CQ	*The Cambridge Quarterly*
ELH	*English Literary History*
ELR	*English Literary Renaissance*
HLQ	*Huntington Library Quarterly*
MP	*Modern Philology*
N&Q	*Notes and Queries*
PBSA	*Papers of the Bibliographical Society of America*
PLL	*Papers on Language and Literature*
PMLA	*Publications of the Modern Language Association of America*
RN	*Renaissance News*
SP	*Studies in Philology*
UTQ	*University of Toronto Quarterly*

ONE. TRAHERNE IN DIALOGUE

1 While the charge of inaccessibility can be found in criticism of both Traherne's prose and his poetry, it is more often leveled at the verse: "Traherne's formal, disciplined poems lack the accessibility, the immediacy of his *Centuries of Meditations*. It is as if the poetic forms were a barrier to the content and we, his readers, can seldom penetrate that barrier" (Elizabeth Jennings, "The Accessible Art: A Study of Thomas Traherne's *Centuries of Meditations*," *Twentieth Century* 167 [1960]: 141.).

2 The most important of the structural studies are Louis L. Martz, *The Paradise Within* (New Haven: Yale University Press, 1964); A. L. Clements, *The Mystical Poetry of Thomas Traherne* (Cambridge: Harvard University Press,

1969); and John Malcolm Wallace, "Thomas Traherne and the Structure of Meditation," *ELH* 25 (1958): 78–89.

3 See especially Douglas R. Jordan, *The Temple of Eternity* (Port Washington, N.Y.: Kennikat, 1972); Rosalie L. Colie, "Thomas Traherne and the Infinite: The Ethical Compromise," *HLQ* 21 (1957): 69–82; and her subsequent chapter on Traherne, "Affirmations in the Negative Theology: The Infinite," in *Paradoxia Epidemica* (Princeton: Princeton University Press, 1966).

4 Clements, in *The Mystical Poetry*, identifies seven major groups of image-symbols: eye, sphere, sun, mirror, king, dwelling place, fountain (p. 44); Alison J. Sherrington, *Mystical Symbolism in the Poetry of Thomas Traherne* (St. Lucia, Australia: University of Queensland Press, 1970), also finds seven: senses, light, water, space, child, king, and marriage.

5 Gladys I. Wade, *Thomas Traherne* (Princeton: Princeton University Press, 1944), 3. At times, of course, this presumed or assumed felicity has been the object of critical censure, as in this comment by Carol Marks: "There is a certain naivete about all this [the "Church's Year-Book"]; it is too simple. All we need do is love 'Simple, Naked Souls,' recognize the true worth of things, and all will be well. . . . In the end, that simplicity diminishes our faith in Traherne's sincere but facile professions. . . . His conviction of man's goodness can inspire us to admiration, perhaps to envy, but not to assent. Opposed in his own day by the theology of Original Sin, Traherne's joyful optimism crashes today against the Berlin Wall, the Vietnamese war" ("Traherne's Church's Year-Book," *PBSA* 60 [1966]: 71–72). See Malcolm M. Day's response to this charge in *Thomas Traherne* (Boston: Twayne Publishers, 1982), 5. Perhaps the most thoroughgoing analysis of Traherne in such blissful and untroubled terms is by Sharon Cadmon Seelig in *The Shadow of Eternity* (Lexington: University of Kentucky Press, 1981), but see also Clements, *The Mystical Poetry*, 180, and Willis Barnstone, "Two Poets of Felicity: Thomas Traherne and Jorge Guillen," *Books Abroad* 42 (1968): 14.

6 *Rethinking Intellectual History: Texts, Contexts, Language* (Ithaca: Cornell University Press, 1983), 14. The extent to which old historicism takes this "detour" is clear even if we assume that Traherne's writings take pains to avoid their own historicity. If they seem to stand, or are presented by Traherne as standing, outside and above contemporary political and theological controversies, we still have not explained this feature: what urgencies require and what gestures mark the apparent historical estrangement? Insofar as that work remains undone, Traherne's text, even on the old historicist's terms, has not really been read.

7 Malcolm Day's recent Twayne study tries to begin this task by offering, in the opening chapters, information that should prove extremely fruitful for further exploration of Traherne in his social, political, and theological contexts. Among other studies that at least point to the general perameters of a New Historical context, see Stanley Stewart's chapter on *Roman Forgeries* in *The Expanded Voice: The Art of Thomas Traherne* (San Marino: Huntington Library, 1970); the several essays by Carol L. Marks, especially "Thomas

Traherne and Cambridge Platonism," *PMLA* 81 (1966): 521–34, and "Traherne's Church's Year-Book"; Sharon C. Seelig's "The Origins of Ecstasy: Traherne's 'Select Meditations,'" *ELR* 9 (1979): 419–31; and Allan Pritchard, "Traherne's 'Commentaries of Heaven,'" *UTQ* 53 (1983): 1–35.

8 "Renaissance Literary Studies and the Subject of History," *ELR* 16 (1986): 8.

9 *After The New Criticism* (Chicago: Chicago University Press, 1980), xiii–xiv.

10 This essay appears in *Literary Theory / Renaissance Texts*, ed. Patricia Parker and David Quint (Baltimore: Johns Hopkins University Press, 1986), 303–40.

11 Two signs of this assumed "objectivity" are the consistent recourse to the definite rather than the indefinite article ("the" rather than "a" context) and a concurrent silence on other, alternative contexts into which the work in question might be situated.

12 *Tropics of Discourse: Essays in Cultural Criticism* (Baltimore: Johns Hopkins University Press, 1978), 89. Compare LaCapra: "*The* context, in the sense desired by Janik and Toulmin, does not exist. The search for it is a quest for a will-o'-the-wisp generated by a questionable theory of meaning. The context itself is a text of sorts; it calls not for stereotypical, ideological 'descriptions' but for interpretation and informed criticism. It cannot become the occasion for a reductive reading of texts. By contrast, the context itself raises a problem analogous to that of 'intertextuality.' For the problem in understanding context—and a fortiori the relation of context to text—is a matter of inquiry into the interacting relationships among a set of more or less pertinent contexts. Only this comparative process itself creates a 'context' for a judgment that attempts to specify the relative importance of any given context" (*Rethinking Intellectual History*, 95–96).

13 "The New Historicism in Renaissance Studies," *ELR* 16 (1986): 19.

14 *Rewriting the Renaissance: The Discourses of Sexual Difference in Early Modern Europe*, ed. Margaret W. Ferguson, Maureen Quilligan, and Nancy J. Vickers (Chicago: University of Chicago Press, 1986).

An anonymous press reader objected to this line of questioning by arguing that "Robert Filmer's *Patriarcha* alone would establish" patriarchy as an historical context of the Renaissance. The *Patriarcha*, however, was written between 1635 and 1642, and not published until 1680, when it was ridiculed by Locke. Belated and contested as it is, I think it overhasty to assume it "establishes" an ideological context in existence eighty or ninety years earlier. The more important issue, however, is what conditions or facts are necessary to establish any given text as articulating an ideological context.

15 I say "paradoxically" because it is precisely on the basis of such blind spots that the New Historicism questions the constructions of the old historicism. That it is enabled by blind spots of its own is a condition rarely acknowledged. To this extent, at least, the claims of critical self-consciousness or awareness seem to me highly exaggerated. I do not mean that any of us is free of a certain blindness, only that a theoretical position that claims such freedom is open to charges of self-deception.

16 *Rethinking Intellectual History*, 35–36.

17 See "The Countess of Pembroke and the Art of Dying," in *Women in the Middle Ages and the Renaissance*, ed. Mary Beth Rose (Syracuse: Syracuse University Press, 1986), 207–26; and "The Cooke Sisters: Attitudes toward Learned Women in the Renaissance," in *Silent But for the Word: Tudor Women as Patrons, Translators, and Writers of Religious Works*, ed. Margaret P. Hannay (Kent: Kent State University Press, 1985), 107–25.

18 "Renaissance Literary Studies," 6, 7.

19 Montrose sees Jonathan Dollimore and Alan Sinfield as the most obvious representatives of the British orientation (Ibid., 7).

20 "The New Historicism," 16–17.

21 (New York: Longman, 1986).

22 "Struggling into Discourse: The Emergence of Renaissance Women's Writing," in *Silent but for the Word*, 256.

23 "The New Historicism," 18–19.

24 "Renaissance Literary Studies," 5–6.

25 *English Poetry of the Sixteenth Century*, 11, 29.

26 That I feel compelled to take up the question of history at all is but the most blatant sign of the pressure the academy exerts on my own choices.

27 Despite their individual differences, the kind of works I have in mind here are Jonathan Goldberg's *Voice Terminal Echo* (New York: Methuen, 1986); Victoria Kahn's "Humanism and the Resistance to Theory," in *Literary Theory / Renaissance Texts*, 379–96; and Charles Whitney's *Francis Bacon and Modernity* (New Haven: Yale University Press, 1986).

28 Obviously, at one level of critical choice, my appropriation of Heidegger, Lacan, and Derrida is no different, methodologically, from the New Historicist's appropriation of Foucault. What is different, however, is that I have tried to bring my "moderns" into more open and active dialogue with the Renaissance text being studied and thus kept *their* historical assumptions and presuppositions in constant view. My own sense is that the New Historicism would benefit by more openly thematizing its Foucauldian commitments and by analyzing more rigorously the presuppositions such commitments require.

29 This is not a hypothetical reader I posit here for the sake of argument, for this challenge was issued by my own "best" reader and colleague, Wallace Jackson. I am both pleased and obligated to record here the debt I owe to his criticism.

30 LaCapra, *Rethinking Intellectual History*, 66.

31 Ibid., 50.

32 Ibid., 18.

33 "The Authentic Discourse of the Renaissance," *Diacritics* 10 (1980): 81.

34 The controversy over the supposed "turn" in Heidegger's career is well known, but I have adopted the pragmatic solution of George Steiner in *Martin Heidegger* (New York: Viking Press, 1979), 3.

35 I say this despite the commendable efforts by Malcolm Day, by Carol L.

Marks and George R. Guffey in their introduction to the edition of *Christian Ethicks* (*CE*) (Ithaca: Cornell University Press, 1968), and by Stanley Stewart in *The Expanded Voice*. Further source-analogue studies of the kind represented in these three works might demonstrate Traherne's originality more dramatically, but I do not believe they would convince many readers of the continuing importance of his thought.

36 This seems to me the unfortunate conclusion of a book like K. W. Salter's *Thomas Traherne*, suspended, as it were, between the impression that Traherne "was a man of intellectual ability thought not primarily a philosopher" and that he "was not a systematic or consistent writer" (*Thomas Traherne: Mystic and Poet* [New York: Barnes and Noble, 1965], 6 and 134). I am much more inclined to agree with, and will try to support, Jordan's assertion that Traherne "has made a consistent, systematic formulation" (*Temple of Eternity*, 5). As the terms mystic and mysticism rarely occur in this study, I should at least note that helpful as they have been in defining Traherne for several generations of readers, I can see no use to prolonging their control over virtually all critical inquiry. To argue, as Salter does, that Traherne is a mystic before he is a poet (p. 113), or that his poetry is "less fine" than the experience (p. 119), does not seem to me to get us very far. Nor do I find much promise in a more contemporary version of those arguments, Nabil Matar's "Thomas Traherne's Solar Mysticism," *Studia Mystica* 7 (1984): 52–63.

37 See Marks and Guffey, *Christian Ethicks*, xxxi–xlvii.

38 Clements offers a fair summary of the current assessment of Traherne's childhood: "There can be no question that the meaning of childhood in Traherne is biblical in origin, mystical in tradition, and symbolic in import" (*The Mystical Poetry*, 8–9).

39 See, for example, Anthony Wilden's comments on Lacan's debts to Heidegger in *The Language of the Self* (New York: Dell Publishing, 1975), 179ff.; and the essays by Edward S. Casey and J. Melvin Woody and William J. Richardson in *Interpreting Lacan*, ed. Joseph H. Smith and William Kerrigan (New Haven: Yale University Press, 1983).

40 See, among other studies, Barbara Johnson's "The Frame of Reference: Poe, Lacan, Derrida," in *Literature and Psychoanalysis: The Question of Reading: Otherwise*, ed. Shoshana Felman (Baltimore: Johns Hopkins University Press, 1982).

41 Cf. Ernest B. Gilman: "In view of the Derridean assault on the 'logocentric' tradition, it may be regarded as perverse to align deconstructive criticism with the defiantly logocentric Protestant polemics of the Reformation" (*Iconoclasm and Poetry in the English Reformation* [Chicago: University of Chicago Press, 1986], 190).

42 All citations of Traherne's published texts are taken from the following editions: *Christian Ethicks* (*CE*), ed. Carol L. Marks and George R. Guffey (Ithaca: Cornell University Press, 1968); *Meditations on the Six Days of the Creation*, ed. George R. Guffey, Augustan Reprint Society 119 (Los Angeles: Clark Memorial Library, 1966); *Thomas Traherne: Centuries, Poems, and Thanks-*

givings, ed. H. M. Margoliouth, 2 vols. (Oxford: Clarendon Press, 1958).

43 See Carol L. Marks, "Thomas Traherne and Hermes Trismegistus," *Renaissance News* 19 (1966): 122—"Again and again, Traherne affirmed man's divinity."

44 Douglas Bush is perhaps the most outspoken proponent of this point of view. "Neither as Christian nor as philosopher does Traherne seem quite mature"; his work contains "a large element of facile, expansive, emotional optimism, the kind of optimism which in the next generations passed easily into deistic sentimentalism" (*English Literature in the Earlier Seventeenth Century* [New York: Oxford University Press, 1962], 158).

45 See especially Clements, *The Mystical Poetry*, and Sherrington, *Mystical Symbolism*, as well as Harold G. Ridlon, "The Function of the 'Infant-Ey' in Traherne's Poetry," *SP* 61 (1964): 627–39.

46 Cf. Traherne's Commonplace Book, where the entry under "circulation" reads: "Tris[megistus] defineth Circulation to be a Motion which is always carried about the same" (fol. 26v).

47 See, in addition to Stewart's *The Expanded Voice*, Joan Webber's *The Eloquent "I"* (Madison: University of Wisconsin Press, 1968).

48 Obviously, the case of Derrida, who is still writing, is quite different from those of Heidegger and Lacan, but in all three cases the status of a definitive "text" is analogous to the problematic status of texts confronted by the critic of Traherne. I would extend this thought a bit further to wonder if the textual complications have not themselves forestalled recent Traherne criticism. If this is so, it may silently attest to the critical commitment of most Renaissance scholars to outmoded notions of "text."

49 See Richard D. Jordan, "The New Traherne Manuscript: 'Commentaries of Heaven,'" *Quadrant* 27 (1984): 76.

50 I am accepting in principle the dating of Traherne's work as set out in Day's *Thomas Traherne*, even though Day suggests that some of the Centuries might have been written a couple of years earlier. Even with that short extension, however, Traherne's poetic career is remarkably compressed. Further evidence on dating Traherne's works can be found in Carol Marks's various articles and in Seelig's "The Origins of Ecstasy," 419.

51 Although both Stewart (*The Expanded Voice*) and Day (*Thomas Traherne*) try to suggest some general outlines of Traherne's artistic development, and despite Carol Marks's rather different attempt to account for a maturing style in "Thomas Traherne's Early Studies," *PBSA* 62 (1968): 511–36, Stewart's conclusion that Traherne's work seems to subvert any purely historical or biographical conceptions of time seems most appropriate (p. 102).

52 My focus on the Dobell poems is, like Clements's book, an attempt to argue both the intellectual coherence and the artistic excellence of this remarkable sequence.

TWO. TRAHERNE AND HEIDEGGER

1. *What Is Called Thinking* (hereafter *WCT*), trans. J. Glenn Gray (New York: Harper & Row, 1968), 50. Heidegger makes essentially the same point in "The Thinker as Poet": "To think is to confine yourself to a / single thought that one day stands / still like a star in the world's sky" (*Poetry, Language, Thought* (hereafter *PLT*, trans. Albert Hofstadter [New York: Harper & Row, 1975], 4). Heidegger, of course, is not the first thinker to have dreamed of this mental possibility, and we might recall Augustine's strikingly similar desire in the *Confessions*, book 10, chapters 8–13.
2. *On the Way to Language* (hereafter *OWL*), trans. Peter D. Hertz and Joan Stambaugh (New York: Harper & Row, 1971), 160. Heidegger is cautious, earlier in this volume, to make clear that he does not mean this singleness literally or narrowly: "we must be careful not to force the vibration of the poetic saying into the rigid groove of a univocal statement, and so destroy it" (p. 64).
3. *OWL*, 160. Compare "site" here to Heidegger's analyses of the "clearing" which the work of art opens and in which that which is both reveals and conceals itself (*PLT*, 53); to the "open" in which poetry lets Being happen (*PLT*, 74); to the "space" language clears for settlement and lodging (*PLT*, 154); and to the "region" that gathers all into an abiding or resting (*Discourse on Thinking* (hereafter *DT*), trans. John M. Anderson and E. Hans Freund [New York: Harper & Row, 1969], 66). Here, as in all the notes to this chapter, comparative references are not meant to be exhaustive; I have merely cited what seem to me to be the most useful or provocative of Heidegger's treatments of a given issue, especially those which appear in the later writings. I have included these references, even at the risk of overburdening the notes, because Heidegger's thoughts on the issues I have selected are never conveniently grouped or systematically developed in a single source.
4. See, for example, his discussion of the *Einblick* that structures the "coming-to-pass" of Being in the disclosure of "the turning," *The Question Concerning Technology* (hereafter *QT*), trans. William Lovitt (New York: Harper & Row, 1977), 44–47. The phrase "comes to pass" renders the verb *sich ereignet*, from *sich ereignen*, "to happen or take place." Heidegger's frequent use of this verb and its even more prominent noun, *Ereignis* or "event," always depends upon the etymological convergence of *er-eignen* (*eigen* = "own," and thus to come into one's own, to come to where one belongs) and *er-augnen* (*Auge* = "eye," and thus to catch sight of, to see face to face). See Lovitt's note on *Ereignis ist eignende Eraugnis* in *QT*, 38, and Joan Stambaugh's similar note in *Identity and Difference* (hereafter *ID*), trans. Stambaugh (New York: Harper & Row, 1974), 14. Other passages linking site to insight occur in *Being and Time* (hereafter *BT*), trans. John MacQuarrie and Edward Robinson (New York: Harper & Row, 1962), 56, 170; in George Steiner's *Martin Heidegger* (New York: Viking Press, 1978), 78–79; and in David A. White's *Heidegger*

and the Language of Poetry (Lincoln: University of Nebraska Press, 1978), 175n. For a typical passage on hearing as distinct from seeing, see *BT*, 206–7. See also Heidegger's discussion of point of view in *QT*, 71–72.

5 *OWL*, 161. In *ID*, the Open is the site in which the Arrival (the *place* in beings where Being presences) and the Overwhelming (the *manner* in which Being reaches beings) appear in reciprocal reflexion, a circling around each other (pp. 17, 64–65, 69). The resulting *aletheia* (truth, disclosedness) is structurally very close, it seems to me, to what Traherne will call "circulation." Heidegger's notion of the "wave" can be related to what he elsewhere calls a vibration of poetry within thinking (*OWL*, 69) or the capacity of language "to sound and ring and vibrate, to hover and to tremble," a kind of rhythmic resonance of echoes and hints rather than audible meanings (*OWL*, 98).

6 In *PLT*, Heidegger writes: "Projective saying is poetry. . . . Projective saying is saying which, in preparing the sayable, simultaneously brings the unsayable as such into the world" (p. 74); in *WCT*, he argues that "every originative and proper naming says the unspoken and in such a way that it remains unspoken" (p. 196). What Heidegger seems to be about in these passages is a distinction between what a poet thinks he is saying (or what we think he is saying) and what language itself lets us hear, as it were, underneath and through his words—something that never quite can be either said or thought. Although he perhaps places too much emphasis on the distinction between speaking and saying, White's analysis of the unsaid and the unsayable is a useful entry into the issue Heidegger is trying to address. See White, *Heidegger and the Language of Poetry*, 40–46.

7 *OWL*, 160–61; see also White, *Heidegger and the Language of Poetry*, 10.

8 *WCT*, 49. As White reminds us, man "belongs (*gehort*) to saying as that apparently unique being who can hear (*hort*) what saying says" (*Heidegger and the Language of Poetry*, 38). I would seize upon Heidegger's notion of listening to authorize my own unwillingness to alter his distinctive terminology. However difficult the terms themselves are, I would rather risk an obscurity that remains within the Heideggerian text than to distort that text even further by introducing obscurities of my own.

9 See Stanley Stewart, *The Expanded Voice: The Art of Thomas Traherne* (San Marino, Ca.: Huntington Library, 1970), 180: "Traherne tr[ies] to make language express the unspeakable."

10 I am well aware that many of Heidegger's critics would take exception to these remarks. Such critics—Terry Eagleton is a convenient example—have never been able to reconcile the Heidegger who attacked technocracy and publicness or who spoke so lyrically of human concern and caring with the Heidegger who supported, even welcomed for a time, the Nazi revolution or who spoke to Karl Jaspers of Hitler's "wonderful hands." When these critics have not—like Eagleton—simply dismissed him with a single reference to fascism, they have consistently accused him of being merely a nostalgic, idealistic, even world-weary aesthete. More valid and more serious, I think, are the positions of Allan Megill in *Prophets of Extremity* (Berkeley: University

of California Press, 1985) and George Steiner in *Martin Heidegger*. Steiner's bold conclusion, in fact, is one I would willingly adopt: that whatever compelled Heidegger to align himself with and to speak for an indefensible historical movement, "there are meaner metaphors to live by" than those offered in his collected writings. For more on Heidegger's relations with the Nazis, see, in addition to the bibliography in Steiner (*Martin Heidegger*, 164), Winfried Franzen, *Martin Heidegger* (Stuttgart: Metzler, 1976), and Karl A. Moehling's unpublished dissertation, "Martin Heidegger and the Nazi Party: An Examination" (Northern Illinois University, 1972).

11 *BT*, 23, 127; *QT*, 56, 104, 109; *OWL*, 20, 155; *WCT*, 106–9; White, *Heidegger and the Language of Poetry*, 137; and *The End of Philosophy* (hereafter *EP*), trans. Joan Stambaugh (New York: Harper & Row, 1973), 59.

12 *ID*, 31; *QT*, 39.

13 *ID*, 58, 68–71; *QT*, xv; *PLT*, 101.

14 William J. Richardson, *Heidegger: Through Phenomenology to Thought* (The Hague: Martinus Nijhoff, 1963), 6ff.; see also Steiner's discussion, *Martin Heidegger*, 66–68, 164.

15 Richardson, *Heidegger*, 6.

16 *QT*, 3–4, 131; *PLT*, 194. Also crucial here is Heidegger's fundamental distinction between what is known or thought *ontically* and what is thought *ontologically*: "ontic knowledge, that which pertains to a given being (*Seiende*), is nearest, while ontological knowledge, that which pertains to being as such (*Sein*), is most remote" (White, *Heidegger and the Language of Poetry*, 60). See also Frank Lentricchia, *After the New Criticism* (Chicago: University of Chicago Press, 1980): "In Heidegger, the 'ontological' (as the being or ground of entities, being which, though not itself an entity, permits entities, as their context, to be encountered as such) is pitted against the 'ontic' (entityhood and the traits of entities, the realm of inquiry for scientists . . .)" (pp. 81–82).

17 *BT*, 32, 62, 67, 119, 180–82, 236, 270, 458; *ID*, 36–37; *QT*, 42; *OWL*, 30–33, 40; *EP*, 79–81; *WCT*, 116; Steiner, *Martin Heidegger*, 81.

18 *WCT*, 9–10, 18, 69, 149; *BT*, 236; *QT*, 32, 131, 154; Steiner, *Martin Heidegger*, 92. Heidegger's notion of man as a pointer needs to be seen in relation to Lacan's ideas about the psychoanalytic subject as a signifier. Although Lacan develops this subject quite differently and derives his terms from Saussure, it seems clear enough that Heidegger's analysis of man as hermeneutic provides Lacan with a crucial philosophical ground.

19 *EP*, 1–8; *WCT*, 161, 172, 186; *PLT*, 65–66, 71; *QT*, 3n.; *BT*, 82, 173–74, 446.

20 *ID*, 9, 11–12, 28; *EP*, ix; *QT*, 57n.; *PLT*, 202–06, 218–19.

21 In Heidegger's terms, "authentic" existence is one in which man remains open to and moving towards his "ownmost" possibilities of being; "inauthentic" existence is one in which man conceals or withdraws from those possibilities by giving himself over to a public "theyness." See *BT*, 82, 220, and Michael E. Zimmerman, *Eclipse of the Self: The Development of*

Heidegger's Conception of Authenticity (Athens: Ohio University Press, 1981).

22 *BT*, 67–68, 82, 88–89, 97–122, 135–38, 141–42, 150, 200, 245, 247, 250, 254, 266–67, 286–87, 305, 403–04, 412–13; *PLT*, 28, 32ff., 65, 165; *WCT*, 65, 187; Steiner, *Martin Heidegger*, 89–90. See especially *BT*, 98: "The kind of Being which equipment possesses—in which it manifests itself in its own right—we call '*readiness-to-hand*.' . . . Dealings with equipment subordinate themselves to the manifold assignments of the 'in-order-to'". Compare, however, Heidegger's other argument that man's use of equipment is a full exercise of worldly concern and historical involvement. See Lentricchia, *After the New Criticism*, 85–86.

23 *BT*, 262, 266–67, 282, 412–13; *PLT*, 39, 45; *WCT*, 16, 187, 191–96; Steiner, *Martin Heidegger*, 89–90. It is important to remember that equipment and thing are not distinct or antithetical entities and that each *manner* of being (or being used) can be authentic or inauthentic. At times readers of Heidegger seem to privilege thing-hood over equipment-hood, as if the latter were a corruption of the former. That interpretation is acceptable only to the extent that one bears in mind the larger question of what his relatedness to either thing or equipment discloses to man about his own Being.

24 *PLT*, 151–54, 173–78, 181, 199–200; White, *Heidegger and the Language of Poetry*, 165.

25 *WCT*, 187, 191, 195–96; *QT*, xiv, 28, 31, 33, 38, 40–42.

26 *PLT*, 33ff., 45, 59. This illustration has been the subject of two equally famous attacks, one by Meyer Schapiro, "The Still Life as a Personal Object—A Note on Heidegger and Van Gogh," in *The Reach of Mind*, ed. Marianne L. Simmel (New York: Springer, 1968), 203–9; the other by Jacques Derrida, "Restitutions of Truth in Painting," in *La Verite en Peinture* (Paris: Flammarion, 1978). For a provocative analogue to Heidegger's conception of world, see Josef Pieper, *Leisure: The Basis of Culture* (New York: Pantheon, 1952), esp. part 2, "The Philosophical Act."

27 *BT*, 204; *OWL*, 62–63, 87–88; *QT*, xix; *DT*, 69; *PLT*, 73, 192, 199; *WCT*, 120; White, *Heidegger and the Language of Poetry*, 22–29, 69.

28 *PLT*, 179; see also 48–49, 149–51, 180; *OWL*, 104; *HLP*, 33n., 54, 70, 93, 96n., 104, 113, 126–27, 184.

29 *PLT*, 44; White, *Heidegger and the Language of Poetry*, 64; Steiner, *Martin Heidegger*, 88–89.

30 *BT*, 91–148, 176, 415, 417; *PLT*, 202–03; *QT*, 43–44; White, *Heidegger and the Language of Poetry*, 65, n.10; Megill, *Prophets of Extremity*, 162–63.

31 *OWL*, 23, 47–53, 93, 107–08, 122–29; *BT*, 55–58; *QT*, xxiv, 10–11, 38n.

32 "Letter on Humanism," trans. Edgar Lohner, in *Philosophy in the Twentieth Century*, ed. William Barrett and Henry D. Aiken (New York: Random House, 1962), 2:271; *PLT*, 132, 215, 227; *OWL*, 5, 22, 26–27, 57, 63; *WCT*, 118–19, 123–24; *ID*, 39; White, *Heidegger and the Language of Poetry*, 20n.4.

33 *PLT*, xiv, 146ff.; *OWL*, 89, 93, 98; *QT*, 11, 28, 33n.

34 *DT*, 69; *EP*, 4; *WCT*, 118–21; White, *Heidegger and the Language of Poetry*, 56–57, 69, 176; Steiner, *Martin Heidegger*, 45–46. While it is beyond the requirements of the present discussion, it is important to remember that behind this "capability of being said" lies Heidegger's entire attempt to rethink temporality.

35 *PLT*, 146, 190–92, 197, 206, 210, 215–16; *WCT*, 118–19, 128; *OWL*, 90, 129; White, *Heidegger and the Language of Poetry*, 37–38.

36 *BT*, 41, 424ff.; *QT*, 64, 159; *OWL*, 196; *PLT*, 75–77; *WCT*, 131; *EP*, 75; Steiner, *Martin Heidegger*, 129; White, *Heidegger and the Language of Poetry*, 166.

37 *BT*, 207; *PLT*, 11; *WCT*, 196, 206; *OWL*, p. 81; *DT*, 69; White, *Heidegger and the Language of Poetry*, 40–46, 70–71, 95, 173. See especially Heidegger's discussion, in *Being and Time*, of idle talk and the they-ness out of which this grows and from which an authentic saying of language must be reclaimed. To some extent, Heidegger's notions can be related to the modern critical theme of defamiliarization.

38 Steiner, *Martin Heidegger*, 67–68.

39 The step-back itself is susceptible to two different interpretations: either a hermeneutic maneuver or a "natural" releasement, as when a piece of equipment breaks. See *EP*, xiii–xiv; *ID*, 49–52; *PLT*, 10, 181, 185; *BT*, 197; *OWL*, 66, 85, 142–43, 146–47, 150–56, 172–98; White, *Heidegger and the Language of Poetry*, 62, 79–81, 87–88, 150–51, 184; as well as Heidegger's various treatments of remoteness, renunciation, and detour.

40 *QT*, xxv, xxix, 23, 48, 88, 100, 106–07, 128, 131, 149; *EP*, 80; *DT*, 46, 63; White, *Heidegger and the Language of Poetry*, 148–50, 169–70.

41 *BT*, 227.

42 *PLT*, 56.

43 *QT*, 42.

44 *BT*, 263.

45 *BT*, 237.

46 *BT*, 344.

47 *BT*, 344.

48 *BT*, 329.

49 *PLT*, 181.

50 *PLT*, 129–30. When we recall that such a "conversion" of the heart is in response to what Heidegger calls man's falling condition, when care is a call of conscience, and when the effect of the conversion is defined as a saving, we can hear behind this text the clear strains of a Christian paradigm. To a critic like Derrida, the existence of such strains is the mark of Heidegger's intellectual failure; to us, it may be taken as an opening upon his relation to Traherne.

51 *PLT*, 151.

52 *WCT*, 139–47; *DT*, 85; *OWL*, 136; Steiner, *Martin Heidegger*, 15, 131, 146.

53 Richardson, *Heidegger*, 601.

54 *OWL*, 135–36, 148; Steiner, *Martin Heidegger*, 32.
55 *OWL*, 136.
56 Although I am much indebted to and admire White's attempt to pin down Heidegger's conception of poetry in *Heidegger and the Language of Poetry*, I do not think his argument will stand. Richardson, in *Heidegger*, simply gives up altogether. My own remarks are frankly utilitarian: I have interpreted Heidegger in ways that seem to me most fruitful for approaching Traherne.
57 *QT*, xxiv, 12–13; *EP*, 19, 55; *PLT*, 59, 159; Steiner, *Martin Heidegger*, 134–35.
58 *PLT*, x, 12.
59 *QT*, 156, 25; *PLT*, 74; *DT*, 69; *BT*, 322; *EP*, 77–78; *OWL*, 59; White, *Heidegger and the Language of Poetry*, 44–46, 80. Obviously, the biblical resonance is important to Heidegger here: poetry is, at some essential or existential level, a sacred act.
60 *PLT*, 218; *ID*, 47; *WCT*, 20, 128, 134–35, 205–06; *OWL*, 69–70, 89–90, 95, 160–61; White, *Heidegger and the Language of Poetry*, 76, 143–47, 154–58, 196ff.
61 *OWL*, 89–90. Compare *QT*, 31, 156; *PLT*, 44, 149–51; *DT*, 82; *WCT*, 118; *EP*, 76; Steiner, *Martin Heidegger*, 129; White, *Heidegger and the Language of Poetry*, 155–56.
62 *After the New Criticism*, 81–100; see also, Megill, *Prophets of Extremity*, 106, 119–25, 145–48, 178–80.
63 Coleridge, "The Friend," cited by Steiner in *Martin Heidegger*, 158.
64 *The Physics*, trans. Wicksteed and Cornford, Loeb Classical Library (London: Wimmilam Heinemann, 1929), 1:295.
65 *The Temple of Eternity* (Port Washington, N. Y.: Kennikat, 1972), 48. One measure of Jordan's haste is the fact that the first entry in Traherne's Commonplace Book is *Aristotle's Philosophie*. Significantly, the first text cited in this passage is the *Physics*.
66 Sharon Cadmon Seelig uses this line and its biblical source (Acts 17:28) to emphasize the "almost blasphemous" inversion Traherne effects in "The Demonstration" (*The Shadow of Eternity* [Lexington: University of Kentucky Press, 1981], 134).
67 Carol Marks, in "Thomas Traherne's Commonplace Book," *PBSA* 58 (1964), 460, notes that "Indwelling" is one of fifteen subjects cross-referenced within the text but not included anywhere in the book. See Commonplace manuscript, f. 65.1. Although it would not be accurate to argue that all of the Commonplace entries represent crucial issues in Traherne's thinking, the knowledge that he intended an extended treatment of In-dwelling is certainly instructive.
68 Seelig, *Shadow of Eternity*, reminds us that Traherne's principal source here is Aquinas's definition of God as pure act (p. 121).
69 Although I argue against any identification of Being with God (or even being with man) in Heidegger's text, such identifications are, at least initially, required by Traherne's. It will remain to be seen whether Traherne can

define Being-as-such in a way sufficient to keep it distinct from any particular being. When I say, moreover, that such identifications are required by Traherne's text, I am well aware that A. L. Clements (*The Mystical Poetry of Thomas Traherne* [Cambridge: Harvard University Press, 1969]), among others, has tried to argue the usefulness of other terminology. And while Clements's own psyche, pneuma, phenomenon distinctions are extremely helpful, my own sense is that it is far more appropriate to adopt Traherne's own terms, Being and being. Jordan offers a general view that is closer to my own: "It could be said that Traherne . . . is always talking about everything. . . . Nothing can be treated in isolation, because any one major part of being, the world, for instance, includes both of the others, man and God. Each of these three is by presence or reflection included in the others" (*Temple of Eternity*, 97–98).

70 This thinking of *both*, I would add, is a better way to discuss what is usually called the paradoxical nature of Traherne's thought. What is labeled "paradoxical" is more often than not what is unthought, for the designation merely throws us back on the unexamined premise of mysticism rather than toward the logic of the seemingly illogical. In these terms, I would also have to disagree with Jordan's assertion that Traherne's systematic "method of thought is . . . the reconciliation of opposites" (*Temple of Eternity*, 24). Reconciliation is precisely the wrong term, for it would collapse difference into sameness, not hold both in relation.

71 Another passage in which Traherne takes up these same subjects appears in *CE*, chap. 9. Here again Traherne is arguing that God's essence is his act and he tries to chart the ways in which God does act. But in the final sentence of the paragraph Traherne radically revises the ostensible subject. I cite the final two sentences to underscore the shift: "His Essence is the Best of all possible Means, by which he attains himself, and by which he is enjoyed. Our Conformity to his Essence is our Way, by a Wise Application of our Souls to that Eternal Act which is his End" (p. 66).

72 See, for the most obvious example, *CM*, I.1. The issue of forgotten knowledge in Traherne should invoke, in addition to the general theories of memory and language developed by Augustine and extended centuries later by Heidegger, the complexities of notions of the pre-existence of the soul. On the latter, see Malcolm Day, "Traherne and the Doctrine of Pre-existence," *SP* 65 (1968), 81–97.

73 See "The Author to the Critical Peruser," "Dumnesse," and "Silence" for representative statements.

74 Traherne's continual plays upon the different grammatical forms of his key words should be compared to Heidegger's similar stylistic penchant. For additional implications of such grammatical play, see chapter four.

75 Obviously, this assertion is somewhat of an exaggeration, as studies by Malcolm L. Day, "'Naked Truth' and the Language of Thomas Traherne," *SP* 68 (1971): 305–25; Ronald E. McFarland, "From Ambiguity to Paradox: Thomas Traherne's 'Things'," *Wascana Review* 9 (1974): 114–23; and Carl M.

Selkin, "The Language of Vision: Traherne's Cataloguing Style," *ELR* 6 (1976): 92–104 will suggest. Still, it is only "somewhat" of an exaggeration: I can think of no single essay that argues systematically the thoughtfulness of Traherne's linguistic choices. More frequently, the problems of disentangling Traherne's own words from those of his brother's emendations seem to be used, often unconsciously, as a justification for avoiding in-depth study of the language of either the poetry or the prose.

76 The notion of the trinity obviously lies behind this passage, but it is interesting to observe that Traherne is unique among mid- to late-century writers in his relative scarcity of trinitarian imagery.

77 I have silently altered Traherne's own text by changing his "object" to Heideggerian "being," but I trust the consistency of his meditation on beingness will countenance such an emendation.

78 Jordan reminds us that the first sixty-nine sections of the Second Century is an extended meditation on "World" (*Temple of Eternity*, p. 89).

79 See the *OED* for the historical etymologies involved here; for the economy implicit in the final meaning, see the further discussion in chapter four.

80 Compare Traherne's statement in the newly discovered "Commentaries of Heaven": "The Light of Glory of it [the World] seems a Sphere into which he enters, out of the Obscuritie of an Eternal Abyss, which is called *Nothing*." I cite from Allan Pritchard, "Traherne's 'Commentaries of Heaven,'" *UTQ* 53 (1983): 19.

81 *EP*, 76.

82 On this paradoxical collapse of sight into sound, to the eternal voice of Truth, see Clements, *The Mystical Poetry*, p. 80.

83 Seelig, in *The Shadow of Eternity*, argues that, for Traherne, "what we are determines what we see" (p. 112). Despite what I have just called Traherne's reflexivity, his more normal emphasis precisely reverses Seelig's point: what we see is what we are! Compare Carol L. Marks's comments on the relationship between sight and insight in "Thomas Traherne and Hermes Trismegistus," *RN* 19 (1966): 129.

84 Although I think this generalization correct enough, it should also be noted that the Felicity poems have more concrete or realistic imagery than those in the Dobell manuscript and, if we can trust the reports several critics have given, other manuscript verse is also more realistic. As we have already had occasion to note, most critics find in this paucity of dramatic and realistic imagery evidence of Traherne's failure as a poet.

85 It is his failure to understand or explore this point that, to my mind at least, weakens McFarland's otherwise provocative article on Trahernean things. See "From Ambiguity to Paradox," *Wascana Review* 9 (1974): 114–23.

86 This, I think, is Traherne's version of Heidegger's step-back.

87 In light of such passages, I would take serious exception to Harold Ridlon's assertion that thoughts "become opposed to 'things' in Traherne's reasoning." See "The Function of the 'Infant-Ey' in Traherne's Poetry," *SP* 61 (1964): 637. Margaret Bottrall, in "Traherne's Praise of Creation," *CQ* 1 (1959),

makes essentially the same point: "Not things, but the thoughts of things are what he values" (p. 130). Both statements betray the critics' wish for particular objects and/or images and their failure to take seriously Traherne's own account of "things."

88 "Exceeding" here hints at the economy of the supplement, a "necessary surplus" that is registered or received as value. See further in chapter four.

89 Compare Heidegger's discussions of indifference in *BT*, 158. In "The Inference," Traherne argues that "*Things* are indifferent" (l. 3), but as the rest of the poem makes clear, the thing that is thought, that appears and is near or present, calls us out of our own indifference. Thus, as Traherne concludes in "Hosanna":

> My Thoughts on Things remain;
> Or els like vital Beams
> They reach to, shine on, quicken Things, and make
> Them truly Usefull; While I *All* partake.
> (ll. 57–60)

90 Augustine, *On Christian Doctrine*, trans. D. W. Robertson, Jr., Library of Liberal Arts (New York, 1958), III.v.9, p. 84.

91 This belonging-together of "every part" within the whole World is a consistent theme of *Meditations on the Six Days of Creation*.

92 At the conclusion of "Bells," Traherne argues that "We must unite / If we Delight / Would yield or feel, or any Excellence" (ll. 75–77); "Misapprehension" specifies that such "uniting" occurs when we understand that because "All things" are "Center'd" in our hearts, "The World [is] set in Man's Heart":

> Of it I am th'inclusive Sphere,
> It doth entire in me appear,
> As well as I in it . . .
> (ll. 51–65)

93 Pritchard calls attention to an analogous passage in the "Commentaries of Heaven": in his article on the Ant, Traherne says "it is never truly seen till it is seen in its Original uses services Relations and Ends" ("Traherne's 'Commentaries of Heaven,'" 17).

94 See "The Author to the Critical Peruser," ll. 37–44; "The Approach," where Traherne summarizes his lack of proper regard as "I careless was" (l. 23); and the passage in the "Commentaries" cited in the preceding note—after describing the various ways we are related to the Ant, Traherne goes on to lament how "we kill it, and pass by without Concernment."

95 Perhaps the best way to approach Traherne's "Thanksgivings" is as acknowledgments of and responses to "all the Care of God" (*CM*, IV.39). Man's own righteousness is thus measured by the capacity of his own care as that is expressed in the gift of thoughtful thanks. And here, of course, Traherne's two privileged terms, circulation and communication, "say" the same thing: that man cares.

THREE. TRAHERNE AND LACAN

1 Anthony Wilden discusses the general debt Lacan owes to Heidegger in *The Language of the Self* (hereafter *LS*) (New York: Dell Publishing Co., 1975), 179–82, 200–202, but William J. Richardson is perhaps the most consistent interpreter of this influence. See his "Lacan and the Subject of Psychoanalysis" and "Psychoanalysis and the Being-question," both reprinted in *Interpreting Lacan*, ed. Joseph H. Smith and William Kerrigan, Psychiatry and the Humanities 6 (New Haven: Yale University Press, 1983), and *Lacan and Language: A Reader's Guide to* Ecrits, co-authored with John P. Muller (New York: International Universities Press, 1982). For Richardson, of course, the turn from Heidegger to Lacan is also a natural one since he is both professor of philosophy and a practicing psychoanalyst. See also, in the Smith and Kerrigan volume, Edward S. Casey and J. Melvin Moody, "Hegel, Heidegger, Lacan: The Dialectic of Desire."

2 *LS*, 45: "the subject is spoken rather than speaking." See also *Ecrits: A Selection*, trans. Alan Sheridan (London: Tavistock Publications, 1977), 65, 86; and *The Four Fundamental Concepts of Psycho-Analysis* (hereafter *FFC*, trans. Alan Sheridan (New York: Norton & Company, 1981), 188, 198.

3 See Lacan on psychoanalytic cure, *LS*, 42, 57, 58, 65, 175; *Ecrits*, 68, 88, 93, 269; Ellie Ragland-Sullivan, *Jacques Lacan and the Philosophy of Psychoanalysis* (Urbana: University of Illinois Press, 1986), 161; and Stanley A. Leavy, "The Image and the Word," in *Interpreting Lacan*, ed. Smith and Kerrigan, 15.

4 In fact, and as perverse as it may initially seem in a chapter employing Lacan, I shall say very little about the Unconscious as such. My aim is not to psychoanalyze Traherne, but to reveal, with Lacan's help, the signifying structures of his discourse. Whether those are also revelatory of his Unconscious is a psychoanalytic rather than a literary question, although even that distinction might be challenged. See the remarks of Shoshana Felman in the collection *Literature and Psychoanalysis* (Baltimore: Johns Hopkins University Press, 1982), 5–10.

5 On Lacan's distinctions between the empty word and the full word, see *LS*, 15–19, 142; *Ecrits*, 40–48; *FFC*, 278; Muller and Richardson, *Lacan and Language*, 70–75; and Ragland-Sullivan, *Jacques Lacan*, 161, 213–14.

6 But see Ragland-Sullivan's important correctives to any naive identification of Lacan as a structuralist in *Jacques Lacan*, 75ff., and 232: "Lacan's epistemology is, in and of itself, a refutation of structuralist and communications theories." I would take this opportunity to applaud Ragland-Sullivan as one of the least reductive of any Lacanian interpreters; her study, in my opinion, should become a standard text on Lacan.

7 "To put it in a nutshell, it seems to me that the 'I think,' to which it is intended that presence be reduced, continues to imply, no matter how indeterminate one may make it, all the powers of the reflection by which subject and consciousness are confounded—namely, the mirage which psy-

choanalytic experience places at the basis of the *meconnaissance* of the subject." This statement is from Lacan's essay on Merleau-Ponty, cited in *LS*, 106. See also, of course, the important chapter on "The Subversion of the subject" in *Ecrits*, 292–325.

8 *LS*, 305–6.

9 *Ecrits*, 300 (see also 128–29, 136, 171, 279, 299).

10 *What Is Called Thinking*, trans. J. Glenn Gray (New York: Harper & Row, 1968), 9–10.

11 K. W. Salter, summarizing a few of the findings of Evelyn Underhill, argues that "the essential fact of Traherne's experience, as he records it, is the change from a world which is centred around his own personality into another and larger universe of being. The early ecstasies of his life . . . centred on himself; but now the sense of 'otherness' disturbs this world" (*Thomas Traherne* [New York: Barnes & Noble, 1965], 41–42).

12 See Juliet Mitchell's account of Lacan's stylistic choice as determined, at least in part, by his rejection of Freud's own attempt to make himself easily understood by a lay and medical public and the paradoxical secularization to which he was subject because of that decision, in *Feminine Sexuality: Jacques Lacan and the ecole freudienne*, ed. Mitchell and Jacqueline Rose, (New York: Norton & Co., 1982), 4. See Lacan's own statements in *Ecrits*, 33; as well as Jane Gallop's analysis in *Reading Lacan* (Ithaca: Cornell University Press, 1985), 31–54.

13 Lacan's unwillingness to fix or totalize any of his schemes or graphs precludes, therefore, any such notion as Heidegger's World (the "relation of all relations"). And this is especially evident in his objection to those who misread his assertion that the Unconscious is structured *as* a language to mean the Unconscious *is* language. See his address and the responses recorded in Richard Macksey and Eugenio Donato, *The Structuralist Controversy* (Baltimore: Johns Hopkins University Press, 1972), 186–200. Lacan's own "slidings," furthermore, makes the task of sketching his key ideas almost impossible without a certain amount of willful *meconnaissance*.

14 I have already suggested, in the opening chapter, that Malcolm Day's Twayne study opens several possibilities for this kind of work on Traherne; but a different example of the kind of project I have in mind here would be a comparative study of the styles, themes, key images, and dictional choices of Traherne and a contemporary like Peter Sterry. Sterry's *Discourse on the Freedome of the Will* (1675) sounds remarkably like Traherne, as even a hasty observation of his plays on the modifications of love, loving, and beloved; part-whole relations; the persistent focus on essence and act; or the complex dialectics of empty/full will reveal. We might well ask, therefore, what historical conditions of theological controversy or discourse incite an Oxford and a Cambridge theologian to adopt compatible idiosyncratic styles? "Compatible" is here an understatement: although I cannot prove it, I have no doubt at all that one of these two men must have read the other's work. (I should point out in passing that Stanley Stewart initially suggests this

possibility, but later renounces it; actually, the initial suggestion was, as he acknowledges, incited by an error in dating the *Discourse*. See *The Expanded Voice* (San Marino: Huntington Library, 1970), 125 and 187. My point is that I think Stewart's first sense of the remarkable confluence of both thought and style here was correct, even if the dating of the published version of Sterry's work—one year after Traherne's death—complicates the question of source-relation.)

15 See Wilden's comments in *LS*, 184.

16 Like Lacan's notion of the Unconscious, neither his statements on signifier and signified nor those on metaphor and metonymy will figure largely in this chapter although I have tried, wherever pertinent, to address these issues in the following notes. In the final chapter, I will try to speak more directly to the question of the status of metonymy in Traherne's text.

17 Freud's text is the important "On Narcissism: An Introduction" (1914), in *Standard Edition of the Complete Psychological Works*, ed. James Strachey (London: Hogarth Press, 1957), 14:73–102; Wallon's essay, "Comment se developpe chez l'enfant la notion du corps propre," appeared in *Journal de Psychologie* (1931): 705–48, and again as *Les Origines du caractère chez l'enfant*, 2d ed. (Paris: Presses Universitaires de France, 1949).

18 Despite her generally shrewd analysis of Lacanian "stages," even Ragland-Sullivan falls into this trap.

19 Ragland-Sullivan, *Jacques Lacan*, 29; see also the comments by Anika Lemaire, *Jacques Lacan*, trans. David Macey (Boston: Routledge & Kegan Paul, 1977), 81; *LS*, 174; and Gallop, *Reading Lacan*, 74–92.

20 Whether the parent is the *real* mother is irrelevant: mother, like father, is a purely structural integer in the Lacanian scenario, a fact frequently overlooked by many of the critiques leveled against his ostensible "phallocentrism" by certain feminists.

21 Actually, *two* misconstructions may occur here: in addition to the normal assumption that the child confuses himself with his reflection, the initial presence of the mother may contribute to another (prior or subsequent?) confusion: "The mother does not mirror the child to itself; she grants an image *to* the child, which her presence instantly deflects. Holding the child is, therefore, to be understood not only as containing, but as a process of referring, which fractures the unity it seems to offer" (Mitchell, *Feminine Sexuality*, 30). On *méconnaissance*, see *LS*, 96–97.

22 *FFC*, 106.

23 See below for Lacan's more complex version of this schema as it appears in the seminar on "The Purloined Letter" (the first essay in the 1966 collection of *Ecrits* [Paris: Seuil]). The present, simplified form appeared first in Lacan's seminar "D'une question preliminaire a tout traitement possible de la psychose" (1957–58) (printed in the 1966 edition of *Ecrits*, 548). For clarity I have maintained Lacan's "Saa'A" rather than the "Soo'O" found in most English translations, but I will reemploy the English *O* when explicating the functions of (m)Other or (o)bject within the scheme.

24 *LS*, 37.
25 *LS*, 107–8; see also Serge Leclaire, "A la recherche des principes d'une psychotherapie des psychoses," *L'Evolution Psychiatrique* (1958), 377–411; Ragland-Sullivan, *Jacques Lacan*, 2ff; and Andre Green's article on "The Logic of Lacan's *objet (a)*," in *Interpreting Lacan*, ed. Smith and Kerrigan, 161ff.
26 Perhaps self-alienation(s) would be the better term, for not only is the child not identical to his reflected image, but the mother holding the child is not the same as her reflected image and the child being held is not the same as either the child himself or the image of himself being held. Each alienation depends upon the child's misperceiving the mirrored image *as if it were real*. "Thus, and this is essential," Lacan argues, "the first effect of the *Imago* which appears in human beings is an effect of alienation in the subject. It is in the other that the subject identifies and even senses himself at first," "Propos sur la causalite psychique," in *Ecrits* (1966), 45.
27 But see his contradictory assertion that "the idea of the mirror should be understood as an object which reflects—not just the visible, but also what is heard, touched, and willed by the child," "Cure psychanalytique à l'aide de la poupée fleur," Comptes rendus, *Revue française de la psychanalyse* 4 (1949): 567.
28 *Ecrits*, 2; *LS*, 135.
29 The image is, of course, both identity and difference: identity being the product of narcissistic identification, difference that of objectification. The human subject enters consciousness only through a variety of such imagistic plays. The language that articulates such plays—I and you, myself and another, child and mother, I and me, etc.—is a subsequent articulation of the already inscribed split in being.
30 *FFC*, 17ff.
31 See the chapter "Of The Gaze as *Object Petit a*" in *FFC*, 67–122.
32 *FFC*, 106.
33 The solid lines here suggest that the impact of the Other upon the *moi* and the registration of that *moi* as imagined object of others is not recognized by the subject even though both incite and direct his discourse toward those others. The solid lines thus represent what in the scopic scenario Lacan calls the screen alienating eye and object, the point of light and the picture that is viewed.
34 See Ragland-Sullivan, *Jacques Lacan*, 44.
35 *FFC*, 115.
36 *FFC*, 106; Macksey and Donato, *Structuralist Controversy*, 192.
37 *Ecrits*, 19.
38 See Emile Benveniste, "Relationships of Person in the Verb," "The Nature of Pronouns," and "Subjectivity in Language," in *Problems in General Linguistics*, trans. M. E. Meek (Coral Gables: University of Florida Press, 1971); and Roman Jakobson, "Shifters, Verbal Categories, and the Russian Verb," *Russian Language Project* (Cambridge: Harvard University Press, 1957).

39 See *LS*, 39, 83, 152–53; *Ecrits*, 104; and commentaries in Lemaire, *Jacques Lacan*, 51; and *Interpreting Lacan*, ed. Smith and Kerrigan, 58, 141, 152.
40 This is suggested, I think, in *LS*, 45, 83, 155, and 161; see also Muller and Richardson, *Lacan and Language*, 18.
41 *Ecrits*, 11.
42 My own sense is that he here relies more on a traditional Freudian interpretation of body fragments as phallic substitutes than on his more typical insistence on a structural system.
43 *Ecrits*, 4–5, 11.
44 See Fredric Jameson, "Imaginary and Symbolic in Lacan: Marxism, Psychoanalytic Criticism, and the Problem of the Subject," *Yale French Studies* 55–56 (1977): 338–95; *LS*, 124; and Ragland-Sullivan, *Jacques Lacan*, 130ff.
45 *LS*, 11, 191, 304; *FFC*, 207; and Muller and Richardson, *Lacan and Language*, 87–88. This point is corroborated, I think, by all of Lacan's late analyses of the phallus and its various functions.
46 On the concurrence of the three orders, see Muller and Richardson, *Lacan and Language*, 245; Gallop, *Reading Lacan*, 162; and Ragland-Sullivan, *Jacques Lacan*, 130–31, 156, 202, 223.
47 Cited in *LS*, 147.
48 See the *Course in General Linguistics*, trans. Wade Baskin (Bungay: Collins, 1974).
49 The three citations are from, respectively, *LS*, 63; *Ecrits*, 86; and *FFC*, 188.
50 "D'une question preliminaire a tout traitement possible de la psychose," *La Psychanalyse* 4 (1958): 18; translation by Wilden, in *LS*, 107.
51 The clearest analysis of Lacan's distinction between ideal-ego and ego-ideals is Ragland-Sullivan's, *Jacques Lacan*, 3, 35, 54, and 80.
52 *LS*, 189; see also Serge Leclaire, cited in *LS*, 143–44, 60.
53 *FFC*, 115.
54 See *LS*, 131, 242; Muller and Richardson, *Lacan and Language*, 22.
55 *FFC*, 215; *Ecrits*, 259, 274; see also Macksey and Donato, *Structuralist Controversy*, 194.
56 *FFC*, 214.
57 That "The Author to the Critical Peruser" has been imported into the Dobell sequence only confirms the point that everyone intuitively recognizes: that Traherne's discourse requires some other.
58 I am only following Traherne in calling this presentation specular rather than auditory, but as he and we will shortly discover, it is both (as the homonyms Eye-I suggest). For another critical treatment of the visual/auditory problems in a presentational poetics, see Joel Fineman, *Shakespeare's Perjured Eye* (Berkeley: University of California Press, 1986).
59 Carol Marks notes that "desire" is one of Traherne's "key words" ("Traherne and Cambridge Platonism," *PMLA* 81 [1966]: 532). Marks also reminds us that "Desire" is one of the entries in the Commonplace Book (although most of this passage refers to what Traherne calls "our naturall desire" of knowl-

edge, not to desire as such).

60 "Solitude" offers a convenient illustration of how the originary scene of abyss/absence/Nothing is replicated in the subsequent history of the self. Here the I begins with the horror of "How desolate!/ Ah! how forlorn, how sadly" he stands; nothing found or seen brings either contentment, rest, or ease. What is found, however, is the force of "A secret Want" (l. 29), the urgings of some "kind of thing I long'd for" (l. 34), and the fact "that I / Did somwhat lack" (ll. 34–35). What the poem then demonstrates is that the compulsive repetition of such lacks "conspire[s]" to create a desire which by its very nature cannot be satisfied. In short, the poem's generative urgency is to assure that everything seen or heard "giv no Answer unto my Desire" (l. 56). Desire, imagining itself as lack, makes certain that it cannot be fulfilled.

61 Traherne, of course, is not the first thinker to imagine desire in these terms. Stephen Greenblatt reminds us that both Richard Hooker and Giordano Bruno, as well as Nicholas Cusa and Marsilio Ficino, explore desire as insatiable. One of Hooker's convoluted sentences is most revealing: "For man doth not seem to rest satisfied, either with fruition of that wherewith his life is preserved, or with performance of such actions as advance him most deservedly in estimation; but doth further covet . . . that which cannot stand him in any stead for vital use; that which exceedeth the reach of sense; yea somewhat above the capacity of reason, somewhat divine and heavenly, which with hidden exultation it rather surmiseth than conceiveth; somewhat it seeketh, and what that is directly it knoweth not, yet very intentive desire thereof doth so incite it, that all other known delights and pleasures are laid aside, they give place to the search of *this but only suspected desire*" (my italics). See Greenblatt, *Renaissance Self-Fashioning* (Chicago: University of Chicago Press, 1980), 295–96n. Hooker's statement is from *Ecclesiastical Polity*.

62 *LS*, 63.

63 See Richardson's essay, "Psychoanalysis and the Being-question," in *Interpreting Lacan*, ed. Smith and Kerrigan, 139–60.

64 Cf. *Ecrits*: "One should try and count the number of substitutions that operate here to bring desire to a geometrically increasing power. A single index would not be enough to characterize the degree. For it would be necessary to distinguish two dimensions in these substitutions: a desire for desire, in other words, a desire signified by a desire . . . is inscribed in the different register of one desire substituted for another" (p. 257). Lacan's insistence on this geometrical logic of desire justifies his further claim that desire itself is the metonymy of the want-to-be, or desire is a metonymy in search of an ever elusive metaphor.

65 Compare *Meditation on the Six Days*: "so neither can the Soul of Man be satisfied with any other thing but with God alone" (p. 83).

66 Malcolm Day argues that Traherne's soul "is so filled with riches that nothing is left for it to desire" (*Thomas Traherne* [Boston: Twayne Publishers, 1982], 50), but I think everything in Traherne's text works exactly counter

to this notion. "On Christmas-Day" would offer a convenient illustration of Traherne's typical subversion of Day's position. Under normative Christian assumptions, the birth of Christ would fulfill desires the wants and lacks occasioned by the Fall have given rise to. In Traherne's poem Christ's birth and death "cloath [man] with new Attires," but these are always and only "new Desires" (ll. 77–78). In short, desire always replicates itself at or on another level; there is always something left.

67 See above, note 64.

68 In "Select Meditations," Traherne writes: "There is in a man a Double selfe" (II.92). This bipartition in being is a frequent subject in the poetry:

> Talk with thy self; thy self enjoy and see:
> At once the Mirror and the Object be.
> ("The Odour," ll. 53–54)
> I my Companions see
> In You, another Me.
> They seemed Others, but are We;
> Our second Selvs those Shadows be.
> ("Shadows in the Water," ll. 61–64)
> . . . how can I chuse
> but love them as my self! . . . my second selves. . .
> thou hast given me my self.
> ("Thanksgivings for God's Attributes," ll. 232–34, 252)

69 And, conversely, an object only re-invokes desire, as Traherne says in "Christendom": "That here to rais Desire / All Objects do conspire" (ll. 100–101).

70 A. L. Clements, *The Mystical Poetry* (Cambridge: Harvard University Press, 1969) reminds us that Eckhart licenses this particular confusion: "The eye by which I see God is the same as the eye by which God sees me. My eye and God's eye are one and the same" (p. 74).

71 In "The Demonstration," Traherne states that "A Miste involvs the Ey, / While in the Middle it doth lie" (ll. 3–4); I take this assertion to be the poet's equivalent to Lacan's unseeable gaze.

72 See Louis L. Martz, *The Paradise Within* (New Haven: Yale University Press, 1964), and *The Poetry of Meditation* (New Haven: Yale University Press, 1954).

73 See Salter, *Thomas Traherne*, chapter 2, "The Spiritual Progress."

74 Martz, *The Poetry of Meditation*.

75 See Clements, *Mystical Poetry*.

76 I must again caution, however, that the narrative I am imposing upon Lacan is an appropriation that he would certainly not allow. My justification is that while I do not intend to deny that Traherne's real, imaginary, and symbolic registers are always concurrently in play, I believe that a willful blindness to that concurrence will reveal an equally viable development.

77 Most criticism has followed Clements in reading the initial voice/self here as

"not split, not divided" (*Mystical Poetry*, 71), but I don't think this view will hold.

78 Both Clements (*Mystical Poetry*) and Stewart (*The Expanded Voice*) discuss the problems of verb tense and the adult speaker recreating his own childhood.

79 I am indebted to a student of mine, John Morey, for this observation and I hope his own work will demonstrate how problematic Traherne's works are for an orthodox Christianity.

80 I refer not to naive romanticizings of Traherne's doctrine of felicity, but to attempts to understand its theological implications. Diane Elizabeth Dreher's *The Fourfold Pilgrimage* (Washington: University Press of America, 1982) is a representative example.

81 *Thomas Traherne: Poems, Centuries and Three Thanksgivings*, ed. Anne Ridler (London: Oxford University Press, 1966), 17.

82 This is but one of several passages in which we can perceive a Traherne who is both reader and rewriter of George Herbert. And that, I think, opens another important approach to Traherne that still needs to be explored. As a speculative entry into such a study I would suggest that many of the changes Philip makes in Traherne's poems may also be the result of a Herbert reading —this time Philip's rather than Thomas's. If we then recall that we have at least five other rewriters of Herbert—Ralph Knevet, Henry Colman, Christopher Harvey, Henry Vaughan, and John Wesley—then we might imagine a concrete test of various contemporary notions of reader response and literary revisionism: seven readers reading a single poet and rewriting him as their own discourses require. This is a task I hope to take up in a subsequent study.

83 See John Calvin, *Institutes of the Christian Religion*, esp. III.24.1, III.10.6, and III.24.8 for a representative reading. Compare Lacan's "every word contains its own reply."

84 The burden of this recognition, if it occurs, is captured in Lacan's assertion that "there's no such thing as an Other of the Other." See "Desire and the Interpretation of Desire in *Hamlet*," in Felman, *Literature and Psychoanalysis*, 25.

85 Note that the syntax itself belies the imaginary illusion in its insistence upon the repetitive and ever present negative: no . . . but, no . . . but.

86 Compare "The World": "What I did see / Seem'd all *Mine Own*" (ll. 87–88).

87 Compare the "Church's Year-Book": "The Dietie Communicating Himself is the father, the virtue by which He communicateth is the Son, Himself Communicated is the H. Ghost" (cited in Marks, "Traherne's Church's Year-Book" *PBSA* 60 [1966]: 61). Stewart, in *The Expanded Voice*, calls attention to a different passage in the same text: "by Communicating our selves we are united to others, give others the Benefit of our selvs, & Enjoy our selvs in being Enjoyed. . . . Because Narcissus like, none can Enjoy Himself in Himself unless he hath a fountain. Nor can any Enjoy themselvs in a fountain; tho they see the Reflexion of themselvs" (p. 124).

88 Again, I am imposing a temporal progression upon Lacan's terms that is

probably unwarranted, but insofar as Lacan's text licenses as well as questions such a progression it seems to me an unavoidable *epos*. The safeguard, perhaps, is to insist that although the symbolic field is somehow fuller and more "conscious" than the imaginary field, the latter is never outgrown, either temporally or psychologically.

89 In this Lacanian context, one might reexamine Traherne's "Thanksgivings for the Blessedness of his LAWS"; as we will see in the next chapter, the essential "law" is an economy of the supplement whereby all things can be prized "according to their value." Although it will take us ahead of the present argument, we might recall that Lacan's interpretation of man's desire as desire of the Other is: "*What value has my desire for you?*" See *FFC*, 192.

90 Since Philip crossed through the two stanzas of "The Apostacy" that appear at this point in the Dobell manuscript as the poem "Bliss," I feel confident in concluding that it does not belong in this sequence. Even if such evidence were missing, the very subject of the poem—Adam's prelapsarian bliss—would suggest that it is seriously misplaced and that it would belong somewhere in the opening series of poems.

91 Despite a bizarre collocation of allusions, Donald Bruce seems to me very close to the Trahernean sense of desire here: "Traherne envisions mankind as smarting from a wound which, delivered by a holy spear like the wound of Amfortas in the legend of Parsifal, will not close, except at the touch of the same spear. Then flame is consumed with flame, and by desire upon desire the lacerations of desire are salved" ("Thomas Traherne, 1637–1674," *Contemporary Review* 226 [1975], 23).

92 Not many critics have seen the sequence as ending in such eucharistic imagery, but Clements is one who does. See *Mystical Poetry*, 184, 187.

93 The fullest study of the impact of Canticles on seventeenth-century poetry is Stanley Stewart's *The Enclosed Garden* (Madison: University of Wisconsin Press, 1966).

FOUR. TRAHERNE AND DERRIDA

1 *Webster's New World Dictionary*, s.v.

2 The two chapters that appear in *Speech and Phenomenon*, trans. David B. Allison (Evanston: Northwestern University Press, 1973), as "The Supplement of Origin" and "Différance" are perhaps the most efficient introductions to these two terms. The first begins: "Thus understood, what is supplementary is in reality *différance*, the operation of differing which at one and the same time both fissures and retards presence, submitting it simultaneously to primordial division and delay. *Différance* is to be conceived prior to the separation between deferring as delay and differing as the active work of difference" (p. 88). As with many of Derrida's favorite words, it is not always clear where implications of one leave off and those of the other begin. It is clear, though, that however *supplement* and *différance* may overlap, they do not attempt to chart the same territory or operation.

3 As Gerard H. Cox notes in "Traherne's *Centuries*: A Platonic Devotion of 'Divine Philosophy,'" *MP* 69(1971): 21, Hooker draws a similar analogy: "The soul of man, being therefore at the first as a book, wherein nothing is and yet all things may be imprinted; we are to search by what steps and degrees it riseth unto perfection of knowledge" (*Ecclesiastical Polity*, I.vi.1).

4 See Derrida's discussion of this analogy in "The Double Session," which appears in *Dissemination*, trans. Barbara Johnson (Chicago: University of Chicago Press, 1981), esp. pp. 184–85. Joan Webber also discusses the analogy in "'I and Thou' in the Prose of Thomas Traherne," *PLL* 2 (1966): 259, as does Stanley Stewart in *The Expanded Voice* (San Marino: Huntington Library, 1970), 103–4, 108.

5 See *Of Grammatology* (hereafter *OG*), trans. Gayatri Chakravorty Spivak (Baltimore: Johns Hopkins University Press, 1976), pp. 157, 183. It should be obvious, in light of the preceding chapter, that Derrida's notions of supplementarity are, if not dependent upon, then remarkably similar to, Lacan's notions of desire. This is especially striking if one were to interpret Lacan's desire literally in terms of language *as writing* (as, that is, the supplement of imaginary speech).

6 This point has been made by many of Derrida's apologists, although detractors still seem not to hear it. Perhaps the fullest version of the categories, as well as an explication of Derrida's project, can be found in Irene E. Harvey's *Derrida and the Economy of Différance* (Bloomington: Indiana University Press, 1986), 112ff.

7 Following Heidegger, Derrida would put the copula under erasure and signify it as the "trace" of *différance*. For a convenient summary of this notion and its relation to Heidegger, see Spivak's introduction to *OG*, esp. xiii–xx, and Derrida's own "The Supplement of the Copula: Philosophy *before* Linguistics," in *Margins of Philosophy* (hereafter *MP*), trans. Alan Bass (Chicago: University of Chicago Press, 1982), 175–206.

8 Thus, what I have termed the supplement of predication is directly related to Derrida's sense of *writing* as the supplement. Traherne's own sense of how an act supplements an idea as the predicate supplements the noun might remind us of Hogarth's assertion, in *The Analysis of Beauty*, that "action is a sort of language which . . . may . . . be taught by a kind of grammar-rules" (cited in Ernest B. Gilman, *Iconoclasm and Poetry in the English Reformation* [Chicago: University of Chicago Press, 1986], 187).

9 *OG*, 167.

10 Ibid., 157.

11 Ibid., 163.

12 Ibid., 150.

13 Ibid., 304.

14 My sense of the importance of the adjective in Traherne's text is influenced by Gaston Bachelard: "I should like to point out the power that an adjective acquires, as soon as it is applied to life. A gloomy life, or a gloomy person, marks an entire universe with more than just a pervading coloration. . . .

And when a philosopher looks to poets . . . for lessons in how to individualize the world, he soon becomes convinced that the world is not so much a noun as an adjective. If we were to give the imagination its due in the philosophical systems of the universe, we should find, at their very source, an adjective" (pp. 143–44). For Bachelard, who calls himself a philosopher of adjectives, adjectives are precisely those marks of interest in an image that increase or announce psychic and phenomenological *value*. The text here is *The Poetics of Space*, trans. Maria Jolas (Boston: Beacon Press, 1969).

15 *OG*, 201.

16 Here I must take exception to Sharon Cadmon Seelig's notion that Traherne inhabits "a world in which the value of objects is inherent" (*The Shadow of Eternity* [Lexington: University of Kentucky Press, 1981], 147). Douglas Jordan seems much closer to the truth when he argues that "the entire value of the physical creation (though not the *being* of it) rests ultimately for Traherne upon the activity of the soul with it," or that value is "more important for Traherne than things themselves" and more important than being (*The Temple of Eternity* [Port Washington, N.Y.: Kennikat, 1972], 33, 78, 82).

17 In this context I would call attention to Barbara Johnson's statement that "the economy of the work of art is thus organized around a signifying surplus that transcends the mere exchange between signifiers and signifieds, between tenors and vehicles." Johnson tries to explicate this thought by recalling some passages from Marx which point directly toward the economy of Traherne's favorite term: "The simple circulation of commodities . . . is a means of carrying out a purpose unconnected with circulation, namely, the appropriation of use-values, the satisfactions of wants" (*Capital* [New York: International Publishers, 1967], 151); "The value originally advanced, therefore, not only remains intact while in circulation, but adds to itself a surplus-value or expands itself. It is this movement that converts it into capital" (Ibid., 150). See Johnson's remarks in *The Critical Difference* (Baltimore: Johns Hopkins University Press, 1985), 36ff.

18 *OG*, 183.

19 In fact, and in relation to a contemporary I have already mentioned, a significant issue for a New Historicist would be to determine exactly why part/whole relations have become so problematic to both Traherne and his Cambridge peer, Peter Sterry. The most consistent likeness between these two writers is their inability finally to name any whole that is not always already subject to the logic of *différance* requiring it to serve as part of a yet larger whole. To what extent, then, despite the theological differences that ostensibly separate Oxford and Cambridge in the 1660s, could we see this problem as arising out of the various totalizing efforts of the age's various grammarians, historians, scientists, and so forth?

20 *Course in General Linguistics*, trans. Wade Baskin (New York: Collins, 1974), 114, 118–19, 120–21. In terms of our own focus, it is important to remember that Saussure's explication of such differences is based upon the

exchange value of coinage; it is, in short, a linguistic economy.

21 *OG*, 303; *Writing and Difference* (hereafter *WD*), trans. Alan Bass (Chicago: University of Chicago Press, 1978), 289–90. Compare also Lacan's notion of the sliding of the signified.

22 See Gregory L. Ulmer, *Applied Grammatology* (Baltimore: Johns Hopkins University Press, 1985): "Metaphor assumes that one of the terms in the comparison has a 'proper' meaning" (p. 33); and Harvey, *Economy of Différance*: "Metaphor is a displacement of meaning from its origin, from the literal meaning, and as such finds a place within philosophical discourse as 'mere adornment,' as a heuristic addition that serves as an illustrative demonstration of a truth beyond itself" (p. 122). See also Derrida's "White Mythology: Metaphor in the Text of Philosophy," in *MP*, 207–72.

23 *OG*, 183.

24 Ibid. Bachelard, in the *Poetics of Space*, also aligns imagination with supplementarity, and he does so by specifically emphasizing the mental *economy* which produces or adds on value: "imagination augments the values of reality" (p. 3); "as soon as the imagination is interested in an image, this increases its value" (p. 152); and "for the imagination, therefore, the world gravitates about a *value*" (p. 171).

25 Cited in *OG*, 186.

26 Ibid., 150, 185–86.

27 Ibid., 311; compare Bachelard, *Poetics of Space*, 86.

28 Is not this tendency toward an expressly literal and dramatic understatement one of the telling features of Traherne's prose that aligns him with both Browne and Burton?

29 See Harvey, *Economy of Différance*, 132, on the notion that the excess must of necessity exceed even itself.

30 Harvey, *Economy of Différance*: "Infinity is that which is *intrinsically* unnameable" (p. 170).

31 Derrida's own interests in margin and limit could perhaps be seen as the central focus of the latest phase of his work, beginning, in 1972, with *Marges de la philosophie* (Paris: Minuit), and continuing through *La Vérité en Peinture* (Paris: Flammarion, 1978), *La Carte Postale* (Paris: Flammarion, 1980), and *Affranchissement du transfert et de la lettre* (Paris: Editions Confrontation, 1982). The fullest study, I think, of this aspect of Derrida's project is Ulmer's *Applied Grammatology*.

32 *OG*, 145.

33 Although the present point does not depend upon any further development of Christ as the supplement, it should be clear that as the Word Christ's relation to God would be susceptible to the same analysis Derrida performs on the supplementary relations between writing and speech.

34 These "superadded Treasures" are a constant theme of the *Meditations on the Six Days of Creation*: see especially 5–6, 33–34, 74, 82. The creation of man, on the sixth day, is the most interesting of these passages, for the initial supplement to man's body, "his own Image," immediately occasions a

multitude of other supplements: enjoyment, use, value, "Obligations, Relations, Education, Pleasure, History, Trades and Service," etc. "God being so marvellous in the creating of them [our bodies] that he hath super-added something to his Image" (p. 74). Here, I think, is a perfect illustration of Derrida's supplement: always already the supplement of a supplement.

35 This logic helps to explain why Traherne, like Derrida's Rousseau, has such an investment in originary scenes and the quest for origins. It is not, therefore, adequate to say merely that Traherne wants to regain a lost innocence; rather, we must emphasize that the scene of loss must continually be restaged in order to produce the want or need that supplementarity requires.

36 I would thus extend the useful comments Stewart makes on what he calls Traherne's "additive style" (*The Expanded Voice*, 67, 70–71, 87, 109): addition is a structural principle not only of Traherne's discursive logic and his syntax, but also of his entire view of existence. Everything in Traherne's world is either "adding to" or being "added to" in the economy he calls circulation.

37 We might note here in passing another registration of Traherne's economy. In the present passage "naked" means empty or void; in the Dobell poems, it generally means full and rich. In both cases, the term itself is neutral: it accrues positive or negative value only as it is read in terms of its own systematic *différance*.

38 See "Plato's Pharmacy," in *Dissemination*, 61–172. For a Traherne analogue to Derrida's *pharmacon*, see *Roman Forgeries* (sig. B6–B6v).

39 *OG*, 71.

40 Ibid., 144.

41 In *Meditations on the Six Days* Traherne makes this point explicitly: all things created before the sixth day "were worthless . . . because they serv'd nothing, and were to no Purpose. . . . [So when man was created] the World became useful in a Moment, which before was unprofitable" (p. 82). Man is the only "Sum of all the Creatures" (p. 84); "all things upon Earth would be of little Value without him" (p. 82). Although Traherne is careful to insert among these declarations the caveat that all things proceed from and end in God, the fact remains that man is the necessary register of all value. On Traherne's use of Pico, see Carol L. Marks, "Thomas Traherne's Commonplace Book," *PBSA* 58 (1964): 458–65; on the possibility that his understanding of man as the *copula* might also be influenced by Marsilio Ficino, see Diane E. Dreher, "Traherne's Second 'Century,'" *N&Q* 26 (1979): 434–36.

42 *Course in General Linguistics*, 66.

43 It should be noted that communication *is* circulation in Derrida's General Economy; see the essay "From Restricted to General Economy: A Hegelianism without Reserve," reprinted in *WD*. Although her focus is on God rather than man, Carol L. Marks, in two separate essays, makes the connection I wish to stress here. In "Traherne's Church's Year-Book" (*PBSA* 60 [1966]) she cites the following passage: "The Deitie Communicating Himself is the father, the virtue by which he communicateth Himself is the Son, Himself

Communicated is the H. Ghost. . . . So is the Same Deitie, as Giving all Things the father, as the Means by which He giveth the Son, as Dwelling in us the H. Ghost: the Three persons being Wholy given, *because each by the Residue, is wholy Enjoyed*" (pp. 61–62; my italics). That "Residue" is exactly the supplement man processes as the capital of the economy of communication. Marks makes a similar point when she argues in "Traherne and Hermes Trismegistus" (*RN* 19 [1966]) that Traherne was convinced that the circulation between heaven and earth expressed a "profit and advantage" that were reciprocal (p. 130). What Marks does not note is the economy expressed in her own terms.

44 Although his terms are necessarily different, Stewart confirms the connections I am drawing here between existential conditions and grammatical categories: "Traherne uses synecdoche in such a way as to subvert the distinction between part and whole. He will suddenly shift from abstract category . . . to particular instance, and back again. The rapidity of the shift, which is frequently accomplished without a tensed verb, functions as an implied copula; the reader can see by such juxtaposition that the particular is the act (or emanation) of an essence" (*The Expanded Voice*, 126).

45 *Equivocal Predication* (Toronto: University of Toronto Press, 1981).

46 *OG*, 163.

47 See Ian Michael, *English Grammatical Categories and the Tradition to 1800* (Cambridge: Cambridge University Press, 1970), 107.

48 Cf. *OG*, 35 on "clothing" as the *différance* of writing/speech. Traherne, in this instance, turns the interior/exterior hierarchy of Derrida's metaphor, even his history of metaphor as such, upside down.

49 Cf. Ulmer's demonstration, via Lacan's conjugations of the verb *aimer*, of the relation between the Derridean supplement and Lacan's desire (*Applied Grammatology*, 205).

50 "What is reflected is split *in itself* and not only as an addition to itself of its image. The reflection, the image, the double, splits what it doubles. The origin of the speculation becomes a difference. What can look at itself is not one; and the law of the addition of the origin to its representation, of the thing to its image, is that one plus one makes at least three" (*OG*, 36).

51 We can here recall that the Möbius strip was one of the "devices" with which Lacan entertained his audiences at the later seminars. See Catherine Clément, *The Lives and Legends of Jacques Lacan*, trans. Arthur Goldhammer (New York: Columbia University Press, 1983), 161.

52 Cf. *OG*, 144.

53 This is an oft-repeated Trahernean maxim. See, for example, *Meditations on the Six Days*, where "to prize every thing according to its Value" is a duty, a law, an obligation, a means to further rewards, and the enabling means of glory itself (pp. 37–38); and the "Thanksgivings," which constantly insist upon this obligation as man's primary duty to God.

54 The following stanza from "Right Apprehension" is a convenient illustration:

> A Globe of Earth is *better* far
> Than if it were a Globe of Gold: A Star
> Much *brighter* than a precious Stone:"
> The Sun *more* Glorious than a Costly Throne;
> His warming Beam,
> A living Stream
> Of liquid Pearl, that from a Spring
> Waters the Earth, is a *most* precious thing.
> (ll. 25–32)

55 As reported in George R. Guffey's *Concordance to the Poetry* (Berkeley: University of California Press, 1974), "more," for example, appears 150 times in the verse; "most" (51); "better" (21); "best" (19); "great" (18); "greatest" (9); "brighter" (5); "brightest" (3).

56 See Harvey, *Economy of Différance*, 128.

57 See *WD*, 93.

58 Whether the arrangement of Dobell may be assigned to Traherne or not, the logic of the placement of "Desire" remains unassailable.

59 For useful surveys of Renaissance attitudes toward the imagination, see William Rossky, "Imagination in the English Renaissance: Psychology and Poetic," *Sewanee Review* 5 (1958): 49–73, and Paul Stevens, *Imagination and the Presence of Shakespeare in "Paradise Lost"* (Madison: University of Wisconsin Press, 1985).

60 See Christopher Butler, *Number Symbolism* (London: Routledge & Kegan Paul, 1970), 6, 30, 34, 75; and C. Stuart Hunter's review essay, "'To read aright': A Sidnean Commentary," *Sidney Newsletter* 5 (1984): 15.

61 The best criticism on Traherne's repetitive style appears in Malcolm Day's *Thomas Traherne* (Boston: Twayne Publishers, 1982), 80–83 and Stewart's *The Expanded Voice*, 70–71, 87. Rosalie Colie, in *Paradoxia Epidemica* (Princeton: Princeton University Press, 1966), comes close to seeing Traherne's obsessive repetitions in the terms I am suggesting: "Traherne could stand not only the total plenitude of creation, but was ever ready to imagine 'more': plenitude for him [and unlike most seventeenth-century poets] was never 'enough'" (p. 155). And here I would also register a slight disagreement with Stewart, who argues that Traherne's repeated "more's" create "a sense of overflowing or fullness of quantity" (p. 136). My own argument would emphasize that "more" is a mark of economic *quality*, not quantity.

62 The continuous registration of "more" is one of the clearest parallels between the known work of Traherne and the recently discovered "Commentaries of Heaven." Here is a brief example from this manuscript: "To be able to see His Omnipresence and Eternity is much, but to be prone to do it is more. To be able to imitat him is much, but to be prone to do it is more. To be able to render unto things their due esteem is much, but to be prone to do it is more. To be able to Enjoy innumerable Millions of Things at any Distances whatsoever is much, but to be so prone to do it, that we can never be

satisfied but when we are Doing it, is abundantly more" (cited in Allan Pritchard, "Traherne's 'Commentaries,'" *UTQ* 53 [1983], 25).

63 Compare Colie, *Paradoxia Epidemica*: "The word 'infinity' might well be selected as the key to Traherne's total devotion" (p. 146). My only quibble with such a conclusion is that it fails to understand how Traherne's infinity constantly escapes any totalization, how it is always already trapped in the economy of the supplement.

64 The Marks-Guffey text is surely in error here in citing, "it added Art unto Power." As I hope is clear by now, power and *act*, not *art*, is the Trahernean signature.

65 For other, representative, examples of the supplementary exchange by which "more" and "infinite" come to intensify each other, see *Poems and Thanksgivings* 237–38, 242, 313–14, and especially 255, where "the unsearchable Excesses / Of eternal Love" are "Infinitely more than infinite . . . for evermore."

66 Compare A. L. Clements's only half-facetious assertion that Traherne's infinity is "without *fin*" and consequently "cannot be . . . de*fin*ed" (*The Mystical Poetry* [Cambridge: Harvard University Press, 1979], 25–26).

67 Compare Bachelard, *Poetics of Space*: "the dialectics of full and empty only correspond to two geometrical non-realities. The function of inhabiting [Heidegger's "dwelling"?] constitutes the link between" the two categories (p. 140).

68 There is actually a third problem if we approach the question of the time frame of the speaker of the poems. Obviously, even though he speaks *as* a child, he is not a child but an adult trying to speak as a child. So doubled always already, the speaker's tense/time at any given point in the sequence is a problem the reader must deal with. However, because it *has* been dealt with, by both Clements and Stewart, I prefer to focus on a different level of the same issue.

69 *Poetics of Space*, xxxiii, 74–90; compare *CM*, V.3; "Dissatisfaction": "In ev'ry House I sought for Health, / Search't ev'ry Cabinet to spy my Wealth" (ll. 9–10); "The City," whose "little Room[s]" and "little privat Cabinet[s]" cannot contain "my richer Wealth" (ll. 40–55); and "A Thanksgiving and Prayer for the NATION," where "Cabinets were made" for the sake of "the Treasures which most we prize" (ll. 31–50).

70 Compare "A Thanksgiving . . . for the NATION"—"The possession of thy Wealth maketh us poor" (l. 201)—and the definition of adoration Traherne records in "Commentaries of Heaven": "Adoration is the Retribution of infinit Bounty, or the Paying back of all Things to God" (cited in Pritchard, "Traherne's 'Commentaries,'" 26). "Paying back," however, is not a typical Trahernean idiom: its more common analogue is "Be Profitable to all that are round about thee" (The Church's Year-Book, fol. 99).

71 *Troilus and Cressida*, II.ii.52.

72 The only competing passage, in order of frequence of allusion, is Psalm 24, which also evokes Traherne's favored term: "The earth is the Lord's, and the fullness thereof."

INDEX

ABOUT THE AUTHOR

A. Leigh DeNeef is Professor of English and Associate Dean of the Graduate School at Duke University. His special fields of interest are Renaissance literature and critical theory, on which he has written four books.

Library of Congress Cataloging-in-Publication Data
DeNeef, A. Leigh.
Traherne in dialogue: Heidegger, Lacan, and Derrida / A. Leigh DeNeef.
p. cm.
Bibliography: p.
Includes index.
ISBN 0-8223-0832-0
1. Traherne, Thomas, d. 1674—Criticism and interpretation—History—20th century. 2. Heidegger, Martin, 1889–1976—Contributions in criticism. 3. Lacan, Jacques, 1901–1981—Contributions in criticism. 4. Derrida, Jacques—Contributions in criticism. 5. Canon (Literature) 6. Historical criticism (Literature) I. Title.
PR3736.T7Z66 1987
801'.95—dc19 87-31952